THE END OF MARRIAGE: WHY MONOGAMY ISN'T WORKING

Dr Julian Hafner

CENTURY

Distributed by
Trafalgar Square
North Pomfret, Vermont 05053

To My Grandfather,
Vic Wray

First published in Great Britain in 1993 by Century
Random House UK
20 Vauxhall Bridge Road, London, SW1V 2SA

Century Hutchinson South Africa (Pty) Ltd
PO Box 337, Bergvlei 2012, South Africa

Random House Australia Pty Ltd
20 Alfred Street, Milsons Point, Sydney, NSW 2061
Australia

Random House New Zealand Ltd
18 Poland Road, Glenfield, Auckland 10,
New Zealand

0 7126 5607 3

Typeset by Deltatype Ltd, Ellesmere Port
Printed in Great Britain by Mackays of Chatham plc, Chatham, Kent

Contents

Introduction: The Compulsory Marriage

In over twenty years as a psychiatrist, few things have surprised me more than the misery caused by bad marriages. I have treated many people who clung fiercely for years to marriages that quite obviously destroyed their happiness and well-being. Often, I was the first person allowed to glimpse the truth that lay beneath a social veneer of marital stability and contentment. During therapy, one or both partners usually talked of feeling trapped in the marriage, unable either to change it or to escape from it. For them, the relationship had become *compulsory*, a term which I use in this book in an attempt to capture the essence of these unhappy situations. I have treated as adults many children of compulsory marriages. Often, they and their parents were seen by outsiders as enjoying a family life that was unusually stable, happy and harmonious. But in reality, the well-being of the child was sacrificed as part of the parents' overwhelming need to remain together and present to the outside world a picture of a united, happy family.

My first real confrontation with these issues was at a social gathering – a small party at a friend's house – a few years before I started training as a psychiatrist. One couple evoked comment because of their obvious affection for each other. Although married for nearly twenty years, they behaved as newlyweds, hugging and kissing in a way that struck me as having a slightly desperate quality about it. When I suggested this to my companion, she accused me of being cynical, adding that she herself thought that the couple's affection was refreshing and romantic.

About a week later, I phoned the friend who had given the party. He sounded upset, and I mentioned this. He told me that the wife of the affectionate couple had yesterday shot her husband dead. I was shocked, and became more so when I heard the apparent reasons for the homicide: the wife had discovered that her husband had been having an incestuous relationship with their sixteen-year-old daughter over the previous seven years. I was very upset, and I thought deeply about how such hideous events could have taken place within a marriage that was widely thought of as a strikingly happy one.

In retrospect, I think that this occurrence made a significant contribution to my later decision to specialize in the marital and family aspects of psychiatry. Further contributions came, I am sure, from my own childhood. I was born during the Second World War, at the outbreak of which my father had enlisted. Apart from three brief periods of leave, he was overseas for six years and I did not see him until I was in my third year. When we were introduced for the first time, I refused, apparently, to acknowledge him, pointing instead to the photograph on the mantelpiece and insisting 'that's my daddy'. From that point on, our relationship was a difficult one. War experiences had psychologically traumatized my father, and he found readjustment to civilian life a major challenge. This made family life stormy at times. It seems that coping with these problems left me unusually sensitive to family dynamics, a sensitivity that was reinforced by a training in psychiatry which placed great emphasis on the marital and family context of mental illness.

Let me emphasize that I am not against the idea of people living as couples. I firmly believe that being in a special, harmonious, mutually supportive and equal relationship can add much to well-being and happiness. But I believe also that comparatively few of us actually live in such partnerships. Instead, we live far too often in relationships characterized mainly by boredom, frustration, resentment – and even danger. Research has shown that in 3–4 per cent of marriages, husbands regularly beat their wives in a way that results in significant injury. Intermittent or occasional physical violence of a serious kind is inflicted by husbands on a further 7–8 per cent of wives. Even more are intimidated by the threat of violence. Commonly, even seriously abused women remain married for years to the men who ill-treat them.

The couples that I have worked with over the past twenty years or so have taught me a great deal about why people stay in bad relationships. What else I have learned comes from academic

2

study, wider reading, and my experience of life outside the consulting room. A single, powerful theme has emerged from this learning: the presence of a pervasive, relentless social pressure on people to marry or live in couples. Marriage and living as a couple – which I shall refer to as *coupledom* – is almost universally accepted as normal and desirable in Western societies. The existence of such a fundamental institution as marriage is simply not questioned by most people. Instead, it is for many their main goal in life. There is a paradox here: the institution of marriage is rarely questioned *because* social pressures to achieve it are so powerful and persuasive. The major aims of this book are to trace the origins of these social pressures, to describe their negative effects, and to suggest some ways of resisting them.

I use a detailed case history in each of the first six chapters, and in Chapters 9 and 10, to illustrate more important themes. These case histories are based on real clients, but names and personal circumstances have been changed to ensure that they cannot be identified. I have also included a bibliography, the contents of which are fairly accessible through bookshops and public libraries. I refer occasionally to articles in specialized journals, giving enough information in the text for these to be obtained by anyone who wishes to do so, although this may require some perseverance from those who do not have ready access to academic libraries. I generally refer to English-speaking nations collectively, although considerable cultural differences exist between them. But, over-all, these differences are outweighed by similarities, and this allows a considerable degree of generalization. In discussing marriage, I include couples not legally wed, but who consider themselves to be married.

I have dealt with some of these matters in a previous book called *Marriage and Mental Illness*. This was written mainly for those in the professions of psychiatry, psychology, social work and psychiatric nursing. Although it has been read by many people outside the mental-health professions, some of the contents are too technical to be of value to those without specialized know-ledge. The present book, which is much broader in scope, is written mainly for people outside the caring professions, although I believe it will also be of interest to those who work within them. I am aware that there has been a spate of popular books in recent

3

years about the tyranny of coupledom. But nearly all of these focus on women's problems. That men's problems are largely ignored is reflected in titles such as *Women Who Love Too Much* by Robin Norwood, and *Why Do I think I am Nothing Without a Man?* by Penelope Russianoff. In this volume I have tried to give equal weight to women's and men's issues.

There is, I think, another problem with popular books in this area. In stating the need for women to change, they insufficiently acknowledge what a huge task this often is. As a result, women who do not or cannot change are at risk of being blamed, by themselves or by others. Books blaming men in the same way have started to become popular. A good example of this is Marilyn French's *The War Against Women*. In the hope of replacing blame with understanding, I have emphasized throughout this book a *historical* approach, so that men and women alike can perceive the full extent and nature of the forces that have shaped traditional attitudes and behaviour.

When I began writing, I had only a bare outline of the book before me. As the project developed, I realized how little I knew about some of the issues that I was grappling with. In order to answer one of my basic questions – why do so many people enter and remain in destructive relationships? – I had to enquire into areas that were new to me, as well as revisiting familiar territory. It became clear that in order to understand couples, I had to clarify the relationship between the sexes in a *general* sense. In writing about this, it was necessary to focus on sex roles and the way in which rigid or stereotyped attitudes to these may have destructive effects on the health of both men and women. While working on the first draft, I realized that the task was becoming an adventure. Like most adventures, the path toward the final manuscript turned out to be risky at times, as well as exciting and rewarding. I hope that the book itself will be an adventure for the reader.

1

Modern Marriage: A Health Hazard for Women

In the Western world, and especially in North America, marriage is as popular as it has ever been. According to the 1988 General Social Survey, over 95 per cent of Americans have been married at least once by the time they reach age forty-five. However, there is a clear trend towards *postponing* marriage. The average age for men at first marriage is now about twenty-six, an increase of some two and a half years since the mid 1960s. For women, age at first marriage has also increased by some two and a half years over the same period, to an average of about twenty-four. Twenty years ago, nearly 30 per cent of women married for the first time at age nineteen or younger; today, this is true of less then 10 per cent.

One effect of this change has been an increase in the number of couples who live together unmarried. But, for nearly all these couples, living together is a postponement of marriage rather than a rejection of the married state.

Although marriage remains very popular, divorce has increased greatly over the past thirty years. The figures vary somewhat between the different Western nations, but the average divorce rate in English-speaking nations is now over 30 per cent. North America has the highest rate, currently at least 40 per cent.

Most divorces are initiated by women. A major reason for this is the change in women's employment prospects over the past thirty years. Because of a huge expansion in the number of jobs available, paid work now exists for most women who want it. Thirty years ago, there were far fewer jobs for women, who were often trapped in miserable marriages because poverty – and enforced separation from their children – was the stark alternative. In suggesting that greatly improved access to paid work is perhaps the most important reason for women's increased willingness to initiate divorce, I do not wish to overlook other factors,

5

such as the Women's Liberation movement. But I believe that the positive effects of Women's Liberation on many women's lives and expectations would not have occurred without the great improvement in their employment opportunities. This important issue is discussed further in Chapter 5.

Now that they are economically free to do so, more women than ever before are choosing to leave unhappy marriages. But many still choose to remain in marriages that are destructive to their health and well-being. Quite how destructive modern marriage can be to women is illustrated by findings from recent research.

Marriage and Psychiatric Disorder

Large-scale, well-designed surveys of the mental health of people living in the community are very expensive. Because of this, very few have been carried out. Recently, however, one was carried out in North America. Called the Epidemiologic Catchment Area (ECA) Program, it was a huge undertaking that involved interviewing a total of about 17,000 community residents in five different locations. The findings, although in many respects surprising, are similar to those of smaller surveys carried out in Europe and in other English-speaking countries. There are no persuasive reasons to doubt their accuracy.

At any one time, over 15 per cent of people living in the community suffer from a recognizable psychiatric disorder – almost one person in 7. Disorders characterized mainly by anxiety or depression are by far the commonest, affecting over 12 per cent of the community. If these figures are surprising, even more so is the finding that *twice as many women as men suffer from anxiety and depressive disorders*.

The ECA survey does not attempt to explain why women are so much more likely than men to suffer from anxiety and depression. But many other studies have clarified this. It is not women in general, but mainly *married women* who contribute to this excess of anxiety and depression: they report levels that are 2–3 times higher than those of their single counterparts. The term 'single' is used mainly to describe women who have not been married. But within this category must also be included formerly married women who prefer to remain unmarried, and who have come to

6

view themselves as single rather than divorced. These women have much lower levels of anxiety and depression than women adjusting to recent separation or divorce.

Several studies have found that young men and women experience very similar levels of anxiety and depression. Women show no increase in psychiatric disorder as they get older – unless they get married. Single women over the age of thirty-five report no more anxiety and depression than single women in their early twenties. But the situation is quite different for single men, who experience more psychiatric disorder as they get older. The picture that emerges from most studies is clear: overall, the mental health of women deteriorates after marriage. But for men, marriage has the opposite effect, enhancing their mental health, or at least protecting them from the psychological deterioration shown by their unmarried fellows.

There is little dispute among social scientists about the reality of these findings. Much more controversial are the reasons for them. A key factor is *employment outside the home*. Most studies have found that married women who do paid work outside the home do *not* suffer from a major excess of anxiety and depressive disorders: they reports levels of 10–12 per cent. The excess is found mainly in married women who have no paid employment outside the home: about 25 per cent of such women report anxiety and depressive disorders. Their poor mental health is revealed even more clearly in several studies comparing unemployed married women with their employed husbands: levels of psychiatric disorder are 3–4 times higher in the women.

Reasons for the high levels of psychiatric disorder in full-time housewives are complex and not fully understood. Perhaps the most obvious one is the simple fact that, for most people, paid employment outside the home is fundamental to their sense of well-being. Because paid work is also a burden, even a tyranny, for many people, its positive effects are rarely looked at objectively. Although there is no doubt about the devastating effect of sudden, forced unemployment, discussions about this almost always focus on its economic impact, emphasizing the financial hardship that families face with the loss of the (usually male) breadwinner's income. There is much less awareness of the negative *psychological* effects of unemployment, especially if it is

7

prolonged. For this reason, I will now outline some of the psychological benefits of paid employment.

The Psychological Benefits of Paid Work

People living in today's English-speaking world are highly mobile, moving freely from city to city and from state to state. They lose day-to-day contact with their relatives and the friends that they have grown up with. Because of this, most employed people look for companionship and friendship at work, and they often base their social life on people they meet while they are working. So, for many people, unemployment means social isolation, or at least loss of their 'social support network'.

Increased social mobility has also meant that work is important for our social status and identity. No longer are most of us born in small towns and villages where everyone knows everyone else, and where matters of social status are common knowledge. Instead, most of us live in suburbs where we know only our immediate neighbours. When we meet people for the first time, we are likely to be defined in terms of our jobs, which have become the main basis for deciding social status. For many of us, job loss means loss of social status and identity.

Many people rely on their jobs not only for social identity, but for personal identity also. Some are so strongly committed to their work role that it has become part of their personality, and such people may become labelled as 'workaholics'. Often, identifying with a work role is intimately connected with overvaluing the role of family breadwinner. Where the two roles combine to provide a sense of identity, purpose and well-being, the effects of job loss are often devastating. Unemployment may lead to an identity crisis with severe, prolonged anxiety and depression that improve only when the identity crisis is resolved.

The loss of economic independence that goes with unemployment is demeaning and humiliating. Reliance on unemployment benefits or welfare, even for a short time, undermines the sense of pride and well-being of people who previously valued their financial independence. Longer term dependence on welfare, or on the financial support of others, can have severe adverse psychological effects from which full recovery may be very difficult.

As well as requiring regular social interaction with other adults, most people need also to keep reasonably busy and occupied. Paid employment provides a structure within which we can keep busy, even if the tasks that we work at are repetitive and monotonous. For the more fortunate among us, work is a varied and exciting challenge that not only keeps us occupied, but allows us to use our creativity and rewards us with a sense of personal fulfilment.

What I have briefly outlined about the benefits of work – and there are doubtless others that I have overlooked – may seem obvious. I make no apology for this, because many of the people that I have talked with about these benefits had previously failed to recognize them. Often, they needed to stand back a little from their work roles and examine them without prejudice. Usually, when they did this, they were surprised at the list of benefits that emerged.

Voluntary Unemployment

Given all the psychological benefits of paid work outside the home, it might be expected that voluntary unemployment is rare. It is, of course, very common, and the overwhelming majority of those who achieve it are married women.

Over the past 10–15 years we have reached a situation where, throughout most of the Western world, the majority of married women are in paid employment outside the home. The precise figures vary from country to country, but in North America and the United Kingdom it is about 55–60 per cent. Australia, a country that is extraordinary for the rigidity of its sex-role structures, lags behind somewhat, but has recently achieved a 50 per cent employment rate among married women.

Although these figures are encouraging, there is still a huge gap between men and women as far as the extent and status of employment is concerned. Many married women are in part-time work, which is often insecure, boring, menial, repetitive, of low status, and has no superannuation, health insurance or sick-leave benefits. Although reliable figures are difficult to obtain, it is probable that fewer than 30 per cent of married women are in full-time paid employment. In contrast, the rate for married men in most Western countries is 80–90 per cent, almost three times that for women. Even if full- and part-time work are combined, the overall employment rate for married men is about 50 per cent higher than it is for married women.

Why Do Married Women Accept Voluntary Unemployment?

It is now rare to meet a married woman who had no experience of being in the work-force before her first marriage. Today, almost all women are in paid employment, usually full time, when they get married.

Of course, women's (as well as men's) attitudes to work vary greatly. Well-educated women who have been to university usually value a career quite highly. They see work as an opportunity not only for financial independence and social status, but also for excitement, challenge and personal fulfilment. At the other end of the spectrum are women, usually poorly educated and from working-class backgrounds, who tend to see work as a necessary evil – at least until they get married. For such women, marriage often seems the only escape from the drudgery and monotony of work that, in the absence of cheap labour, would be done by a machine. In such circumstances, marriage and the chance of voluntary unemployment usually seem very attractive.

The views of most young single women lie between these two extremes. Such women have graduated from high school and are usually working full time in jobs that they quite enjoy. These jobs are generally of modest status: even in the 1990s, in almost all work settings, the more senior posts are held mainly by men. The only significant exception to this is the health-care industry, especially nursing.

It is young women in jobs of average status and pay who agonize the most about voluntary unemployment after marriage. This is because both paid work and voluntary unemployment appear to be fairly attractive options for them. For nearly all, the decision about whether or not to accept voluntary unemployment does not have to be made until after childbirth. However, since over 90 per cent of married women have children, it is a decision that nearly all must make.

Child-raising and Voluntary Unemployment

In Western society, the pressure on married women to take primary responsibility for raising their own children, ideally as full-time mothers, is very strong indeed. It comes as a complete surprise to most Western women that other societies have a different view of child-raising. This difference is most marked in developing countries, where married women are far too valuable as an economic resource to devote much of their time to child-raising. They remain full-time in the work-force throughout their adult lives. The task of raising their young children falls mainly on those who cannot do hard physical labour, or who have not yet learned to do highly skilled work. It is therefore the elderly and children aged seven to twelve who carry out most of the child care.

It is true that the environment of women in developing countries is mainly rural, and that they live mostly in villages and other small communities. It is also true that their work is usually in the fields close to their homes, or in the village itself. They do not experience the geographical separation between home and work that occurs in Western society. None the less, their primary commitment to work is a very real one, to which the direct personal care of their children *must* be secondary. If they did not work, they would not eat, and neither would their children. Even during the first year of their lives, the children of these women do not stop them working full time: the women continue their tasks as usual, with their babies attached to their backs or waists.

Historically, the situation was not greatly different in Western society. Before the Industrial Revolution, the great majority of Westerners lived in small villages where they worked at home or nearby. Child care was shared among family members as a routine aspect of working life. After the Industrial Revolution, the bulk of the population came to live in towns and cities, and paid work generally required men and women to leave home for offices, mills and factories.

The destructive effects on women of these profound social changes are discussed at some length in Chapters 5 and 6. At this point I will refer only to the dilemma that has arisen for women with young children. In order to work outside the home they must grapple with varying degrees of guilt and conflict about the idea of not raising their own young children on a day-to-day basis. For some, the idea of handing over the care of their children to someone else is totally unacceptable. Others see it as a valid option, providing the quality of 'other care' is satisfactory. Nearly all Western women agree that it is highly desirable to look after their own children on a virtually full-time basis until they are at least a year old. In English-speaking countries, over three-quarters of married women actually achieve this. To do so, they must join the ranks of the voluntarily unemployed. Not all women are adversely affected by the unemployment that they choose, or must accept, in order to become full-time mothers. But many are. The reality of this is illustrated by the following case history.

Case 1: Mary's Suburban Dream

Mary was twenty-eight when she came to see me. An attractive, neatly dressed woman, her carefully applied make-up did not hide the fact that she looked tired and depressed.

When I asked her to tell me about the problems that had brought her to see me, tears immediately started to flow down her cheeks. She apologized, and I reassured her that it was quite all right to cry in front of me, and that we had plenty of time to talk. She didn't need to start telling me her story until she was ready.

After a minute or two, although she was still weeping a little, Mary began. 'I'm really depressed, nearly all the time,' she said. 'But what makes it even worse, I don't know *why* I'm so depressed. I feel so *angry* with myself for being depressed, so utterly stupid. After all, I've got everything I ever wanted – two lovely children, a nice home, no money worries. Yet I sit home and cry.'

At this point, Mary hesitated and looked at me very directly. 'Just in the past few weeks I've felt suicidal. I don't really want to kill myself – I couldn't do it to the children. But I'm worried that I might do something on impulse.'

Naturally I took Mary's disclosure very seriously. After further discussion, we agreed that the chances of her attempting suicide on impulse were not high. She was reassured enough to feel that she could manage to cope with any suicidal thoughts and impulses, especially now that she had decided to seek help for her depression.

Family Background

I then asked Mary to tell me a little about her family background. She began by describing her mother:

'I suppose I've always had a bit of a love-hate relationship with my mother. She's always expected me to be perfect. But whenever I did my best at anything, she was never quite satisfied. Often, she was critical of my efforts. So I was always trying to do better, to get some praise from her.'

Mary's mother, Susan, had been working as a sales assistant in a small town when she met George, Mary's father. George was a mining engineer, and had become involved in oil exploration. His work required a great deal of travelling around the country, and this continued after they married, when Susan was twenty-two and George was twenty-five.

Initially, Susan and George travelled together. When Susan was twenty-four, Mary's brother Michael was born; Mary was born eighteen months later. There were no other children. For about five years or so after Mary's birth, Susan and George had no home of their own. Although George was earning good money, he still had to move around the country, and it made more sense to save his earnings rather than buy a house. Susan did not work outside home.

Finally, the family settled in a good suburb of a city with a population of about half a million. Susan expressed a wish to get a job, now that the children were older. George was strongly against the idea. He had a traditional view of family life, and believed that children needed a full-time mother until they were well into their teens. He also thought that it would reflect badly on his position as family breadwinner if Susan worked: people would think that he was unable to provide adequately for his wife and children.

After a few arguments, Susan surrendered to George's viewpoint. But she became increasingly bored, resentful and frustrated, and took out these negative feelings on Mary, although she spared Mary's older brother. As we have seen, the main effect of this on Mary was to leave her feeling that she was never quite good enough, in spite of her best efforts. She coped with this by becoming perfectionistic and over-meticulous. These traits proved helpful at school and Mary, naturally bright, did quite well academically.

Work

Sadly, Mary's academic success was wasted. Her father believed that education was useless for women, who should be content with marriage and children. Although Mary's mother had a different view, the role model that she provided for Mary was one of full-time mother and housewife, and she never openly expressed any dissatisfaction about this role to Mary. And so, even though Mary graduated well from high school, she had no interest in a career. She wanted only to marry and have children. To Mary, a job was simply an interlude before marriage.

But Mary was intelligent and highly conscientious. She did so well in the department store that she had joined (like her mother) as a sales assistant, that she was rapidly promoted. By age twenty-two she was a buyer in the store's fashion department. She greatly enjoyed her work, which she found stimulating and challenging. She valued her financial independence, and had an active and enjoyable social life.

Marriage and Motherhood

Mary met Frank through a mutual friend, and immediately felt a strong attraction to him. He was twenty-seven, three years older than Mary. They married ten months later; a year after that Sarah was born.

Frank had a well paid job, which, together with the couple's combined savings, allowed them to get a manageable mortgage on a pleasant house in a good suburb. Mary had carried on working until a month before Sarah's birth. She told all her family and friends that she was delighted to stop work and really looking forward to being a full-time mother and housewife. Frank, like Mary's father, had traditional views about women's roles, and fully agreed with Mary about the importance of her being a full-time mother.

Mary had a long, difficult and painful labour that finally required a Caesarean section. Although she was delighted to have a baby daughter, the mild postnatal 'blues' that she considered natural never really wore off.

The suburb where the couple lived was remote from Mary's

friends, nearly all of whom she knew through work, and who tended to live closer to the city centre. Since most of them were still working, they soon lost interest in seeing Mary, who was preoccupied with raising Sarah. Remarkably quickly, Mary found herself virtually friendless. But she suppressed her feelings of rejection and sadness, and hid her loneliness by trying hard to be the perfect mother and housewife.

Sarah was a demanding baby, waking up frequently at night, and feeding poorly. Frank insisted that Mary dealt with Sarah at night, refusing to get up because he needed to be fresh for his work, which was often demanding and tiring. When he got home in the evenings he expected Mary to wait on him and prepare a cooked supper even though she was usually far more exhausted than he was. He had no interest in looking after Sarah, believing that this was 'women's work'. Mary's mother, Susan, had finally defied her husband and got a job, which kept her so busy that she had little time or energy to make the fifty-minute trip to Mary's house. In fact, Mary had found her mother's initial attempts to help her so intrusive that she was relieved rather than disappointed about her later lack of involvement. But this left Mary even more isolated: by the time Sarah was six months old, Frank was the only adult Mary saw at all regularly. When he came home, Mary craved his emotional support and companionship. Tired as he usually was, he wanted only to sit down and watch TV, be fed, and have any other needs met by Mary until it was time for bed. Once in bed, lovemaking was a rare event, but both Mary and Frank were too tired and preoccupied to miss it much.

The Struggle to be Perfect

Mary had always totally rejected the idea that she was, or ever would be, a 'career woman'. But her great success at work meant that, without realizing it, she had become one. Because Mary still saw her job as simply an interlude between marriage and motherhood, she did not consciously grieve its loss, even though it also meant losing her social status, her contact with colleagues and friends and her financial independence.

Mary buried all her negative feelings about giving up her job. Those that she couldn't bury she transformed to positive feelings

15

about her new role as a full-time wife and mother, into which she redirected all the perfectionistic drive and energy that had been crucial to her success at work. Idealizing her new role, she was determined to be a perfect wife and mother.

Mary had all the usual mechanical aids to housework, which she could have completed rapidly each day. But her perfectionism attached itself to the house and she became obsessed with order and cleanliness. Some days she spent hours washing and scrubbing areas that were already spotless.

Sarah started to walk at eleven months, and Mary became over-concerned about her picking up germs. She also found herself constantly tidying up after Sarah, whom she increasingly resented because of the disorder she brought to a house that Mary struggled to keep in a state of perfection. She expected her daughter to look and behave as perfectly as the house, and found herself screaming at Sarah whenever the little girl fell short of these impossible expectations. She also smacked Sarah quite often, sometimes very hard. She buried her guilt and self-disgust about this by putting even more time and energy into the struggle for perfection.

Mary told Frank nothing about these problems. She wanted him to see her as the perfect wife, and she worked very hard at preserving the image of a perfect marriage – an image that she needed for her own psychological stability. Frank, brought up to believe that men and women led naturally different lives, had little interest in how Mary spent her day. He assumed that she enjoyed her 'easy life', about which he frequently made disparaging comments, adding to Mary's guilt and frustration. He rewarded her perfectionism by praising her for the domestic order and cleanliness that prevailed. Frank had no interest in a social life beyond his work, and Mary was too tired and preoccupied with Sarah and household cleanliness and order to want to do any entertaining. She discouraged any contact from neighbours for similar reasons, preserving her social isolation.

Because Frank believed that Mary was happy, he suggested that they have a second child as a companion for Sarah. Mary, still clinging to the idea that happiness and fulfilment lay in being a perfect wife and mother, agreed. A son, Harry, was born when Sarah was twenty months old.

16

Rather than relieving Mary's unhappiness, as she had hoped, Harry added to it. Keeping a perfectly clean and tidy home became even more of a struggle. But Mary was not a quitter. She kept at it, and might have continued indefinitely but for the following episode.

Domestic Violence

One morning, Sarah was being particularly irritating while Mary was attending to Harry, who had just learned to walk. Mary lost control and hit Sarah across the head really hard. The little girl slipped and banged her head against the edge of a cupboard, cutting her forehead.

When Frank got home, he saw the sticking plaster on Sarah's forehead and asked her what had happened.

'Mummy hit me,' said Sarah.

Frank didn't believe his daughter, but he none the less questioned Mary about it. She denied it, but something in her manner made Frank persist. At first, Mary got angry, and then she suddenly burst into tears.

'Christ, you don't know what it's like being cooped up all day with two young children. Yes, I did hit her, she got on my bloody nerves. I hate her sometimes. It's all right for you. You're out all day. You meet people. You're a success, people admire you. I'm just a housewife. You don't understand *anything* about my life.'

Instead of feeling sympathy for Mary, Frank got angry. He started to shout at her, and Mary yelled back, now out of control. She screamed and raged, letting out all the anger and frustration that she had struggled for so long to hide from Frank and from herself. She accused Frank of being selfish and inconsiderate, even suggesting that he was having an affair. In turn, Frank got more and more angry until finally he too lost control – and slapped Mary as hard as he could around the face. She fell over.

The argument stopped. Frank had never hit Mary before, and both were utterly astonished by his violence. Neither spoke to one another until the next morning, when Frank tried to apologize. Although Mary accepted his apology, she did not forgive him. Her image of perfection was shattered. She became more and more

17

depressed, and thoughts of suicide began to trouble her. It was at this point in her life that Mary had come to see me.

Therapy

Mary's first attempt at seeking help had been to consult her family physician, a man in his fifties who, like Mary's husband Frank, had a traditional view of sex roles. He agreed with Mary that she had no reason to be depressed, because, after all, she had everything that she had always wanted. He prescribed an antidepressant drug. Mary experienced bad side-effects from the medication and stopped taking it. Her lack of improvement prompted her family physician to refer her to a psychiatrist with whom he had been to medical school. But this man was due to go on sabbatical leave, and so Mary ended up seeing me instead.

It rapidly became clear that Mary blamed herself for her depression and related problems. This self-blame was strongly reinforced by Frank who could see no reason why she should not be perfectly happy, and by her family physician who shared Frank's views. Because Mary was so socially isolated, she was never exposed to different ideas. It had never seriously occurred to her that she had very good reasons to be depressed, and that these reasons were a result of her environment.

The main tasks of therapy were to help Mary understand the reasons for her depression, and to then help her make any changes in her life that were necessary. During the first five sessions, held once a week, she came to acknowledge just how much she missed her paid work. She came to realize how totally unsuited she really was to the role of full-time mother and housewife. As an intelligent, well-organized and energetic woman, she could in reality complete her domestic tasks in a small fraction of the time available to her. But rather than do this, and then seek other activities outside the home, she had been trapped by her value system – a system that commanded her to be a 'perfect mother'. To Mary, a perfect mother was a full-time mother who sacrificed her own needs, interests and pursuits for the sake of her children and husband.

Mary came to understand how unrealistic was the expectation that she be fulfilled by the exclusive company of infants. Mary had

a lively intelligence and a need for conversation and companionship that could not possibly be met within her domestic role as she
conceived and practised it. But, because of her idealization of the
role, and her identification with it, she had failed to see that what
she cherished so much was the real cause of her unhappiness.

I had suggested that Frank be involved in therapy, but Mary
initially resisted the idea: she was not ready for a direct assault
upon the idea that her marriage was perfect. As well, it took her a
great deal of courage to tell me about the reality of her domestic
life, especially her maltreatment of Sarah. To share this with
Frank would have risked his hostility rather than his understanding. Mary was still totally dependent on the idea of being Frank's
wife. Because she felt unable to survive without him, she was
unwilling to risk alienating him or otherwise threatening their
marriage. If she could fix *herself* up, she thought, then the
marriage might be restored to perfection.

Will This Marriage Survive?

After six individual therapy sessions, Mary agreed to invite Frank
to join us. Over the next three conjoint sessions, he learned about
the realities of Mary's life and the inevitability of her depression.
Mary had decided that she wanted to return to work, initially part-
time. Here she was unusually fortunate: she had been so highly
regarded by her former employers that they were happy to have
her back on a part-time basis; and there was an excellent child-
care centre at the department store, where both Sarah and Harry
could be well cared for while Mary was working.

When Frank heard about Mary's plans, he became angry. To
him, Mary working part time was tantamount to her abandoning
her role as wife and mother. How, he demanded, could she
possibly give the children the care they needed, and meet his
needs also, if she was working outside the home?

Mary's initial reaction to Frank's anger was to abandon her
plans to work outside the home. However, within a few days she
became very depressed again, and Frank began to realize that he
had to endure either a depressed wife or a working wife. His
hostility turned to grudging acquiescence, and Mary started work.

Once she began working outside the home, Mary's depression

19

rapidly resolved. Her obsession with domestic perfection receded, and she suggested to Frank that they use some of her earnings to pay for someone to come in and do the routine domestic chores.

This suggestion evoked another outburst of rage from Frank, who insisted that Mary continue to personally fulfil her domestic obligations – even though he did almost no housework himself. By now, however, Mary's self-esteem had increased enough to release her from the idea that she could not survive without being married to Frank. Free from the tyranny of this false idea, she stood her ground.

Frank threatened divorce – a theat that he had previously used effectively to keep Mary in line. This time, she said that she had consulted her own lawyer. She asked an astonished Frank if he had looked carefully at what a divorce would cost him, financially and emotionally. Frank's bluff had been called. For the first time, he began to really listen to what Mary was saying, and to take her views seriously. He became willing to compromise further.

Gradually their relationship became more equal, and a genuine companionship began to emerge. When Harry was two years and three months old, Mary decided to resume full-time work. To her surprise, Frank supported her. He then astonished her by saying that he planned to change his job to a less demanding one, so that he could share the task of child-raising more equally with Mary. Although it would mean he had to take a drop in salary, this would be more than compensated for by Mary's income.

At this point, Mary and Frank decided that they didn't need any more contact with me. In fact, I had seen them only three times in the previous year. Although I have no further professional contact with them, I have heard that they are still together.

Implications of the Case

Mary's case illustrates many of the issues that married women must grapple with if they are to avoid becoming depressed or even developing a psychiatric disorder. I will briefly summarize the most important of these.

Trapped by a Rigid Belief System

Traditional Anglo-Saxon culture is still the major force shaping attitudes and behaviour in English-speaking countries. An important historical influence on Anglo-Saxon culture was the feudal system, a rigid hierarchy in which the authority of the Lord of the Manor was absolute. The Lord of the Manor delegated authority to the male head of each household, creating a powerful and pervasive patriarchy within which women and children had few rights. Because authority was absolute, it was futile to question the social order, or the beliefs that sustained it.

Although the feudal system has been replaced by democracy, all societies have a powerful tendency to preserve traditional beliefs and values. A large number of people in English-speaking countries still cling to beliefs that have their origins in feudal times. One of the most powerful of these beliefs holds that women do not have equal rights with men. Even in North America, with its celebration of democracy, these beliefs still prevail. If anyone doubts this, let them recall the defeat of recent attempts to change the American Constitution to give women fully equal rights. Conservative women's groups were crucial in defeating the Equal Rights Amendment. This suggests that women themselves agree with the idea that they do not deserve to be fully equal with men.

The idea that women's rights and needs are secondary to those of men is profoundly destructive. Unless women challenge this idea, it will continue to reinforce all the other beliefs about women, and especially the idea that a woman is somehow incomplete without a man to protect and support her. If these false beliefs persist, women like Mary will continue to be trapped in homes within which their suburban dream has become a nightmare.

The Pitfalls of Medical Help

The medical profession is highly conservative. Many doctors, especially older men, have very traditional views of women's roles. Such doctors are unlikely to see that married women not working outside the home often have many reasons to be depressed and anxious. Instead they will usually agree with the suffering wife that it is somehow *her* fault that she is depressed. This belief is backed up with a prescription for tranquillizers or antidepressants: taking medicine is a clear message that it is something *inside* that has gone wrong.

Sadly, psychiatrists and other mental-health workers are not immune from such beliefs. The still very popular psychoanalytic or Freudian approach can be particularly unhelpful to married women trapped in unhappy domestic situations. The focus of psychoanalytic therapy is initially on childhood events rather than what is happening in the here and now. This historical focus may actually reinforce patients' self-blame (at least to begin with), and make it less likely that they will be able to recognize and confront the real issues in their lives. For these reasons, married women in difficult domestic situations should be very careful in their choice of therapist.

The Power Struggle Within Marriage

Once married with children, women like Mary tend to define themselves through their roles as wives and mothers. These roles become basic to their sense of identity. A challenge to the role is a challenge to the basic sense of self. It is this which makes it so difficult for women like Mary to challenge the beliefs upon which their lives rest. Rather than confront marital problems, they tend to deny them or blame themselves for their occurrence.

It is natural and commonplace for women with a traditional view of gender roles to marry men who have similar attitudes. Research shows clearly that men tend to be more conservative than women regarding gender issues. Within a marriage of two people who share the same traditional belief system, there is little to challenge the basic assumption that the wife is subordinate to her husband.

When a crisis leads to a request for professional help, an opportunity is created for unhelpful beliefs to be confronted. Usually, because the wife is much more vulnerable to psychiatric symptoms, or because she takes the responsibility for 'repairing' the marriage, she is the first to enter therapy. If she is fortunate enough to find a therapist who is sensitive to women's issues, then it is inevitable that therapy will begin to challenge the rigid beliefs about sex roles that have constrained her thus far.

Once this starts to happen, conflict with the husband is almost inevitable. Generally, husbands should be involved in couples therapy early on, but this is not always possible. Sometimes, it is definitely not appropriate. Even if it is, many therapists have been trained exclusively to conduct individual therapy, and are unable or unwilling to offer a couples approach.

Working through these issues together in therapy is the best way for most couples to resolve them. Even when this happens, conflict is inevitable: the husband will not easily relinquish the assumption of superiority within the marriage. It is not uncommon for husbands to refuse to change their views. When this occurs, the wife's situation is unlikely to change much unless she finds the courage to leave the marriage or at least creates for herself the option of doing so.

Husbands who are willing to change their views often benefit enormously. By sharing domestic and work roles more equally with their wives, they can often reduce the time that they spend in their breadwinner role. Where their jobs are boring or difficult and frustrating, this can only be to their benefit.

I recently read a newspaper article about a married man who had no less than three jobs: he worked a total of over eighty hours a week. His wife, the mother of two teenage children, did not work outside the home. She complained about the financial pressures that forced her husband to work so hard. It had apparently never occurred to either her husband or herself that *she* might go to work. So rigid was this couple's belief system that it seriously threatened the husband's health and well-being. But it was easier for the couple to continue in this self-destructive way rather than change their beliefs.

The journalist who wrote the article made no attempt to point out that an obvious solution to this couple's dilemma would have been a degree of role-sharing. Instead, he took the couple's view that they were the victims of an uncaring government that made it more difficult for couples to survive on a single income. He tacitly supported the idea that the wife should not work outside the home. This is just one example of the many ways in which the media tend to reinforce a traditional view of gender roles.

Mother Care Versus Other Care

The question of the best care for young children is probably the issue that causes most difficulty for women trying to create more flexible gender roles. Social pressures on women with pre-school children to be full-time mothers are still almost overwhelming. Mothers who work are unfairly blamed for a whole range of social ills, from juvenile delinquency to drug addiction.

There has been a fair amount of research comparing 'mother care' with 'other care'. The facts are quite clear. There is no evidence that, beyond the age of about twelve months, alternatives to mother care are harmful to children. If anything, the reverse is true: for example, good child-care centres offer a range of opportunities for children's personal growth and development which are beyond a mother on her own.

As Mary's case illustrates, full-time mothers almost inevitably become irritable and frustrated with their young children to the point of screaming at them, and smacking is common. This makes the mother feel guilty, the more so when she has an idealized, unrealistic view of motherhood that requires her to be constantly patient, affectionate and nurturing. Out of this guilt emerges a determination to try even harder to be a perfect mother, with inevitable failure. This leads to a vicious cycle whereby feelings of guilt and inadequacy increase together with frustration and irritability. As part of this, the children are exposed to a confusing mixture of solicitude and anger. Their own irritability increases, making it even more difficult for the mother to manage them. The problem then escalates further until help is sought or some other outside intervention occurs. In such situations, it is usually better for children to see less of their mother, although this suggestion may increase the mother's sense of guilt and inadequacy, initially at least. If, while away from her children, the mother can do things that restore her sense of usefulness and well-being – and, for most women, this means paid work – then she will become far more effective at meeting her children's needs when she is with them. The children can only benefit from such an arrangement.

Sex-role Beliefs, Paid Work and Compulsory Relationships

Recent research has helped to clarify the relationship between the level of psychiatric disorder married women experience and their attitudes to paid work. Married women employed outside the home *by choice* show the lowest level of psychiatric disorder. At about 5 per cent, it is comparable to that reported by their husbands. Women who do not wish to work outside the home, but who do so for compelling financial reasons, report a level of psychiatric disorder of 20–25 per cent. Of those women who choose a full-time domestic role, some 30 per cent report psychiatric disorder. *The highest levels, at least 40 per cent*, are reported by women who would prefer to work outside the home but who remain full-time wives and mothers *because they feel compelled to do so*. Most commonly, these feelings of compulsion arise from their own or their husbands' unrealistic, stereotyped beliefs about the maternal role.

Such findings underline the importance of paid work outside the home to the well-being of married women. Those who reluctantly work outside the home for purely financial reasons report less psychiatric disorder than those who choose a full-time domestic role. This suggests that even in women who experience conflict over it, work outside the home exerts a positive effect that is strong enough to outweigh the negative effects of this conflict. Of course, the nature of paid work is important in determining its contribution to psychological well-being. Common sense suggests that full-time work of a physical, repetitive, boring and menial type is of limited benefit for married women. If full-time work means returning home exhausted and irritable, and then having to carry out domestic chores, part-time work is likely to be a better choice. This dilemma is one faced mainly by working-class women with limited education. Recent research has confirmed that in such circumstances, part-time work has greater psychological benefits than full-time employment.

Women who choose not to work outside the home generally have a traditional attitude to sex roles. It is clear that they frequently experience depression and anxiety in relation to the demands and constraints of full-time motherhood. But when they do, they tend to blame themselves. Because they have identified

25

so strongly with idealized, stereotyped notions of motherhood and wifeliness, they believe that adherence to such ideas is the only path to happiness. The possibility that these ideas are actually causing their depression and anxiety rarely occurs to them. Husbands generally share their wives' views; in fact, they tend to be even more traditional. As a result, both wife and husband agree that the wife *should* be happy. After all, she has everything that she always wanted: children, a pleasant home, and a hard-working, reliable husband – of whom she probably sees very little. The husband often blames the wife for not being happy. This adds to her own guilt and self-blame, and these in turn add to her depression and anxiety. Trapped in a vicious cycle, her depression, guilt and self-directed anger increase progressively until she finds a way to interrupt the circular process.

Although such women may recognize, especially after some counselling or therapy, that a full-time domestic role is unhealthy for them and their children, guilt paralyses them. It stops them from departing from the traditions that have been instilled in them, especially if these traditions are firmly endorsed by their husbands. Any deviation from stereotyped roles not only creates guilt in women with traditional ideas of marriage and mother-hood, it threatens their idea of *togetherness*. This notion is often fundamental to them. It is based on the idea of the mother as the emotional and practical centre of domestic life. But this idea works only if the mother is there as a facilitator, encouraging children to become more independent as they grow older, which means accepting that she will see progressively less of them. For many women with traditional sex-role beliefs, togetherness means not only emotional harmony and intimacy between themselves and family members, but the frequent presence of family members around them. If togetherness so defined is absent, these women tend to blame themselves. They believe that more closeness will arise naturally if they improve their performance of traditional roles. If this does not happen, they blame themselves even more for the lack of togetherness in the family. This adds yet another twist to the vicious cycle of depression, anxiety, guilt and self-directed anger that is so often present.

Some women in this situation become so desperate that they demand togetherness. They demand it from their children and they demand it from their husbands. Of course, togetherness cannot be created on request: it must arise spontaneously. Demands for togetherness often create an effect opposite to that intended, with family members withdrawing from the wife-mother. This is especially true of sons and husbands, whose socialization tends not to make it easy for them to experience togetherness as an intimate, emotional experience. Married women in this situation may become very depressed, or may develop other severe psychiatric disorders. This stops them from carrying out their domestic roles adequately, at least in terms of their own very high standards. Because a full-time domestic role is central to their adjustment and well-being, failure to carry it out properly adds to their depression, anxiety and sense of failure. Eventually, they may become chronic psychiatric patients, attend-ing a clinic or private psychiatrist and spending regular periods in a psychiatric hospital. By this stage, they have exchanged a full-time domestic role for that of a psychiatric patient. As chronic patients they are able to achieve a measure of togetherness, but it is motivated by family members' concern for their health rather than by a spontaneous desire. It is compulsory rather than voluntary.

It is clear that women with strongly traditional sex-role beliefs are those at most risk for compulsory relationships, of which chronic psychiatric disorder is a common surface manifestation. Such women are at increased risk for a whole range of relationship difficulties, including domestic violence and morbid jealousy. Once their relationships have become compulsory, the chances of escaping them are remote. The only realistic solution to these problems lies in prevention. But social pressures reinforcing traditional sex-role attitudes are still very powerful, and the true facts about sex-role issues are extraordinarily difficult to obtain. For example, although there is overwhelming evidence for the psychological benefits to married women of paid work, this knowledge is not widespread in the community. Instead, attitudes to married women's employment are determined largely by myths and stereotypes, frequently reinforced by the popular media. The most potent and destructive of these myths concerns the belief that young children suffer if their mothers work outside the home. Although what objective evidence exists suggests that the reverse is generally true, awareness of this evidence in the community at large is very limited. The true facts about mother care versus other care and the benefits of paid work are obscured from most women. The extent to which this occurs has surprised and puzzled me ever since I first discovered it in my clinical work. It is a mystery that I attempt to solve in the chapters that follow, particularly in Chapter 6. The issue is a crucial one, because without full and free access to the facts, there can be no valid decisions and no true freedom of choice.

2

Men Who Cannot Live Without Women

Although women experience psychiatric disorder nearly twice as often as men, the situation is reversed for physical disorders. Death rate is the ultimate measure of physical health: in Western countries, men's annual death rate is *double* that of women. In other words, twice as many men than women die each year. Although there are slight differences between the various Western countries, Western men die at an average age of 72–73, whereas women die at an average of about 79–80. The gap is about *seven years*, and this gap has remained remarkably constant over the past three decades.

Why are men so accepting of these seven lost years? Why are they not demonstrating on the streets demanding the right to live as long as women? Why, when women live an average seven years longer than men, are Western societies increasing the emphasis on specialized women's health centres? If death rate is the most important index of health, then it is men rather than women who need more health care. The remarkable fact that men do not get this extra health care, and seem not to want it, is a paradox that will be explored in this chapter.

There are many reasons why Western men die younger than Western women. But there is one basic underlying theme: men, in general, do not take enough care of their physical or emotional health. One major reason for this is that men expect (or allow) women to do it for them. Of course, it is unrealistic to allow someone else to take responsibility for one's own physical and emotional health, and this is why the arrangement does not work. The failure of this arrangement is one of the most sinister and destructive aspects of the current relationship between men and women.

Men Who Deny the Feminine Within

Men's failure to take enough responsibility for their emotional and physical health originates in their denial of the feminine within them. To understand this, it is necessary to comprehend how children are socialized in Western society, and to be aware of how greatly this process differs for men and women.

In Western societies, young children are raised almost exclusively by women. Infant boys naturally identify with their primary care-givers – usually their mothers or other female relatives. As part of the normal process of psychological development, young boys incorporate within themselves, or *internalize*, the attributes of those with whom they spend most of their time. This process of internalizing mainly female attributes is central to psychological development in the first four years of boys' lives. As a result, they come to strongly *identify* with their mothers.

For most boys, exclusive care by their mothers, or by other women in a domestic setting, comes to a sudden end when pre-school or kindergarten starts at age 3–4. Suddenly, little boys must learn to relate to other children and adults in a fairly large group. They move from the relative privacy of their homes to the public arena. Because gender differences are so marked in English-speaking countries, little boys are expected to behave in public quite differently from little girls, and to associate mainly with other little boys. As part of this, they must quickly abandon or suppress their primary identification with the mother. Instead, they must identify with men, and strive to behave, feel and think as they believe little boys should. This means becoming more aggressive, assertive and independent. It also means strongly suppressing any tendency to show timidity, fear or anxiety, to shed tears, or to be overtly caring and affectionate.

For a boy who has a warm, close relationship with his father, or with another male figure, the task of abandoning the basic identification with his mother is not insurmountable. Gradually, he comes to identify with his father or the equivalent man in his life, and to internalize many of his attributes. These internalized 'masculine' attributes slowly and systematically blend with the earlier 'feminine' ones. This lays the basis for a robust, positive sense of personal identity in which male and female elements are adequately balanced.

The sequence of events is quite different in boys who have little or no intimate contact with their fathers or equivalent male figures. Sadly, this probably applies to the majority of boys in America and other English-speaking countries. Surveys have repeatedly shown that the average father spends only a small fraction of his time directly relating to his children. Often, fathers relate to their children indirectly, through their wives. In such circumstances, when a young boy seeks to reduce his identification with his mother, he has no adequate male figure with whom to identify. He cannot internalize the male attributes of a father who is a real person, with foibles, weaknesses, fears and anxieties that are both endearing and frustrating. As a result, he cannot blend internalized male attributes with his pre-existing female ones.

The Suppression of the Inner Self

To resolve this dilemma, boys in such a situation rely on *images of manhood* obtained from the media and from popular mythology and fiction. These images are unreal; they are idealized, one-dimensional distortions of manhood. In the formation of such images, all the 'macho' or stereotyped aspects of manhood tend to be exaggerated. The emphasis is on sporting and financial success, power and control. When these images are internalized, they cannot blend with earlier female internalizations. They are too harsh and rigid. Instead, *these earlier female internalizations are ruthlessly suppressed*. They are totally incompatible with the false, stereotyped images of manhood that displace them.

Once this crucial process of suppressing internalized female attributes occurs, a constriction of the personality begins. There is great difficulty in exploring or acknowledging the inner self, and especially in acknowledging tender, caring feelings, or feelings of weakness and dependency. As part of this, there is nearly always a rigid adherence to stereotyped, fixed beliefs about male and female roles. Such beliefs are termed *sex-role stereotypes*. I will outline shortly the destructive effects on men's health of sex-role stereotypes.

The development of personal identity in women is very different, because they are rarely required to abandon or suppress their primary identification with their mothers. For them, the task

31

of internalizing male attributes is a less fundamental one, which means that it is generally somewhat easier for women to develop a robust personal identity than it is for men (see *The Reproduction of Mothering* by Nancy Chodorow). Of course, women have their own difficulties in identity formation, and I will discuss some of these in Chapters 6 and 9.

Destructive Effects of Sex-role Stereotyping

A 'stereotype' is a rigid and oversimple way of seeing a person that is based not on the *true* qualities of that person, but on the characteristics attributed to the group or class to which the person belongs. The commonest stereotypes relate to race, age and sex roles.

The Civil Rights movement in America has challenged the habitual use of racial stereotypes, at least in public. Movements such as Grey Power are challenging our negative stereotypes about old age. But, although Women's Liberation has been a vigorous social force over the past twenty years, negative stereotyping of women remains widespread in public and private. This is mainly because sex-role stereotypes are so deeply ingrained in English-speaking societies that they are unconsciously accepted by men and women alike. This makes it difficult for many people to understand that their use is destructive. The following anecdote demonstrates this.

A boy and his father had an automobile accident in which the father was instantly killed. The son survived with severe injuries and was rushed to the nearest hospital that had facilities for major surgery. The senior trauma surgeon was called to examine the boy, but on doing so said, 'I cannot operate on this boy because he is my son.'

When asked to explain this, nearly everyone refers to step-fathers or adoptive fathers, rarely arriving without help at the correct answer: the surgeon is the boy's *mother*.

Occupational stereotyping, exemplified by the automatic assumption that trauma surgeons are men, is just one aspect of a pervasive, persistent sex-role stereotyping that seeks to rigidly and narrowly define women's behaviour and place in society. The destructive and limiting effects of this on women are fairly obvious. Much less obvious are the destructive effects of sex-role stereotyping on men, but they are even more harmful. I will now outline some of them.

Denial of dependency

Men who have stereotyped ideas about sex roles believe that men are basically tough, independent creatures who are well suited to manage in the world alone. The reality is different. Such men actually rely greatly on the presence of women to preserve their image of themselves as strong, powerful and independent. They form relationships mainly with women who are as stereotyped in their beliefs as they are. Such women are happy to adopt a submissive posture which allows them to feel protected by the image of the strong man that they themselves have helped to create.

The need for highly stereotyped men to have a woman dependent on them comes from their suppression of the feminine within. Suppressing the feminine is hard work. It requires constant vigilance for the threat from within of anything regarded as 'feminine'. This includes thoughts and feelings of weakness, vulnerability, fear, anxiety, uncertainty, dependency, tenderness and warmth. When the process of suppressing unwanted psychological attributes becomes habitual or fixed, it is technically known as repression but, to avoid unnecessary confusion, I will use only the term suppression. The constant presence of a dependent, stereotypically feminine woman is vital to this process of suppression. By being 'super-feminine' this woman carries her male partner's femininity as well as her own. She allows him to project his denied femininity on to her. In turn, her denied 'masculine' attributes can be projected on to him, and he therefore carries her masculinity as well as his own.

Men are much more dependent on this arrangement than women. Without the constant presence of a female partner they have to confront their buried feelings, or to experience the *emptiness within* that is the result of ruthlessly suppressing their feminine attributes. This feeling of emptiness is sometimes experienced as a sense of imminent fragmentation of the psyche, which is profoundly frightening. Men will do almost anything to

33

avoid it. Women are less likely to experience this inner emptiness or sense of psychic fragmentation, because they generally have no need to suppress their primary identification with their mother.

Murder-suicide

Strongly stereotyped relationships often end in violence. If the woman seeks to leave the relationship, the man's denial of his dependency makes it impossible for him to openly state his need for her. Instead, he will often use violence or threats of violence to keep her in the relationship. It is now common to read in the media reports about men who kill the women who have left them, and then kill themselves: the murder-suicide. This is the ultimate in men's denial of dependency: unable to openly express his profound need for the woman, such a man kills her in order to obliterate the pain of not possessing her. But, because he cannot live without her, he then kills himself. For women, living with such a man is the ultimate form of compulsory relationship.

Drug Abuse

When women are worried or depressed, they usually cope by talking about their problems to other women, although this becomes difficult or impossible if they are socially isolated. Talking generally makes them feel better, and often leads to constructive solutions. Men who are worried, stressed, or in a state of personal conflict are much less likely than women to openly discuss their problems and acknowledge related feelings of depression and anxiety. If they do, they are far more likely to talk with a woman than with another man. But instead of talking, men tend to try and *avoid* the emotional pain and sense of vulnerability that accompanies open and honest discussion of personal problems. They often cope by *distracting* themselves from their painful thoughts and feelings, or by *suppressing* them using drugs, especially alcohol. This is partly because they find their inner world an alien, confusing and frightening place.

The Epidemiologic Catchment Area survey mentioned in Chapter 1 has shown that alcohol abuse or dependency is over five times more common in men than it is in women. Abuse of, or dependency on, illicit drugs such as cannabis, amphetamines and cocaine, is nearly three times more common in men.

Alcohol abuse in men is encouraged further by the stereotype that it is manly to drink. For many stereotyped men, the only way they can feel close to other men is to drink with them. Obviously, using alcohol or illicit drugs to manage personal problems is a bad strategy, since it not only fails to solve the original problem, but adds to it through the profoundly destructive effects of drug abuse.

The abuse of drugs, including alcohol and tobacco, is a major factor in shortening men's lives. Nearly all the causes of death that afflict men more commonly than women are strongly related to the abuse of alcohol, tobacco and illicit drugs. This crucial topic will be discussed more fully in Chapters 3 and 4.

Health Care and Diet Problems

A marked division of labour over health-care matters exists in most marriages. This division of labour ranges from the obvious, such as preparing 'healthy' food, to the more subtle matter of emotional health. Even in the 1990s, married women take nearly all the responsibility for preparing household meals. The media, and especially women's magazines, put enormous emphasis on healthy eating. It is now common for people to believe that 'we are what we eat'. According to this belief, unless we eat healthy food, we cannot be healthy ourselves.

The reality is quite different. For example, a recent study found that permanently adhering to a diet aimed at keeping blood cholesterol at recommended levels would increase the average person's life span by only 3–4 months. But the belief in 'healthy foods' has become so widespread that many people directly equate food with health. As a result, married women who prepare the family meals often feel directly responsible for the health of their husbands and children. Buying and preparing so-called healthy food is often very time-consuming. It can become something of a tyranny for the married woman who feels that she must do it. And it can become even more of a tyranny for the family who feel compelled to eat the products.

The net result of women's attempts to get their children and husbands to eat 'healthy' foods is sometimes destructive. Husbands come to resent constant harassment to abandon tasty fried food and meat in favour of less palatable salads and vegetables. Because husbands themselves are not active participants in the process, but feel that it is imposed on them, they often acquire a negative attitude to healthy eating. For example, when their wives are not around, they may binge on forbidden foods – and feel guilty about it. Although this may briefly increase their blood cholesterol, this effect is much less important than the weight increase that occurs if forbidden foods are indulged in regularly. Scientists are generally agreed that obesity, especially when marked, significantly reduces life span.

If married men and women took more equal responsibility for food preparation and cooking in the home, this absurd situation would largely cease to exist. Men could become much more interested in the whole debate about nutrition, and, as a result, would be better able to choose their diets in an informed and rational manner. They would not feel dependent on women to do it for them.

Men whose self-image is a stereotyped one of toughness and invulnerability will often abuse their bodies through excessive physical work or violent sports. They may deny or overlook symptoms of injury until they can barely function. If they finally become partially disabled, and unable to work or play sport in their usual way, they commonly develop severe depression and anxiety which interacts with their physical disabilities. These men often expect their wives to devote themselves to looking after them and, where wives are willing to do this, the husbands not uncommonly become chronic invalids. But the origins of their invalidity are as much psychological as physical.

As with healthy eating, women who feel responsible for their men's physical health may make it difficult for them to take on this responsibility for themselves. Because of this, such men will continue with unhealthy lifestyles or doing things that are bad for their health – knowing that their wives will nurse them if they become ill or incapacitated. More seriously, because they have not personally explored issues about their health, these men find it very difficult to cope with symptoms of potentially fatal illnesses such as heart disease or cancer. They tend to deny or ignore these symptoms – just as they deny many of their feelings – until they have a heart attack, or until the cancer is too far advanced for treatment to be effective.

Homophobia

Homophobia means a fear of homosexuals or of being a homosexual. It is very common in men generally, and almost universal in men who have a sex-role stereotyped view of human relationships.

The essence of homophobia is the habitual suppression of warm, tender, loving feelings, especially towards men. Stereotyped men fear strong feelings of this kind towards anyone, whether man or woman. Such feelings threaten to expose the feared, rejected feminine within. However, they are usually manageable when felt towards a woman – although they may never be *expressed*, which is, of course, a complaint that women have about men in general. But if they are felt toward another man – panic ensues!

This panic that men often experience when confronted for the first time with tender, affectionate feelings toward another man is so common that it has its own clinical term – predictably enough, 'Homosexual Panic'. In a sex-role stereotyped world, men are not supposed to have tender feelings, especially toward each other. Stereotyped men who have this experience believe it to be an abnormal, deviant one that is 'feminine'. In their stereotyped world, this means homosexual, a notion that evokes fear and disgust.

Not only do stereotyped men panic about such dangerous, 'deviant' feelings, but they struggle to avoid experiencing them with men again. Especially, they avoid social situations where they are alone with another man for any length of time. This makes it impossible for them to develop close intimate relationships with other men. This also means that they cannot learn from their less stereotyped peers about other ways of relating to men. Worst of all, these men are left feeling that only women can be close, intimate companions – yet another factor that encourages stereotyped men to be dependent on women, a dependency that they are compelled to deny.

Sex-role stereotyping has other harmful effects on men's emotional and physical well-being. These include the preoccupation with being competitive and 'successful', even if this means working extraordinarily long hours, to the exclusion of all other interests; the need to be constantly in control, and to have power over others; and difficulty in acknowledging or expressing feelings, or in allowing others to freely express them. The following case history illustrates many of the negative effects of sex-role stereotyping on men.

Case 2: The Hollow Man

Michael's mother Cathy was an attractive woman of great intelligence and ability. As a child, she had a passion for music, but this was not appreciated or encouraged by her family until her maternal grandmother returned from overseas and came to stay with them when Cathy was eleven.

Cathy's grandmother persuaded Cathy's parents to buy her a piano, and from then on Cathy played and practised as often as she could. Her talent was recognized by her piano teacher, herself a woman of great musical ability. With her support and guidance, Cathy obtained a place at a prestigious music college. Here, she quickly became recognized as one of the most promising students. Her teachers and peers assumed that she would proceed to a successful career as a concert pianist.

Cathy was well on the way to this when, aged twenty, she met Stephen at a party. They both felt an immediate strong attraction to each other. Cathy had worked so hard at her music that she had almost no social life, mixing only with her small circle of college friends and acquaintances. She had not found the time nor inclination for a sexual relationship. But meeting Stephen evoked within her feelings that forced her to recognize the powerful sexuality which she had previously suppressed.

The effect of this on Cathy was profound. The passion that she had felt toward her music was transferred on to Stephen. She lost interest in her studies and, instead of practising, thought constantly of Stephen, craving to be with him. Stephen was four years older than Cathy and quite sexually experienced, but even he was surprised – and flattered – by Cathy's fierce sexuality. Sometimes they made love all night. The next day, even if Cathy had the desire to practise, she was too exhausted and distracted to do so.

Cathy's teachers were horrified at the change in her. Instead of being supportive and understanding, they were critical. They threatened to suspend her unless she attended and practised regularly. This made Cathy bitter, and she had mixed feelings about resuming her studies, when after a few months, her passion for Stephen began to exhaust itself. And so, when Stephen suggested that they get married, Cathy saw this as a welcome alternative to returning immediately to music college. But she was sure that she would resume her music career, probably some-where else, when her life was more settled.

Although Stephen was an attractive, sensual man, he was less intelligent than Cathy. He was ambitious, but his job was rather boring and not well paid. The couple bought a house soon after getting married, and money was short, so Cathy worked full time as a receptionist in a nearby motel. When Cathy was twenty-three, Michael was born. He was a small, sickly baby who failed to thrive and frequently suffered from ear and chest infections. Cathy was constantly preoccupied with Michael's health, especially after he stopped breathing and went blue one afternoon when he was four months old. Although he started breathing again spontaneously, he was admitted to hospital for observations. Although the paediatrician could find nothing wrong, he was unable to reassure Cathy and Stephen that further episodes would not occur.

As a result, Cathy was in a state of perpetual anxiety about Michael, and her own health suffered. This stopped her from resuming part-time work as she had planned. Stephen was forced to change his job for one that allowed him to earn more money, but the only one that he could find required very long hours. He left home early in the morning and returned, exhausted, late in the evening. Cathy had to carry the entire burden of looking after Michael and the home.

None of the couple's parents was able to help them financially, and money continued to be very short in spite of Stephen's long hours at work. When Cathy's cheap piano finally deteriorated beyond repair, they could not afford to buy a replacement. The chances of Cathy resuming her musical career appeared more and more remote, and she became increasingly disappointed, resentful and despondent about this.

Michael's Overprotection

Michael's health improved steadily from about fifteen months. By age two he had become an attractive, lively and intelligent child, healthy apart from a continuing proneness to chest infections. Cathy found that devoting herself to Michael lessed the pain that she felt about the loss of her musical career. Instead of dreaming about becoming a success herself, she began to dream about Michael's success.

Stephen had coped badly with Michael's poor health as an infant. Believing that the child might well not survive to his first birthday, Stephen had protected himself from the pain of anticipated loss and grief by detaching himself emotionally from Michael. But when Michael's health improved, Stephen was unable to feel close to him, probably because Stephen's own father had been cold, remote and critical toward him. Often, Stephen was irritated and disturbed by Michael's presence. Michael sensed this, and withdrew emotionally from his father. Because of his poor relationship with Michael, Stephen welcomed Cathy's willingness to take exclusive responsibility for Michael's upbringing.

Even though Michael's health continued to improve, Cathy was grossly overprotective of him. She would not allow him to mix with other children in case he caught infections from them. He saw almost nothing of his father, for whom he had little affection. His mother was virtually his sole companion.

Initially, Cathy had dreamed that Michael would become the famous pianist that she had once hoped to be. But the child was not the least bit interested in music, and appeared not to have inherited his mother's musical ability. Cathy was angry and resentful about Michael's lack of interest, but she disguised her anger toward him by increasing her overprotectiveness. Michael sensed his mother's heavily disguised hostility toward him, and managed his feelings of rejection by clinging to her. The time that Cathy and Michael spent together was rarely spent constructively

40

or having fun. Cathy's overprotectiveness served only to imprison Michael, and to stop him from forming relationships with other people. From a psychological perspective, it meant that the personal attributes that he had internalized were the feminine ones of his mother, with whom he strongly identified.

The Learning of Machismo

Reluctantly, Cathy enrolled Michael in school when he was five. Predictably, he was much more comfortable relating to the girls in his class. On the first day, he joined the girls at their play. Although silently puzzled, they were happy to let him play with them. In the afternoon, some of the little boys called him names like 'faggot', 'wimp' and 'sissy'. Although Michael didn't understand what they all meant, he knew that they were critical and hostile terms, and he went home confused and distressed.

When Michael told Cathy about his first day, she became angry. 'Of course you mustn't play with the girls, you stupid boy. It's not healthy. You must play with the boys tomorrow.' And the next day, Michael played with the boys. But he didn't understand or enjoy their rough games. He looked enviously at the girls playing games that were much more interesting. Of course, each time he showed an interest in playing with the girls, he was ridiculed by the boys.

To cope with his inner confusion and anxiety, Michael began to behave like the other boys. He started to tease and disparage the girls, and emulated those of his male peers who seemed to be most successful at being little boys. These were inevitably the more aggressive and dominant ones. Michael took on these attributes, and exaggerated them. Within a few months, his transformation was complete. He had become aggressive and unruly, constantly competing with other boys for attention from the teachers and for leadership of the 'gangs' that formed and re-formed. He had ruthlessly suppressed all the attributes within him that he now regarded as 'womanish' and totally unacceptable. His natural feelings of warmth, tenderness and compassion had been buried deep within him. Instead, when he had feelings at all, they were mainly of anger or fear. But Michael came to regard fear and anxiety as 'unmanly', and so he struggled to bury those feelings also. Sadly, what Michael thought to be proper 'manly' behaviour was, in reality, a rigid stereotype, a boyhood version of 'machismo'.

At home, Michael's behaviour changed also. He began to distance himself emotionally and physically from his mother, and became disobedient of her. He looked to his father for clues about how boys should behave and feel. But Stephen had got into the habit of working very long hours, including weekends, and Michael saw almost nothing of him. When they were together, Stephen still felt awkward and uncomfortable with the boy, and he tried to avoid spending time with him. They never played together or went on trips alone.

Not having a father or any other adult male with whom he could identify, Michael internalized the 'masculine' attributes that he saw portrayed on TV and in the comics. He continued to ruthlessly suppress any aspects of his inner world that he regarded as weak or feminine. His inner life came to consist mainly of day-dreams about becoming a rich, powerful and famous man.

Cathy had become chronically depressed, but she did not realize it. She had been pregnant twice more, but had miscarried on both occasions. These losses had increased her sadness and depression. When she and Stephen finally agreed to have no more children, Cathy was too depressed to play any role for herself other than that of full-time mother and housewife. Although Stephen sometimes resented the very long hours that he worked as the sole family breadwinner, he had ceased to enjoy family life. He found Cathy's company irritating and depressing. He disliked spending time with his son. Work, although rather routine and dull, was actually a welcome alternative to spending time at home.

In spite of her chronic depression, Cathy struggled to exercise her lively intelligence. She read widely, and played a little on the piano that they had been able to afford when Michael was six. Michael himself continued to show no interest in music. Cathy had no social life. The women in her neighbourhood who worked tended to look down on her as a full-time mother, assuming that they would have nothing in common. But Cathy found the other full-time mothers boring and tedious, because their lives appeared to revolve around domestic and social trivia.

Having such an empty, unfulfilled personal life, Cathy started to live by proxy, through her dreams about the success of her son. She had finally accepted that he wouldn't be a famous pianist, but now she dreamed of him becoming a successful politician.

His mother's dreams, and her constant encouragement of him to be competitive and successful, fuelled Michael's own fantasies about power and fame. He did very well at school in sport, and was also good academically. The only time Michael's father took any interest in him was when he had a sporting or academic success. This added further weight to Michael's belief that he had to be constantly competitive, and that winning was everything.

Love and Early Marriage

Michael got into a prestigious college and did well enough to enter a famous graduate school that groomed people for business careers. He had grown into a tall, strong, handsome young man. Very attractive to women, he had become a womanizer, with a reputation for sexually exploiting women and then ruthlessly discarding them. But towards the end of his time at business school, he met Jane, a strikingly beautiful woman who was studying for a nursing degree. They fell in love and married a year later, when Michael was twenty-three and Jane twenty-two.

Jane did not really enjoy nursing. In fact, she was strongly ambivalent about the whole idea of a career for herself. Once she and Michael were married, she readily abandoned her own personal aspirations and began to live for and through Michael. She dreamed of being the wife of a rich and powerful man, and devoted all her time and energy to helping Michael achieve these goals.

With both of them working together at the same goals, Michael's business career flourished. At thirty, he was already wealthy. Although the couple by then had two children, a boy and a girl, they were cared for by a series of live-in nannies, and they saw little of their parents. In his early thirties, Michael got involved in politics and by thirty-five he had become a prominent figure, tipped by many for high office.

Michael had lost interest in Jane sexually only two or three years after they married, and they made love only occasionally. Like his father, he worked very long hours, and had little time or energy for sexual relationships, although he had two brief affairs that he kept secret from Jane. He ended those with the same emotional detachment and ruthlessness that enabled him to be so successful in business and politics. Jane had been so busy helping Michael build his career that she had not greatly missed the sexual side of their relationship. But she was sexually possessive of Michael, and would have been shattered to discover that he had been unfaithful to her. Although Michael knew this, at thirty-six he allowed himself to begin a third affair, this time with a beautiful young woman not unlike a younger version of Jane. Strive as he did to remain emotionally detached from her, he became more attracted to the woman than he planned. He took risks. He was indiscreet. One evening, Jane paid an unexpected visit to his office. She found Michael and the young woman making passionate love on the sofa-bed that Michael kept in an adjoining room.

Jane stormed out of the office in a rage. She immediately rang her lawyer and told him to file for a divorce. The lawyer suggested that she think again about this, because of Michael's public image. Having calmed down a little she agreed to hold off for a while, although she told Michael that she was filing for a divorce and wanted him to move out of the house at once.

Through abject apologies and repeatedly begging forgiveness, Michael persuaded Jane to withdraw her divorce threat and allow him to continue living under the same roof. His public image was safe. But his private life began to fall apart.

The Downward Spiral

Jane withdrew all her emotional and domestic support for Michael. She also withdrew, over a period of weeks, from almost all her commitments to entertain and to attend public meetings on his behalf. She attended only those functions that were absolutely crucial to Michael's business activities and political campaigning. Although Michael was able to compensate for this by employing other people, he could not replace his wife's emotional and domestic support. He was used to Jane attending to his smallest personal needs: over the years, she had learned to anticipate most of them. Now, he found himself having to organize his clothing and meals in a way that had never been necessary before. But the

44

thing he missed most acutely was Jane's constant emotional support and her adulation of him, especially her belief that he was a special, brilliant, almost superhuman man who would inevitably become a famous leader. For the first time in his life he did not have a woman who was constantly present and who lived for him and through him; a woman who had abandoned her own personal aspirations and placed them on him; a woman willing to make endless personal sacrifices on his behalf – as long as he was on target to become a rich and successful man, a famous leader of the people.

Michael was devastated by the loss of Jane's support. He began to experience acutely frightening feelings of emptiness and inner fragmentation. These feelings were almost impossible to describe, but he felt as if he was about to physically implode. Although he knew this couldn't happen in reality, the feeling was so strong that reason was suspended and he feared that it might actually happen. So distressing and disturbing were these episodes that he found himself begging to die rather than experience them for a moment longer.

Michael refused to accept an emotional basis for these episodes and thought that he had a brain tumour. He told his physician that he had severe headaches, and wanted a brain scan. This proved normal but, rather than reassuring Michael, the negative finding made him think that he was going insane.

Michael alternated between emotional numbness and panicky fearfulness. Always a fairly heavy social drinker, he began to drink alone in order to block out his frightening feelings of emptiness, inner fragmentation and panic. His performance deteriorated, and this began to arouse public comment. Unable to cope with this, he drank even more heavily and started to abuse the tranquillizers prescribed by his physician. He became depressed. He stopped looking after himself. He accosted young women in bars. He was arrested for drunk driving. Finally, he allowed himself to be admitted to a private psychiatric hospital. He still clung to the hope that the destruction of his private life would not become public knowledge. Of course, it did, and the press made much of his 'breakdown' and psychiatric hospitalization.

Michael spent fourteen weeks in the psychiatric hospital. So heavy had his alcohol intake been that over a week was required just to manage the symptoms of acute alcohol withdrawal. It was discovered that Michael's alcohol abuse had caused a gastric ulcer, which had been bleeding. He needed medical treatment for this. While in hospital, his panic attacks subsided and his depression lessened. When he left, he had arranged to see a local psychiatrist (myself), initially on a twice-weekly basis. Jane had agreed to have him home.

Therapy: Filling the Emptiness Within

When Michael entered my consulting room for the first time, he was thin and haggard. He had grown a beard that made him look a little sinister. There was no trace of the raw energy, ambition and talent that had taken him so far in business and politics.

Michael told me that he had abandoned his political aspirations. Given the widespread prejudice toward those who suffer from mental illness which exists in English-speaking countries, he believed that he would never again have enough credibility to be successful as a political candidate. Although his business interests had been adversely affected by his fall from grace and his absence in hospital, he had been able to preserve a core business that was not very demanding on his time, and which provided an adequate income for him and his family. He explained that Jane had found a renewed interest in her career, and was currently doing a nursing refresher course. Once registered, she planned to resume full-time work. While talking about this he experienced a mild panic attack, and this allowed me to suggest a link between his panics and Jane's increasing independence from him.

Michael was able to explore his dependence on Jane and his denial of it – a denial that had been successful until Jane actually withdrew from her traditional role of supporting Michael. Although the feeling of inner emptiness or numbness continued to distress Michael, he gradually came to recognize feelings of compassion, warmth, tenderness, weakness and dependency that he had long buried. Initially, he experienced some of these feelings towards me, which, because of the professional, structured setting in which it occurred, made them less frightening than they would have been otherwise. After learning to talk about them he began to experience them towards others, including Jane

46

and his children. He even began to feel more positively about his mother, whom he had previously regarded as a neurotic, troublesome nuisance. Most surprising of all, he started to become interested in music, and took up playing the piano. He no longer regarded such interests as 'feminine' and beneath his dignity.

As Jane spent more time on her career, Michael spent more time looking after the children and performing domestic chores. To begin with, he had found it painfully difficult to be warm and loving with the children. However he gradually learned that experiencing and expressing such feelings was not dangerous and unhealthy, but a genuine and necessary aspect of being a reasonably mature, flexible man.

Michael ceased therapy after about eighteen months. He felt that he was no longer a 'hollow man'. He believed that he had come to acknowledge and even to value those 'feminine' attributes that he had previously tried to deny and bury. As a result, he was much less aggressive and competitive, and no longer so dependent on Jane for his emotional well-being. Overall, he felt happier, and was enjoying a range of activities and interests far broader than when he had been obsessed with success and achievement. He looked forward to the future, but not for the public status and recognition that he had previously craved. Instead, he planned to continue developing his friendships, family relationships, hobbies, and other interests. To Michael, success was now a personal, private thing that had little to do with the wealth, power and public acclaim that had once meant everything to him.

Implications of the Case: Prominent Men Model Sex-role Stereotypes

It might be thought that the problems of sex-role stereotyping that led to Michael's downfall are rare among successful and prominent men. In 1983, a paper called 'The marriage of the "collapsible" man of prominence', by H. Bird, P. Martin and A. Schuham, appeared in the prestigious *American Journal of Psychiatry* (140: 291–5). This paper was based on a study of sixteen men who needed urgent psychiatric treatment because they were in a state of acute emotional crisis and unable to function. These men were among the most successful in American society. Five were presidents of major public corporations; four were very successful and wealthy businessmen; two were prominent attorneys and one of these was also a politician; and three were senior, highly respected physicians or surgeons. All were regarded by their communities as wealthy and powerful men, and were easily recognizable in the local media.

The authors of the paper pointed out that all these men had ceased to function when their wives tried to relinquish or modify stereotyped roles that required them to live for and through their husbands. The men themselves appeared to have rather rigid, stereotyped views of sex roles.

In spite of a great deal of therapy, four of the marriages ended in divorce. Of the remaining twelve, nine were improved and three unchanged. Therapy did not focus on sex-role issues, but appears to have been aimed at restoring the men to their previous circumstances. This approach may have created guilt in their wives about their attempts at increased independence and self-determination. Therapy that specifically challenged the couples' sex-role stereotypes may have been more successful, but such an approach is still uncommon in psychiatry.

In conclusion, the authors of this exciting paper suggest that 'the marital relationship of men of prominence is a key determinant of their psychological functioning . . . a breakdown in this relationship results in dire consequences not only for the husband himself but for the community.'

I think that the implications of the paper go well beyond this conclusion, important though it is. It is to be expected that men of prominence often have a sex-role stereotyped view of personal relationships. In order to achieve prominence, they must devote themselves almost exclusively to their professional endeavours. They have little or no time to be involved in domestic or child-raising activities. This means that their wives are required to play an actively supportive role, inevitably abandoning or postponing their own personal aspirations. In a very real way, prominent men, and perhaps especially politicians, are providing powerful role models that endorse sex-role stereotyping.

This is of much concern to anyone who seeks a more balanced society with greater role-sharing and equality between men and women. But there is an even more worrying aspect to it. Sex-role stereotyping in men requires the suppression of 'feminine' attributes such as emotionality, anxiety, fearfulness, dependency, compassion, affection and tenderness. If our male leaders have learned to suppress such attributes within themselves, does this explain their apparent willingness to go to war?

Declaring a war inevitably means death, destruction and human anguish on a vast scale. For example, during the latest (1991) major war in the Middle East, ostensibly aimed at overthrowing Iraq's expansionist president, over 100,000 Iraqi soldiers were killed or seriously injured by overwhelmingly superior forces that were mainly American and British. Making decisions to unleash such horror must surely require the capacity to bury deeply any feelings of compassion and tenderness for those members of the human race who happen to be on the opposite side. If the ability to do this is intimately linked with sex-role stereotyping, then a reduction in stereotyping should decrease the willingness of a nation to declare war on another. I will develop this important theme in Chapter 7.

3

The Weaker Sex

In my attempts so far to trace the origins and effects of compulsory relationships, several themes have emerged. The most important concerns sex-role stereotypes, which seem to be intimately connected with compulsory relationships. Not everyone is greatly influenced by sex-role stereotypes. Most vulnerable to them are those with identity problems. For such people, using stereotypes to create a map of the social world protects them from having to deal with the reality of its intricacies and complexities. But those who regard stereotypes as an accurate reflection of social reality create for themselves a world that is harsh and inflexible. This is mirrored in their social life, and they are likely to form compulsory marriages or other forms of compulsory relationship. Children from such families tend to become as dependent on stereotypes as their parents, and in turn are likely to form compulsory relationships when they grow up. The link between sex-role stereotyping and compulsory relationships appears, than, to be a circular and mutually reinforcing one.

As I outlined in Chapter 2, men have greater problems than women in achieving a robust sense of personal identity. This makes them more susceptible than women to sex-role stereotyping and some of its destructive effects, and these contribute to men's raised mortality rates. If survival is a measure of strength, then men, not women, are the weaker sex. As we established in the previous chapter, Western women live, on average, about seven years longer than Western men. Such a remarkable fact deserves more detailed consideration, and this is the main object of the present chapter. Most of the figures quoted come from the USA, but, with the exception of higher American homicide rates, data from other English-speaking countries are very similar.

Men's Excess Mortality

Mortality rates are calculated as the number of deaths each year per 100,000 people. Overall, men die at twice the rate of women, but there are important differences across age groups. This is well illustrated in Table 1, based on the 108th edition of the *American National Data Book and Guide to Sources*.

Table 1. Annual Deaths per 100,000 People for Different Ages

	15–24	25–34	35–44	45–54	55–64	65–74	75–84
Men	152	190	287	667	1,650	3,660	8,300
Women	53	70	140	352	914	2,100	5,130

From Table 1 it is clear that in the age group 15–24, men die each year at *3 times* the rate of women: in other words, 30 men die for each 10 women. In the 25–34 age group, this ratio falls slightly to 2.7:1. This means that each year, 27 men die for every 10 women. In the 35–44 age group the ratio is 2:1. Thereafter, it falls slightly each decade until it reaches 1.6:1 in the 75–84 age group. Although the *average* mortality rate for men is over twice that for women, the excess mortality is much higher in younger men. But mortality rates in the younger age groups are comparatively low. This explains why, in spite of an average death rate twice that of women, men's life span is only 7 years less.

To understand why men do not survive as long as women, it is necessary to look at specific causes of death. Table 2 shows the seven causes of death that account for most of men's excess mortality.

Table 2. Main Causes of Men's Excess Mortality Rate

Cause of Death	Annual Death Rate per 100,000 People	
	Men	Women
Suicide	21	5
Homicide	14	4
Lung cancer	55	18
Motor vehicle accidents	29	10
All other accidents	27	13
Cirrhosis of liver	18	8
Heart disease	248	125

Table 2 shows that suicide, homicide and lung cancer are responsible for the greatest excess of male deaths over female deaths, with a ratio of 3:1 or more. Next are motor vehicle and other accidents, cirrhosis of the liver, and heart disease, all with a ratio of 2:1 or greater.

Suicide

Figures on suicide must be treated with caution. Different countries – and even different states – have different attitudes to suicide, and the means of gathering and defining the statistics vary widely. None the less, the following facts are in little dispute.

The overall suicide rate is at least *4 times* higher in Western men than in Western women. It has undoubtedly increased in young men age 15–25 over the last three decades. The increase varies greatly from country to country. Overall, it is at least 100 per cent, and is probably higher. In the USA, the suicide rate of 15–25-year-old men has at least *doubled* over the last thirty years: Currently, it is about 23 each year per 100,000 people. The rate among young women has remained fairly constant, and may even have decreased slightly: at present it is about 5 each year per 100,000 people.

Although the suicide rate among young men has increased, and is now over 20 each year per 100,000 people, it is still much lower than the rate in old men. For men age 65–74, the annual rate is about 33 per 100,000. For women in the same age group it is about 7. For men age 75 and over the annual rate is about 54 per 100,000; for women of this age, it is less than 6. *Men age 75 or more are nearly 10 times more likely to commit suicide than women of the same age.*

Even though the suicide rate among old men is at least double that for young men, the media has focused on the problem of suicide in the young, and especially in teenagers. This is understandable: there are few tragedies greater than the death of a healthy teenager, with the loss of so many years of promise ahead. There has been much concern recently about 'copy-cat suicides', usually of young men. In these, the methods employed are similar to those in suicides recently reported in the media. This has led to suggestions that there be a ban on reporting suicides in the popular media. A more democratic and realistic approach has been proposed, namely that *alternatives* to suicide are emphasized in conjunction with every media report. In this way, young people contemplating suicide may become aware of more constructive solutions to their problems.

In choosing an example of media-reported suicide, I have selected an account first published over twenty years ago in a German newspaper, but recently translated and reproduced in an article by R. F. W. Diekstra in the Journal *Crisis* (1989, Vol 10: 16–35):

> It was around noon on 12th August 1969 that 19-year-old Jurgen Peters climbed the ladder on the outside of a water tower in the German city of Kassel. By the time he reached the top, a number of people were already gathering at the foot of the tower, wondering and guessing what the young man was up to.
>
> It soon became clear that he intended to jump all the way down in an attempt to take his own life. Earlier that morning, Jurgen had been fired by his boss, a local garage owner, for whom he worked as an apprentice mechanic. The reason had been that, upon being asked to test drive a client's car, he instead had gone joy riding and in the process had severely damaged the car as well as two others.
>
> Bystanders called the police, who in turn called the fire department for assistance. A fire ladder was put out to the top of the tower, and one of the firemen tried to talk Jurgen out of his plan, without success, however. Then a girl he had been dating and liked very much was asked to talk with him. She succeeded in persuading him to give up his attempt.
>
> While stepping from the water tower onto the fire ladder and starting his descent, a couple of young men watching the scene began yelling: 'Hey coward, you don't even have the guts to jump, do you?' and similar provocative remarks. One could observe Jurgen hesitating, interrupting his descent. Then all of a sudden he climbed up the ladder, hopped on the top of the tower and almost in one movement jumped off it. He died on the spot.

To read such a report is profoundly distressing. Rational response is almost impossible. But, as Diekstra points out, Jurgen's suicide was a public event, observed by several people. This is very rare, and it makes the suicide unusually instructive. Jurgen's climb up the tower was an impulsive reaction to his car accident, which had caused him deep humiliation, the loss of his job, and the prospect of a major financial burden well into the future as he paid for the cost of the damage he had done. That he had not made the final decision to kill himself is suggested by the ability of his girlfriend to persuade him to start climbing down the tower. Only when two young men accused him of cowardice did Jurgen change his mind and jump to his death. Diekstra suggests that Jurgen jumped partly to prove that he was not a coward, and that this 'macho' attitude to suicide in young men contributes to its relatively high rate.

Although there is a fair amount of professional literature on the subject of suicide in the young, written mainly by sociologists and mental-health workers, its true causes remain uncertain. It remains a comparatively rare event, even in young men. Because of this, it is almost impossible to predict, so that our knowledge of preceding events is nearly always retrospective and reliant on the accounts of others. In spite of these limitations, it is possible to identify some of the factors that make young men so much more prone to suicide than young women.

One of the most important is *choice of method*. The following figures are based on suicide figures as a whole, but they are equally applicable to the young. In the USA, 65 per cent of men use firearms (including explosives, used by a very few) to kill themselves. This method is used by about 40 per cent of women. Only about 14 per cent of men use poisons, whereas these are used by nearly 40 per cent of women. Some 15 per cent of men and 13 per cent of women use hanging or other means of strangulation. About 7 per cent of men and 9 per cent of women jump from heights, drown, or electrocute themselves.

Firearms, used more commonly by young men than by young women, are far more likely to be fatal than poisons, which are used more commonly by young women. As a result, suicide attempts by young men – and by men in general – are more likely to be successful.

Men's choice of method is, of course, influenced by cultural factors. The collection and use of firearms is, in most Western countries, an essentially male activity. It is an aspect of the male sex-role stereotype, and is a prime example of how stereotyping contributes directly to men's excess mortality.

Additional cultural factors thought to be responsible for the relatively high suicide rate in young men relate to sex-role issues. The social pressure on young men to be successfully competitive in a highly visible way is very great. Young men who commit suicide often have a history of self-defeating behaviour, frequently linked with alcohol and drug abuse. At the same time, they appear to have a rather limited view of what constitutes success, which they see very stereotypically in terms of wealth, power and social prominence. It is likely that the gap between the way that they see themselves and the way that they would like to be is very great. Despair about ever bridging the gap between reality and their hopes and dreams is probably a significant factor in precipitating the final act.

Although we know little for certain about the real causes of suicide in young men, we probably know more about suicide in old men. The old are more likely than the young to be suffering from recognizable clinical depression. This is true also of middle-aged men who kill themselves. While young men who commit suicide are also likely to be clinically depressed, this may be obscured by other psychiatric disorders, especially 'Borderline Personality Disorder'. Although old men who kill themselves often have a history of depression, many do not. In these cases contributing factors include social isolation, loneliness, fears of declining physical and mental health, and especially the fear of becoming dependent on someone else. Because men's socialization puts so much emphasis on physical activity and prowess, men are much more sensitive to the age-related decline in physical strength, endurance and agility. Fears of losing their physical robustness interact with fears of becoming dependent, and this interaction may generate an overwhelming sense of helplessness and hopelessness. At such a point, suicide may seem a realistic option. Many of these problems have their origins in men's denied dependence on women and in related sex-role stereotyping.

Clearly, suicide in old men is a huge social problem that has been largely ignored. It is yet another example of how the health and well-being of men in modern Western society tends to be taken for granted. If old women committed suicide at nearly 10 times the rate of old men, I think that feminists and other concerned women would recognize the issue as one of major importance, and try to draw public attention to it. But because the ratio is reversed, and men are the main casualties, the problem is overlooked. I will explore some reasons for this in later chapters.

Homicide

The overall homicide rate among American men is 14 each year per 100,000 people. This is much higher than in any other Western country. Tragically, it is overwhelmingly a problem of Black Americans. In Black men, homicide occurs at the staggering annual rate of about 50 per 100,000; in Black women, it is about 10 per 100,000. The annual rate in White men is about 8 per 100,000, and in White women about 3 per 100,000. Clearly, the ratio of homicide deaths between Black men and women, at 5:1, is even higher than it is for Whites.

Nearly all Black homicides occur in cities where massive social problems are the main cause of this frightening destructiveness. But the male:female homicide ratio of 5:1 is a reminder that even in this profoundly deprived cultural context, sex-role issues are crucial.

In cities, Black American culture has a strong matriarchal theme. Even more exclusively than White children, Black children are raised by women. Once they are old enough to attend high school, they are thrust into an aggressive environment where 'macho' behaviour among the boys is very prominent. In adapting to this, young Black boys must suppress their primary identification with their mothers even more fiercely than their White compatriots. As a result, sex-role stereotyping and its negative affects, especially homicide, are even more prominent among American Blacks than among Whites.

Motor Vehicle and Other Accidents

Men are killed in motor vehicle accidents nearly three times more frequently than women. There is, of course, an overlap between deaths by motor vehicle accident and deaths by suicide. A proportion of deaths in automobile crashes is undoubtedly deliberate, and in some cases it is impossible to tell whether

56

the fatal incident was accidental, deliberate or a combination of both.

Nearly half of the men killed in automobile accidents have alcohol in their blood, often at high levels. This is especially true of men under twenty-five, among whom motor vehicle accidents account for a majority of deaths.

The overall rate of death by violence in men age 15–34 years is over 110 each year per 100,000 people. For statistical purposes, causes of violent death comprise suicide, homicide and all accidents. Alcohol and other drugs play a major role in all these violent deaths. It has been suggested that the rate of male deaths from any form of violence would be reduced by nearly 50 per cent if alcohol was somehow eliminated. Alcohol is also a major factor in the other main causes of excess male mortality, to be discussed next.

Lung Cancer, Heart Disease and Cirrhosis

Although young women now smoke cigarettes as much as young men, older men are still two or three times more likely to smoke than older women. In young women, many of whom are obsessed with the need to be slim, smoking is seen as a means of curbing appetite. Because their desire to be slim outweighs their desire to be physically fit, many young women ignore or deny the well-established health dangers of smoking in order to achieve the body weight that they believe is essential for sexual attractiveness. This is an example of how *women's* physical health is directly undermined by sex-role stereotyping.

Paradoxically, sex-role stereotyping has recently had a marginally positive influence on young men's smoking. Because of their media-fuelled obsession with sport, many young men have a strong desire to be physically fit. Often, this desire is stronger than the desire to conform to the 'macho' image of smoking so effectively portrayed by the 'Marlboro Man' genre of advertisements. As a result, smoking in young men has decreased somewhat in recent years.

Older men continue to smoke at relatively high rates, although increasingly this is true only of those in lower socio-economic groups. Here, stereotypical pressures and traditions still outweigh educational input about the health dangers of smoking.

The link between cigarette smoking and lung cancer is now so firmly established that only the tobacco companies and a few scientific eccentrics argue that it does not exist. Less well established, and not so widely publicized, is the link between cigarette smoking and cardiovascular conditions, especially heart disease.

Recent research has suggested that a *combination* of smoking and drinking alcohol is much more destructive to health than either habit pursued independently. The key to this is *carbon monoxide*, a gas that is present in tobacco smoke in high concentrations. When carbon monoxide is absorbed into the body, it slows down the rate at which alcohol is broken down into its various by-products prior to being eliminated. This means that the harmful effect of alcohol and its by-products on the tissues is greatly increased. So potent is this effect that it may be a significant factor in lung cancer as well as cardiovascular disease and cirrhosis of the liver. It is, of course, well known that a high level of alcohol intake alone is sufficient to cause cirrhosis of the liver, although a lack of certain vitamins probably speeds the process up. There is still some medical controversy about the relationship between alcohol and vitamin deficiencies in causing cirrhosis.

Most heavy smokers are heavy drinkers also. Such people, mostly men, are at very high risk indeed for diseases of the lungs, heart and liver. So much so that this behaviour must be regarded as suicidal, or at least quasi-suicidal. According to the Epidemiologic Catchment Area survey, such quasi-suicidal behaviour is widespread in men. Combining all age groups, 5 per cent of men, but less than 1 per cent of women, are dependent on alcohol at a level that meets the usual criteria for alcoholism. The highest rate of alcoholism (6.2 per cent) was found in men aged 25–44. Over 2 per cent of men regularly abuse illicit drugs, with the rate peaking at 4.8 per cent in the 18–24 age group. If figures on cigarette smoking are included, then at least 10 per cent of men are regularly abusing drugs at a level that represents extreme danger to their health. To this quasi-suicidal behaviour must be added overt suicide and suicide disguised as motor vehicle or other accidents. Some of the behaviour associated with acquiring AIDS, an overwhelmingly male disease, must also be regarded as quasi-suicidal.

It is, then, absolutely clear that men's excess mortality is caused largely by overtly self-destructive behaviour or by diseases to which self-destructive or unhealthy lifestyles make a major contribution. Devoting expensive health-care resources to the treatment of diseases that appear to be the result of unhealthy lifestyles is causing increasing conflict among those who fund and deliver our health services. This conflict adds impetus to the next stage of my enquiry, namely the origins of men's self-destructiveness.

The Origins of Men's Self-destructive Behaviour

Men's self-destructive behaviour has long concerned those who have written about the human condition. Clearly, there is a strong link between sex-role stereotyping and self-destructive behaviour. Freud explained it in terms of a Death Instinct, although his ideas about this were challenged later. Freud's approach was essentially a clinical one and, in the same vein, I will start my enquiry with a case history.

Case 3: The Cowardly Lion

Richard was referred to me by his family physician, who was concerned about his heavy drinking, depression and anxiety symptoms. Richard presented as a handsome man who looked a little older than his forty-one years. Slightly above average height, he was about two stone overweight. His face showed signs of chronic fatigue and anxiety. During our first interview, he made no attempt to obscure the extent of his alcohol abuse; indeed, he seemed to take a perverse pride in the amount of his intake, while at the same time emphasizing how destructive had been the effect of alcoholism on his life.

As Richard's story unfolded, it seemed that he was a classic underachiever. He had been very bright at school, but had rarely applied himself to his studies, and had left high school without graduating. His problems with drugs had started when he was fifteen, at which time amphetamines were readily available in the neighbourhood. Initially, he used them only occasionally, in an attempt to escape from his chronic depression and anxiety. But by the time he was seventeen, Richard was dependent on them. His drug abuse had contributed to his academic failure, and this added to his chronic depression, poor self-esteem and sense of unworthiness. Drugs became the only way of relieving these negative, unpleasant feelings. When he turned eighteen, Richard began to replace amphetamines with alcohol, and from about age twenty he relied mainly on alcohol to help him manage his feelings of depression, anxiety and, increasingly, self-disgust.

Because he was good-looking, charming and intelligent, Richard managed to get fairly good jobs, although his lack of qualifications placed limitations on the kind of work he was offered. Invariably, his drinking caused problems at work, and he was usually dismissed for incompetence. Although Richard blamed his problems on his alcoholism, he blamed himself for not being able to overcome it. Gradually, his self-esteem became lower and lower, and his self-dislike greater and greater. From his early thirties, Richard became chronically suicidal, and he had been close to killing himself on a number of occasions. I discovered soon after we started therapy that he had tried to end his life some three weeks before our first interview. He explained that he had drunk a bottle and a half of bourbon and then filled the bath. He stood in the bath holding an electric radiator, and then dropped it into the water. Just as the radiator fell in the water, the electric cord reached its full length and the power plug was pulled from its socket in the wall. Although there was a great deal of hissing and steaming, there was no electrocution. Richard regarded his survival as a small miracle, and this introduced a gleam of hope into his life. It was this gleam of hope that led him to seek psychiatric help through his family physician.

Family History

Richard's father, James, had been a hotel manager, and was himself a very heavy drinker. But although his drinking had disrupted family life, it had not greatly interfered with his career, and he retired at sixty-five quite comfortably off. Richard recalled domestic violence in his childhood. When drunk, his father tended to become aggressive and abusive toward his wife, Martha. Occasionally, the abuse extended to physical assault, and on at least two occasions Martha had been badly beaten by James. But she never made any attempt to leave what seems to have been a compulsory marriage.

Richard and his sister, four years his senior, were also abused, but much less so than their mother. For Richard, the pain of seeing his mother hurt and humiliated was far greater than the pain of the abuse that he suffered himself. James, when he was sober, tried to be friendly toward Richard, but Richard, very aware of his father's sudden changes of mood, did not respond. Unable to identify with his father, he internalized stereotypic male attributes that required him to harshly suppress the feminine qualities internalized earlier from his mother. Richard's identification with his mother was unusually strong, and the task of suppressing the feminine aspects of his identity was a profoundly difficult one. It required him to adopt strongly sex-role stereotyped attitudes and behaviours, and as these 'macho' characteristics became established, they contributed to his adjustment problems at school. Since attempting to suppress unwanted feelings was the only way he knew how to manage them, it was natural to try this technique to ward off the feelings of depression that emerged strongly soon after puberty. But the depression persisted and became chronic, until he discovered that amphetamines offered respite.

Marriage

Richard married Jenny when he was twenty-two and she twenty. They had met at a party, where Jenny had first seen Richard on his own, propped up against a wall. She felt an immediate attraction, and wandered over to talk to him. Jenny misinterpreted Richard's shyness as silent strength, which increased her sense of attraction toward him. She made an effort to interest him. Flattered by the attentions of this attractive young woman, he stopped getting drunk and became charming and responsive. Only five months later, they got married.

Jenny's father was an alcoholic. He had tended to abuse her when drunk but, in a remorseful way, had tried to be warm and affectionate when sober. Together with her mother, she had waged a long war against her father's alcoholism, but to no avail. In the course of this, she had decided to become teetotal. But, as is

61

often the case with the daughters of alcoholic men, the need to fight alcoholism by proxy remained strong within her.

Richard had managed to obscure his alcohol problems from Jenny during their brief courtship, but they became obvious soon after their marriage. From then on, their relationship revolved around Richard's alcohol problem. Jenny constantly exhorted Richard to stop drinking, and tried a whole range of strategies aimed at helping him do so. Many of these, such as hiding his car keys, had a punitive element. Overall, Jenny's attempts to reduce Richard's drinking had the opposite effect.

The couple had no children. Investigations had shown that Jenny had fertility problems, and the chronic marital difficulties removed any incentive for her to try and remedy these. Also, Jenny was concerned that if she had children, they might become alcoholics like her father and husband. In a sense, Richard became Jenny's child. He was very dependent on her, and this was partly a transfer of dependency from his mother. But his macho self-image required him to deny this and, instead of feeling dependent on Jenny, he felt mainly anger and resentment toward her. These negative feelings revolved around the way in which she reacted to his drinking problem.

The Death of Richard's Mother

Richard's mother died suddenly and unexpectedly of a stroke when he was thirty-one. He coped with this by totally denying its emotional impact. He shed no tears. Instead of grieving his mother's death, he increased his alcohol intake in an attempt to suppress all his painful feelings. As is quite common in such situations, about a year after his mother's death, Richard began to experience episodes of acute panic. These panic attacks were a reaction to the 'emptiness within' associated with the extreme suppression of internalized feminine attributes, a process that I have outlined in the previous chapter. They were precipitated by the first anniversary of the death of Richard's mother, a time of great turmoil in his unconscious mind. Some of the attacks were associated with severe palpitations, which initially led Richard to fear that he was dying of a heart attack. Others were associated with a profoundly frightening sense of impending psychic fragmentation. Richard described these in terms such as, 'I feel as if I'm going to mentally disintegrate', and 'It's like a complete mental blackout, a total confusion'. These feelings suggested a brain tumour to Richard, or some other disease that might cause him to have a stroke like his mother. Several years were spent pursuing fruitless medical investigations, during which time Richard's panic attacks and associated symptoms came to cause as much concern within the marriage as his drinking, which continued unabated. Richard's anxiety symptoms had a vital function within the relationship: *they helped to create a compulsory marriage*. Richard felt as if he could not survive without Jenny to care for him; and Jenny felt that she could never abandon a sick man.

Therapy

Once I understood enough about Richard and his problems to plan therapy, I suggested Jenny take part in the process. But Richard preferred to continue seeing me on his own. I then proposed that unresolved grief about his mother was a major factor in his panic attacks, and that his continuing abuse of alcohol was closely connected with his attempts to control these panics, or to ameliorate their effects. Unfortunately, using alcohol in this way actually increased the chances of panics occurring, setting up a vicious cycle.

Initially, Richard strongly resisted the idea of a relationship between his panics and unresolved grief. But he was compelled to reconsider the notion when we established that his first panic attack had occurred the day after the first anniversary of his mother's death. Even more convincing was the discovery that his abortive suicide attempt with the electric radiator had occurred the day before the 10th anniversary of her death. At the time, he had not been consciously aware of the anniversary. But his unconscious mind included a timing mechanism that had located it unerringly. Such events are not uncommon in clinical psychiatric practice. Once he was convinced, Richard began the challenging task of mourning his mother's death. This involved getting in touch with buried feelings of loss, sadness and anger, expressing them, and letting flow the tears that he had previously been unable to shed. He worked at this task hard and courageously, and, within four months, the task was largely completed. His panic attacks decreased in frequency and intensity, and then disappeared. But his alcohol abuse persisted. Freed from the constraints of a compulsory marriage by the resolution of Richard's panic disorder, Jenny began threatening divorce unless he stopped drinking. Predictably, this threat increased Richard's alcohol intake, and the marriage appeared in jeopardy.

Father's Death

Just at this time, Richard discovered that his father was dying of cancer. James had moved to another state, and Richard saw very little of him. His initial reaction was to dismiss the significance of his father's impending death. But, with the support of Richard's family physician, I suggested that he visit his father. When he returned from a brief stay, he announced without emotion that his father probably had only a few weeks to live. To my surprise, he then told me that he planned to take leave from his job (which miraculously he still held) as soon as it could be arranged, in order to go and care for his dying father. This he did. He was with his father for five weeks before he died. On his return, Richard told me about the experience in some detail.

When he went back for his final visit, Richard found his father almost too weak to walk. A nurse had been coming in regularly to help him cope, and to ensure that he had sufficient supplies of pain-killing drugs. Richard discharged the nurse, and took over caring for James. Even though James was weak and near death, he still enjoyed a glass of beer. He wanted to drink it in what was, for him, the most natural setting – a bar. Each morning, Richard put James in his wheelchair and took him down the street to the nearest bar, which was in a hotel. So weak and frail was James that he would often take two hours to finish a half pint of beer. Initially, waiting for his father to get through two half pints was an ordeal for Richard, but, to his amazement, he found that James soon accumulated a small group of acquaintances who clearly enjoyed his company. The dying man became something of a celebrity.

As he talked with James, Richard realized that he had never known his father. For the first time, James talked openly and freely about his own childhood, and about the hopes and dreams he had as a young man. Richard learned that as a child, James had been horribly abused by his own father, who also had a major alcohol problem. He began to feel sympathy and understanding for his father, and even love.

James described the night his father died: 'At 4.00 a.m. I woke up. He was thrashing around in bed, completely incoherent. For over an hour I tried to help him, then I drifted off to sleep through exhaustion. I dreamed that I was taking him to a quiet place, and suddenly I woke up. He had just died. He was free of all that pain. I put my arms around him and wept. But I felt a sense of relief as well as sadness.'

Richard organized and attended the funeral before his return home. It was clear to me that he had largely worked through his grief. As we were talking about this, he mentioned that his father's family physician had said that James 'showed true grit' in coping with a painful death. Richard then added, 'I wish some of it had rubbed off on me'. At this point I was overwhelmed by a sense of sadness, and shed a few tears. Richard asked what had upset me, and I replied by asking him if he had seen the movie *The Wizard of Oz*, or read the book. He had not, and so I described the Cowardly Lion from that marvellous story. This lion insisted that he had no courage, even after successfully undertaking the most courageous deeds. I told Richard that he was just like the Cowardly Lion. He then shed a few tears himself.

I finally asked Richard about his drinking, and he said, in a rather surprised manner, that he had virtually stopped. He explained that while sitting for hours in the bar waiting for his father to finish his beer, he had been forced to learn controlled drinking. Having to look after his father meant that he needed to remain sober. After his father's death, he found, to his astonishment, that he could restrict himself to one or two drinks a day, and that on some days he did not drink at all.

I followed Richard up for a further four months, during which time his self-esteem steadily increased, and his drinking steadily decreased. His marriage had improved, although Jenny was beginning to develop psychological problems of her own now that Richard's problems were no longer occupying her attention. She had sought help for these from another therapist. We finally ceased therapy when both Richard and I agreed he no longer had a problem with alcohol. Although he still had a very poor opinion of himself, and made frequent self-denigrating comments, he believed that therapy could not help him in this regard. Instead, he wanted to prove to himself that he was a worthwhile person. With this in mind, he had enrolled in night school to gain some professional qualifications. He knew that this would be a real challenge, but he was determined to succeed. I thought that he would.

Implications of the Case

Richard's case illustrates clearly how self-destructive behaviour can emerge from a background of family abuse. It demonstrates the intimate and complex relationship between self-destructiveness and sex-role stereotyped behaviour and attitudes. It shows also the extreme persistence of self-destructive behaviour, and how its origins must be examined and resolved before enduring changes are likely. In Richard's case, marital interaction contributed to the persistence of his alcoholism, which in adulthood was the most obvious sign of his self-destructiveness. Less obvious was the self-disgust, which was so intense that it required him to punish himself relentlessly.

Richard believed that he was a worthless, cowardly failure. These harsh judgements were made in comparison with an ideal that was highly stereotypic. For Richard, success could be measured only in tems of occupational achievement and the acquisition of wealth and social status. By these criteria he was a complete failure.

In reality, Richard was a very courageous man. But he was reluctant to acknowledge this, perhaps because mourning his mother's death and helping his father die with dignity were not on his list of worthwhile achievements. By the time his father died, Richard had come to understand and forgive him, which allowed him, finally, to identify with him. These changes meant that Richard felt more complete as a person, and also helped him to relinquish some of his stereotyped beliefs.

Generalizing from one case requires great caution. None the less, most men who are severely and persistently self-destructive have many features in common with Richard. Few have the chance to redeem themselves through acts of courage and heroism. But acknowledging the true extent and nature of self-destructive behaviour, and seeking help for it, are themselves often acts of great courage.

My approach to understanding Richard and his self-destructiveness has been basically psychoanalytic. This approach, informative though it is, cannot do full justice to the social context of human behaviour, nor to its biological or historical components and antecedents. It must be supplemented by other approaches. The most relevant of these is the emerging field of *ethology* – the systematic study of animal behaviour in the natural environment. Studies in this area have already yielded rich insights into human behaviour and its aberrations.

An Ethological Perspective

It was Konrad Lorenz, one of the pioneers of ethology, who first drew widespread attention to the concept of *territorial behaviour* and its fundamental importance in understanding the structure of human societies.

Territorial Behaviour

Territorial behaviour became fundamental to the survival of almost all species because it was so efficient. Once a particular species has found a 'niche' for itself in the food chain, its members compete mainly *with each other* for available food supplies. If each scrap of food in a particular area was competed for by all the members of the species who happened to be present, the amount of energy required for its struggle would be enormous. In fact, more energy would be expended than could be replaced by the available food. The result of this would be the failure of the species to survive.

Nature devised a brilliant alternative to fierce competition for every scrap of food – the concept of *territory*. Mating pairs were required to defend an area of territory – whether it was land, sea, or air – within which they had relatively free access to their basic food supplies. The energy required to maintain a territory was not very great, because the animal kingdom evolved a whole set of rules that strictly governed territories and territorial behaviour.

These rules are demonstrated frequently in most suburban back gardens – by many species of birds, and especially by domestic cats, who are often fiercely territorial creatures. Observing them shows just how efficient is their territorial system. If a cat intrudes into the territory of another, the two animals indulge in *ritual threatening behaviour*, with growling, hissing and baring of teeth and arching of backs. In most instances, the intruding animal retreats without a fight, leaving the defending cat (usually a male) free to roam and feed in its own territory. If fights do occur, although they are often savage, they are invariably brief, and very rarely do they result in major or permanent injury. Once re-established, the territory can be maintained simply by marking its borders with the resident's characteristic odour, usually transmitted through urine. The resident can then put most of his energy into the basic survival task of hunting for food.

One of the main reasons for the extraordinary expansion of the human species throughout the world has been the ability of human groups – whether they be the primitive hordes of our early history or later clans and tribes – to be fiercely aggressive to other human groups. This fierce aggression was necessary because food supplies were very scarce for long periods of time. This was especially true during the last Ice Age, when conditions over much of the planet were unbelievably harsh. The groups that survived were those that contained men who were physically strong and aggressive enough to maintain territories and to hunt successfully within them. But survival also required the harnessing and control of this strength and aggression so that it was not directed at members of the same horde or clan. The social groups that survived were only those that had learned to channel aggression mainly outward, on to competing groups.

To protect clan members from fighting and killing each other, a system of *hierarchies* developed. This was a modification of the basic territorial system. But instead of competing for territorial rights, individual males competed for status within the social hierarchy. Put more mundanely, they competed to establish a 'pecking order'. As a result, instead of fighting constantly for social status and the privileges that went with it, these rights were established on a relatively stable basis.

Submission Gestures

It is at this point that we can begin to understand the origins of men's self-destructive behaviour. The first and most important clue lies in the occurrence of *submission gestures*. These gestures are almost universal among mammals. They evolved in order to prevent fighting between members of the same species from becoming too destructive. If, after every fight over territorial boundaries, an animal was badly or fatally injured, then the species would be unlikely to survive. Human beings have evolved a range of submission gestures, of which the most obvious are lowering the head, bowing, and kneeling, all of which expose the vulnerable base of the neck. Submission gestures work only because they guarantee that the conflict will not immediately be resumed. In socially cohesive animals living in groups, where simple flight from the territory is not a viable strategy, this required the evolutionary development of brain mechanisms that powerfully inhibited aggressive behaviour. These brain mechanisms, technically known as *behavioural inhibition systems*, are fundamental to much of man's self-destructive behaviour.

In common with other animals, much of the basic circuitry of the human brain is designed to allow aggressive behaviour to be rapidly and effectively initiated. Rather than design new brain circuits, nature has achieved other patterns of behaviour by reversing or modifying the output from those brain circuits that drive and organize aggressive behaviour. In social animals, *being submissive means a redirection of aggression from the external to the internal*. In certain circumstances, this internal redirection of aggression can result in self-destructive behaviour.

Internalized Aggression and Self-mutilation

In the case of captive primates, it is not uncommon to see a young male biting itself on the arm or leg, apparently in extreme frustration. Occasionally, severe self-mutilation results. This behaviour usually occurs after a young male has been involved in a status challenge with an older, larger male. In spite of submission mechanisms, such challenges are very dangerous for young males; they occur mainly in captivity, a constricted environment that encourages social aberrations. Self-biting is an excellent example of the internalization of aggression. Paradoxically, it is often a

69

self-protective behaviour, because it may be an alternative to a quasi-suicidal attack on an older, stronger male. This has helped to ensure its evolutionary survival.

Human beings indulge in a wide range of spontaneous self-mutilating behaviours. Mild self-mutilation is quite common. It includes nail-biting, pulling out one's hair (an activity which, when compulsive, rejoices in the name of trichotillomania), and pinching and punching oneself. More severe are those activities seen quite commonly in people psychiatrically diagnosed as having a 'Borderline Personality Disorder'. These activities usually involve compulsive cutting of arms, wrists and other parts of the body. Extreme but well-documented examples of self-mutilation include self-amputation of fingers, hands, feet, or tongue; enucleation of eyeballs or testicles; and cutting off other parts of the genitals. These extreme examples are fortunately quite rare, and the victims are usually suffering from a clearly recognizable psychiatric disorder. They are almost all men.

Of course, the ultimate expression of internalized aggression is successful suicide, which is much more common in men than in women. This is precisely what we would predict from the idea that self-mutilation is the result of internalized aggression. Men are socially conditioned to be far more aggressive and competitive than women. Inevitably, part of this aggression becomes re-directed inwardly, and relatively high suicide rates are but one tragic consequence of this.

Instinctive Behaviour

We have seen that a basic, instinctual drive towards physical aggression, especially in men, has been a fundamental part of the human species' success in dominating this planet. Many kinds of instinctive behaviour must be *frequently repeated*. If they are not, the urge to carry out the behaviour gets stronger and stronger until it may become unmanageable. This is most obvious with basic instinctual drives such as eating, drinking and sexual activity. It is less evident with more complex instinctive behaviours such as the drives to explore, to maintain territorial integrity, to take risks, to hunt and gather food, to clean the nest, to groom and be groomed, or to compete for social status. But most of these instinctual drives, even the complex ones, need regular repetition, the absence of which leads to an increase in emotional and bodily tension. One way of managing this increased tension is to take mood altering drugs, of which the most popular is alcohol. We are now in a position to understand the relationship between the aggressive/competitive drive in men, and their self-abuse using alcohol and other drugs.

Competitive Behaviour, Drug Abuse and Increased Mortality
In modern American society, and in other societies without a rigid class structure, competition between men is highly valued. It is regarded as fundamental. To be socially healthy is to be competitive. Increasingly, competition is occurring also between women, and between women and men. The struggle to achieve a balance between competitive and submissive drives is a fundamental one. Freud called it the struggle between Life and Death instincts. Generally, the higher a man's social status, the more successfully has he expressed his competitive instincts; his need to inhibit or suppress them will be relatively low. In men of low social status, the opposite is true. Although such men have been less successful in expressing their competitive drives, social and instinctual pressures force continued repetition of them. This means that the brain mechanisms which inhibit or suppress competitive behaviour are persistently active also. Because this involves a redirection inward of the aggressive drive, these men are at relatively high risk for self-destructive behaviour. As well, a lack of opportunities to successfully express the competitive drive increases the likelihood of raised emotional and physical tension. This combination of raised tension and inward turning of aggression is a major factor in men's self-destructiveness. It explains the link between alcohol and self-destructive behaviour. Alcohol is used to relieve tension, but because it has a disinhibiting effect, it actually increases the chances that self-destructive behaviour will occur. Of course, habitual abuse of alcohol, especially when combined with smoking, is highly self-destructive in its own right.

Many other drugs are used to relieve emotional tension and feelings of despair and frustration about social position and opportunities. The most destructive of these drugs are those that are taken intravenously. Abuse of intravenous drugs such as heroin is overwhelmingly a problem of those of low

71

socio-economic status. In fact, a whole subclass has been created that revolves around the distribution and abuse of narcotics. Paradoxically, use of intravenous drugs reduces the sense of social alienation experienced by people who live on the fringes of society. Self-injection of drugs, especially when sharing needles, is a high-risk activity that generates a strong sense of social bonding and belonging. Tragically, the price paid for this feeling of belonging is often death.

Social class strongly influences the whole range of self-destructive behaviours. Working-class men are far more likely to smoke tobacco than middle- or upper-class men. In fact, smoking has now become quite rare among professional men. Deaths from all the causes listed in Table 2 are more common in lower than in upper socio-economic groups. This difference is reflected in the shorter life span of working-class men. Social class differences in death rates from cardiovascular disease are particularly striking. Negative lifestyle factors appear mainly responsible for this. Working-class men have proved relatively resistant to educational input about the link between cardiovascular disease and an unhealthy lifestyle. They have tended to ignore information about the dangers of tobacco smoking, excessive alcohol intake, and obesity; and about the benefits of regular exercise and a balanced diet. Of course, economic factors are relevant here: a tight budget makes it difficult to afford food that is both 'healthy' and appetising.

Unfortunately, no amount of propaganda about lifestyle changes will alter the basic reality of working-class men's lives. Working-class men are, by definition, at or near the bottom of the social hierarchy. Because of this, increased levels of emotional tension and inwardly directed aggression are inevitable. As a result, it is far more difficult for working-class men to reduce self-destructive behaviour than it is for middle- and upper-class men.

High blood pressure is a major contributor to heart attacks and strokes. There is good scientific evidence that problems with competitiveness and aggression are important causes of high blood pressure, at least in men.

It seems that men who habitually suppress their aggressive impulses are more likely than others to develop high blood pressure. This is a reminder that suppressing competitive drives may lead directly to health problems, without the intermediary of overtly self-destructive behaviour such as drug abuse.

Sex-Role Stereotyping, Sexual Competition and Aggression
Competition between males for females is fundamental to the survival of most mammalian species. It ensures that only the strongest, fittest and most aggressive males are able to find a mate. The attributes of the competitively successful male are genetically passed on, increasing the chances of the species continuing to function successfully in its particular environmental niche. In other words, sexual competition between males ensures that only the stronger and more aggressive males pass their genes on to subsequent generations: *it is fundamental to the genetic integrity and development of the species, which are vital for its long term survival.*

Competition between males over social status or the 'pecking order' serves a complementary purpose: it preserves the everyday structure and survival of the species by ensuring that the social group as a whole is able to compete successfully with other social groups. Sexual and social competition are inextricably intertwined. An increase in sexual competition will result in a corresponding increase in social competition, and vice versa. So far in this chapter I have discussed mainly social competition. But the intensity of sexual competition in a society is a crucial factor in determining the overall level of competitiveness and aggression. When the overall level of aggression in a society or a nation is high, it tends to be projected outwards. One result of this is conquest of other nations, and territorial expansion. In this regard, the major English-speaking nations have an extraordinary record. Out of a tiny island (Britain), the English, from the sixteenth century on, spread their culture and language throughout the world. This remarkable expansion, which was fuelled by a desire for wealth through trade and increased access to natural resources, was achieved mainly by warfare. English-speaking nations have been centrally involved in almost all the major wars of the past two centuries, and they remain among the most heavily armed and best prepared for battle.

I recognize that long before the creation of the British Empire, the Roman Empire exerted a comparable cultural and military influence. The Spanish Empire, at its height, had power that was almost as great. It is likely that all major colonial nations have shared many of the social qualities of Britain at the peak of its colonial influence. In continuing to restrict my discussion mainly to English-speaking nations, I am not suggesting that the characteristics revealed are necessarily unique to them.

What are the qualities of English-speaking societies that, historically at least, have made them so aggressive and expansionist? Of course, there are many, and a comprehensive discussion of them is beyond the scope of this book. I shall focus mainly on sexual competition and its contribution to overall levels of aggression and competitiveness. In the next chapter I will show that there is a close link between sex-role stereotyping and the maintenance of sexual competition. Because of the intimate connection between sexual and social competition, sex-role stereotyping helps to maintain the latter also. By helping to sustain competitiveness, sex-role stereotyping has become of crucial importance in preserving the traditional social structure of English-speaking nations.

4

Sexual Competition

Sex and the Sedentary Lifestyle

The technological advances of the past century or so have liberated Westerners from physical toil. Before the Industrial Revolution of the nineteenth century, 90 per cent of Westerners survived by working the land. Their days were filled with hard physical toil, and they had little time or energy to pursue activities that were not directly concerned with physical survival.

Now, less than 10 per cent of Westerners directly work the land. Those that do rely on machines to do most of the work. Few of us who live in America, the United Kingdom, or other English-speaking countries have jobs that require hard, prolonged physical labour. For most of us, *lack* of physical activity is more of a problem. Gymnasia, fitness centres and aerobics are part of a huge industry that has emerged to help us combat the negative effects of a sedentary lifestyle.

Any society that has been based for thousands of years on hard physical labour finds it profoundly difficult to adjust to a life of physical inertia. New outlets are needed for energy and drive that were previously expended in physical tasks basic to survival.

A major outlet is increased sexual activity. One of the first observers of this was Sir Solly Zuckerman who in 1932 published an influential book called *The Social Life of Monkeys and Apes*. His work was based mainly on studies of animals in captivity. He noted that they spent a great deal of their time in sexual activity, or in sexual competition. He concluded that sexual bonding and related activities were fundamental in preserving the structure of complex primate societies.

Since Sir Solly's time, skilled observers have spent time living and working in the natural environment of apes and monkeys.

75

These dedicated scientists have shown that the high level of sexual activity observed by Sir Solly was a characteristic only of captive animals. In the wild, sexual activity was relatively infrequent, because the daily struggle to survive took up so much time and energy.

Modern Westerners have much in common with Sir Solly Zuckerman's captive apes and monkeys. Very little of our energy is required for basic survival. Most of us live in small houses or apartments in which we feel, at least some of the time, confined and claustrophobic. Many of us feel captives of routine and boring work even though having no paid work at all would be even more of a dilemma. These constraints, together with the absence of regular physical labour from our lives, have resulted in a great increase in the amount of time and energy that we devote to sexual matters.

New ways of coping with this increased sexuality have not been popular. Instead, people behave in traditional ways sexually, and this has created new problems. For example, we cling fiercely to marriage: over 95 per cent of Americans have been married at least once by the time they reach forty-five. The percentage is not much lower for other English-speaking countries. Sexual dissatisfaction is a major factor in marital disharmony and breakdown, and will continue to be so until we change our attitudes and expectations about sex within marriage.

Almost all of us expect our marriage partners to be sexually faithful, and most of us struggle hard to be faithful ourselves. Biologically, this is an absurd situation: ethological and cross-cultural studies suggest that both the male and female of our species are intrinsically polygamous. The origins of patriarchy are intimately connected with the need to control female sexuality (this is a major theme of Chapter 5). The expectation of fidelity is usually combined with the idea that a married couple should be able to fully meet each other's sexual needs indefinitely. This notion is sustained by numerous books on the subject, the most popular of which tend to focus on the physical techniques of sex rather than its social and emotional context. An emphasis on physical techniques often gives rise to false expectations about sexual performance, with inevitable frustration and disappointment.

76

The huge increase in the amount of time and energy devoted to sexual matters has had repercussions throughout society. One of the most obvious effects is in the area of *sexual competition*. Many of us, and especially the young, devote much of our free time to the process of attracting and keeping sexual partners. Huge industries, and especially the popular media, sustain this process and are sustained by it themselves. There is also an indirect contribution to the process of sexual competition. Of vast proportions, it concerns *social status*. Raised social status, especially for men, increases the chances of finding an attractive sexual partner. Sexual competition and the fight for social status have become linked inextricably. Although we have come to accept this linkage, it is in fact an extraordinary one that is far less evident in non-Western cultures. It has many negative effects, usually mediated through sex-role stereotyping. To fully understand these, it is necessary to trace the social origins of sexual competition.

Mating and Courtship Rituals

In the earliest human societies, courtship or mating rituals were often collective, occurring at particular times of the year. Most rituals were based on imitating birds and animals, and this extended to the use of ornamental masks and other clothing. Where these ritual adornments have survived to the present day, they are often striking in appearance. Much time and effort goes into their construction, suggesting that even in the Stone Age, men put much of their spare time into sexual competition.

It is no coincidence that men often mimicked the actions and plumage of birds in their courtship rituals. The brilliant plumage of birds is primarily concerned with sexual competition. Birds that survive alone or in mating pairs, rather than in flocks, have special problems of survival and reproduction. A major difficulty for young birds is simply finding a mate. In these species, ritual fighting between males over females has been largely replaced by *direct appeals to the females themselves*. Those males with the most brilliant and extravagant plumage are those most likely to attract a mate. If two males are attracted to the same female, she will probably choose the one with the most brilliant plumage. There will be no need for aggressive sexual competition between the two males – competition that may lead to the injury of one or both, reducing the chances of survival of an already scarce resource.

The ethologist Konrad Lorenz has shown that sexual competition by appealing directly to the female is not without its dangers. He describes a species of bird that had adapted successfully to a wide range of environments. Living mainly in mating pairs, it had become numerous. Sexual competition increased, but the species relied on its traditional method of mate selection, namely the display by males of brilliant tail feathers. Through the evolutionary process of natural selection, which favoured the survival of genes responsible for the most extensive and luxurious feathers, the species eventually became so encumbered by plumage that flight was impossible. Unable to fly, the species was greatly reduced in numbers by predators, and now struggles to survive. As we shall see, excessive sexual competition can be destructive for human beings as well as for birds.

Modern Westerners have greatly extended the use of ritual adornment in their courtship and mating customs. Expensive designer clothes and footwear have now become fundamental to the social and sexual attractiveness of young men. Although the labels on these garments are small, their ritual significance is great. Fashions change frequently and rapidly, ensuring the survival of yet another industry that is based primarily on sexual competition. Older men may be less susceptible than the young to designer clothes, but an expensive suit remains a potent symbol of social status and wealth.

Combining Direct and Indirect Sexual Competition

The human species is unique in combining two quite different forms of sexual competition. We have borrowed from birds the idea of ritual adornment. This allows men to attract women without requiring them to compete aggressively with each other. Ritual adornment is an example of *indirect* sexual competition. But rather than use this non-aggressive method of mate selection on its own, we have combined it with the tradition of two males fighting each other – direct sexual competition.

Western man has extended indirect sexual competition far

beyond the use of ritual adornment. It now includes a whole range of additional symbols, the main object of which is to demonstrate wealth and social status. Expensive cars are among the most potent of these symbols. The dream of owning one sustains many a young man. The crucial point is that social status and its symbols have become a fundamental aspect of indirect sexual competition. This means that *visible signs of social status* and *direct competition between men over women* have become inextricably intertwined in our dating and courtship behaviour. The implications of this idea are profound. In particular, it helps to explain the intimate link between social and sexual competitiveness in today's Western world.

The Fight for a Mate

Men who have not married by the time they reach forty or so are viewed with suspicion in Western society. They are also very rare creatures, especially in the USA where, as we have seen, over 95 per cent of men marry at least once before age forty-five. It is widely assumed that men who never marry are homosexual, although this view is based on prejudice rather than on facts. Homosexual men are the victims of even more prejudice than middle-aged bachelors. It is therefore not surprising that many homosexual men marry in order to obscure their homosexuality, sometimes as much from themselves as from the public gaze. Ridiculous as it may seem, men are required to marry in order to show that they are not homosexual. Put slightly differently, they must marry in order to prove that they are not sexually or socially deviant. For these and many other reasons, the pressure on American men to marry is overwhelming. Australian men experience a similar level of pressure, and it is only slightly less in the United Kingdom.

The social pressure on women to marry is also very strong, but it is slightly less than that on men. Because of the high frequency of destructive wars and battles in the history of the English-speaking world, the death rate of young men has often been many times that of young women. There is a long tradition of women who have been unable to find husbands, not because of any personal deficiencies, but because so many young men had died on the battlefield. In large part because of this tradition, society accepts unmarried women more readily than it does unmarried men. It is not automatically assumed that unmarried middle-aged women are homosexual, even if two of them live together. Relatively free of such prejudice, it is slightly easier for women than it is for men to avoid the tyranny of coupledom.

Not only do Western men feel compelled to marry, but they are required to be the active partners in the search for a mate. Although women are becoming more active in the dating process, sex-role stereotypes still demand that men take the initiative and ask women out, rather than the opposite. Of course there are many individual exceptions to this, but that is not the point. The real issue concerns the *expectations* that are placed on men, the fulfilment of which is seen by many men as an essential part of their masculinity.

In modern America, finding a mate or a steady girlfriend involves men in the fiercely competitive *dating* process. Dating is a fundamental aspect of American life, and it includes elements that are highly ritualized. In many ways it is just as ruthless as the fierce mating rituals between males of other species from which it partly derives. Ideally, dating requires competition between males to be indirect rather than involving fisticuffs or other direct, open displays of aggression. But fights between young men over women are, of course, very common.

Much of the energy that used to be expended on the daily struggle to survive is now directed into the dating process. Young American men often start dating in their early teens, and continue the process until they believe that they have found their ideal partner, or at least the best possible one. This means that many men devote nearly ten years of their lives to this complex and demanding process. Countries such as England and Australia that have lagged behind America in this regard are fast catching up.

For men, increasing their social status and wealth is a fundamental part of the dating game, since increased social status means a better chance of securing a physically attractive and charming wife. Even after marriage, most American men continue to work hard at improving their social and occupational status.

The values that preserve the dating game, with its fierce competitiveness, are essentially *external* values. They rely on *appearances*: on physical attractiveness, and on social status and visible signs of affluence and occupational success. Sex-role stereotypes are also based on appearances, on the superficial, on the image rather than the reality. Without sex-role stereotypes, which help create idealized images of social and sexual perfection, the dating game could not be played.

Of course, many people learn to reject values based on the superficial. But the power and intensity of those forces that create and maintain sex-role stereotyped attitudes is very great. For many young people, beliefs based on the superficial become so much a part of their value system that they can never abandon them. This produces casualties among the socially successful as often as it does among those who appear to achieve little. We give little thought to those men who lose at the dating game, to its casualties, or to those who do not even take part in it. The losers are the men who are poor, not very intelligent, who lack education, are physically unattractive, and who lack any redeeming qualities such as charm or the ability to amuse and entertain. How do these men live their lives? The following case reveals the experiences of one such man.

Case 4: The Boy Who Kept Making Mistakes

When John came to see me for the first time, I asked him to tell me something of his childhood. He said that he could remember nothing before the age of eight. I replied that this was very unusual, adding that I had none the less worked previously with a few clients who had similar gaps in their memories of childhood.

A short, slight man, John initially avoided looking at me. As the interview progressed, he became more relaxed, and ventured a few shy glances. He was not unattractive, especially when he smiled. John had a long history of petty crime, but had managed to escape any custodial sentences. Now, at twenty-three, he had been caught stealing a car while on probation. He was remanded on bail. While waiting in the court to have his case heard before a judge, he had gone into the toilet. A court officer noticed that he had been in there longer than usual, and went in to check that he had not absconded. He found John hanging by his scarf from a pipe in one of the cubicles.

John was unconscious when the officer untangled him from his scarf. Fortunately, the pipe from which John tried to hang himself was too low for him to be fully suspended from the ground. In fact, it was only an accidental rotation of his body that had made the suicide attempt so nearly successful.

The attempted suicide was taken very seriously by the authorities, and John spent a few days under observation in a public psychiatric facility. When he finally came before the judge, a psychiatric report was available. On the basis of this, the judge agreed not to sentence John to prison on condition that he had psychiatric treatment. He was also allocated a new probation officer.

Psychiatric treatment at the request of a court is particularly difficult. It is often not clear whether the client is really motivated to work at therapy. For this reason, I very rarely take on clients in such circumstances. But I agreed to assess John because I happened to know his probation officer, whom I liked and trusted. She told me that she thought John genuinely wanted to look at his problems and try to find a way out of his self-destructive lifestyle. She added that he seemed intelligent, and might be able to do something worthwhile with his life if he got sufficient support and encouragement.

I knew from working with similar clients in the past that my chances of success were not good. I knew also that if John was going to benefit from therapy, it would be very hard work for both of us, and that it would probably take at least twelve months to achieve any real progress.

Our first session went quite well. I accepted that John could not remember anything of his life before he was eight years old, and we agreed to start from there. This is what unfolded over the next two sessions.

Trying to Please Mother

John's earliest memories were of living with his mother, Margaret, in a small weatherboard house in a poor outer suburb of a medium-sized city. He attended the local primary school. He was an only child.

John was constantly in trouble. He told his mother that he

wasn't as bad as other boys, but was picked on unfairly by the teachers. It seemed that he was partly correct in this assertion. There were boys in the school who behaved a lot worse than John – but they didn't get caught. It seemed that whenever John did anything against the rules, he was caught.

Because John was intelligent, and because he loved his mother and wanted to please her, he sometimes did very good school-work. But at other times he made foolish errors, or misunderstood questions, so that his often lengthy answers were valueless. This created great frustration in those teachers who had taken the trouble to get to know John. They could see that he had ability, but he made so many mistakes – often ridiculously simple ones – that his work was rarely acceptable.

John struggled to do well at school, but success eluded him. He still believed that the teachers victimized him, and that they marked him down unfairly because of this. He mixed very little with the other children. Although he felt lonely and isolated, he was so frightened of being rejected that he avoided the other children rather than ask to join them.

At age twelve, John made friends with a group of boys who were already in trouble with the law. He was not particularly attracted to these boys, but they were willing to spend time with him and he felt more comfortable with them than he did with the other students. But the price for belonging to this group – which called itself the Ferry Street Gang – was to break the law. John did – and, of course, he got caught the first time. His friends ran away and escaped.

The crime was not a very serious one. It involved John in stealing goods from a store while the store-keeper was distracted by two of the other boys in the gang. John was caught because he made the mistake of running the wrong way, and ended up trapped in a small store-room. The worst part for John was the police officer telling his mother what had happened. She burst into tears, and then became very angry. She told him that he was a wicked boy and that she hated him. John was utterly devastated at this rejection by his mother, whom he had so desperately tried to please for as long as he could remember.

From then on, John gave up trying to please his mother. He gave up trying to succeed at school. He spent most of his time hanging about on the streets with his gang, who began to replace his mother as a source of emotional support. He felt unwanted at home. His mother had not forgiven him for getting in trouble with the police, and was critical and hostile towards him. She had also increased her abuse of alcohol, which was already a problem. John blamed himself for this.

The Incompetent Delinquent

John tried hard to be a good gang member. But he kept making stupid mistakes. He was more of a liability than an asset. Although the other gang members liked him and wanted to involve him in their delinquent activities, they left him behind when they were attempting anything serious. Because of this, John was not caught doing anything other than minor misdemeanours. Most members of the gang spent time in corrective institutions, but John was just given warnings, often by police officers on an informal basis. He felt bad about being such an incompetent juvenile delinquent, but his mistakes had the paradoxical effect of keeping him out of real trouble with the law.

Gradually, John's relationship with his mother improved. Although Margaret made no secret of the fact that she was very disappointed in him, she allowed him to continue living at home. John dropped out of high school just before his sixteenth birthday. His mother was angry and distressed, but their relationship survived. After nearly nine months of unemployment, John got a job pumping gas at a local garage. He began to save some money, and became more reliable and regular in his habits. His mother began to entertain a shy hope that he might, after all, make something of his life. What she did not know was that from the age of seventeen, John had started taking illicit drugs on a regular basis.

Drug Abuse and Petty Crime

John had dabbled with drugs in his early teens, but had never been a regular user. Once he started working at the garage, he had an income. He could afford drugs. But the real reason for his developing habit was his sense of inadequacy and failure. He felt a

84

sense of despair about ever doing anything right, about ever being successful. When he looked back on his short life, all he could see was a succession of stupid mistakes, of lost opportunities, of wrong decisions. He blamed others for most of these, in an attempt to protect himself from feelings of guilt. But he was none the less tormented by a sense of guilt that revolved around the ways in which he had disappointed his mother. He felt unbearably envious of the obviously rich people who stopped at the garage to have their limousines filled with gas. He felt lonely, but was too shy and insecure to approach girls for a date. He spent a lot of time day-dreaming about beautiful women. He fantasized about being rich enough to attract them through displays of wealth and power. The more he dreamed of these things, the more of a failure he felt when confronted with the reality of his life.

Although John was no longer a member of the Ferry Street Gang, which had disbanded itself, he still had contacts in the world of drugs and petty crime. He started meeting with a group of regular users, and began taking drugs again himself. Although some members of the group injected themselves with heroin whenever they could get it, John used mainly amphetamines and 'crack'. He injected himself occasionally, more to establish his credentials with the group than because he enjoyed it.

The group included a young woman called Tammy whom John found very attractive. Under the influence of 'crack', he made a pass at her, and she responded. They started an affair, which was John's first sexual experience. His depression and guilt vanished as he became absorbed in this relationship. He fell deeply in love. John and Tammy began to spend more time together on their own than with the other group members. They planned to share an apartment together.

Tammy's drug habit was much worse than John's. She was addicted to heroin, and sometimes worked in massage parlours, strip joints, or even on the streets, to pay for her habit. John hated the idea of Tammy selling herself. He promised to maintain her supply of heroin if she agreed to stop prostituting herself. To do this, John had to supplement his income. He became involved in a car-theft syndicate. For over two years he earned enough money to support Tammy in her habit. He was able to afford to rent a small apartment that they shared. John himself continued to take mainly amphetamines and 'crack', injecting himself only occasionally.

After two years in this relationship, Tammy became restless. She started working in a massage parlour again. John found this out by chance, and was very angry and upset. After this, their relationship began to deteriorate, and John began making mistakes in both his legal and illegal jobs. He came to the attention of the police, was put on probation, but reoffended. Put on probation a second time, the judge made it clear to John that a further offence meant prison.

At the time that John made his bungled attempt at committing suicide, he believed that he was going to prison. His relationship with Tammy had virtually ended. He could see no point in living. Once again, his habitual tendency to make mistakes had the paradoxical effect of saving him – this time from successful suicide. Had he chosen to hang himself from a pipe a little higher up the wall, he would almost certainly have died. Had he not actually twisted around while trying to suspend himself from the lower pipe, his attempt would probably have failed entirely. The court official would have found him unharmed in the toilet cubicle, and would doubtless have regarded this futile attempt as a gesture not to be taken seriously. But because he nearly died his attempt at suicide was taken very seriously, and led to him having psychiatric treatment rather than a prison sentence.

Therapy

During the fourth therapy session, I made an error of judgement. I suggested to John that he was an intelligent young man, and I asked him why he thought that he had not made very constructive use of his abilities so far in his life.

What I intended to be a firm but sympathetic confrontation was interpreted by John as a harsh attack. But he did not tell me this. Instead, he failed to attend the next interview. I rang his probation officer, and she told me that she was very worried that John was about to go back to stealing and stripping down cars. Because I felt partly to blame, I made an effort to contact him by phone, and was successful. I apologized for my tactlessness, and asked John to attend his next scheduled appointment. He did, and he pointed out that if I could make mistakes and admit them, then perhaps he could learn something about making mistakes from me! I accepted this rather back-handed compliment, and we were then able to start talking about John's self-destructive behaviour.

As part of this, John agreed to try and recall something of his childhood before age eight. He was adamant that he had no first-hand recollections, and very few second-hand ones, because his mother refused to talk about his earlier childhood. Their few surviving relatives lived in different states, and John had little contact with them. They had been unable or unwilling to help John with his memory problem.

I suggested that John try once again to get his mother to help fill in the gap in his memory of childhood. When he raised the matter with her, she became upset and weepy, and refused to discuss it.

After a total of twelve sessions, although we had established a fairly good working relationship, and John had not resumed his illegal activities with automobiles, therapy became bogged down. John's feelings of guilt were getting stronger, and he was still taking amphetamines and 'crack' spasmodically. He was beginning to see that his proneness to make mistakes was part of a general, mainly unconscious, self-destructive tendency. But the origins of this tendency remained a mystery.

It seemed that events in his early childhood might hold the key to some real understanding of John's problems. But knowledge of these events was denied us.

After much deliberation, I suggested that John have an amytal interview. This involves the slow, graduated intravenous infusion of sodium amytal. This potent drug has the capacity to relax some people to such an extent that unconscious barriers to the recall of painful memories are lowered. It is a risky procedure that I use very rarely.

About ten minutes into the interview, John started to talk: 'My father. There's something about my father. I see him coming through the door. It's dark outside. He must be coming back from work. He's walking unsteadily, his breath smells like it does when he's been drinking a lot. I look at him. He stops and shouts, "Stop staring at me, brat!" I start to cry. My mother comes in from the kitchen. "Stop picking on the boy," she yells at my father. "I'll pick on the little shit if I want to," he yells back. I start to cry more, and my father turns toward me, raising his hand to hit me: "Shut up, or I'll really give you something to cry about, you little turd!" My mother yells some more, and my father turns back toward her.'

At this point of the interview, John starts to tremble a little, and sheds a few tears. I ask him if he wants to stop. He wants to carry on. He starts talking again.

'I see and hear it all so clearly. It's as if it's happening again right now. I hear my father yell at mother again: "Right, you sodding bitch, I'll have you." He walks toward her. She goes back into the kitchen. I run up to my father and try to stop him going into the kitchen. He knocks me over and walks on. I crawl after him. I see my mother pick up a long, sharp knife. She threatens Father with it, but he just carries on walking toward her. They struggle. He tries to take the knife from her. She slips and falls, and he falls on top of her. I'm screaming so loud that my voice gives out. Suddenly, it's quiet. My father gets up. My mother doesn't. I see blood on the floor. I see the handle of the knife sticking out of my mother's side.'

John stopped talking. He started to weep. He sobbed and sobbed for about ten minutes. Then he went to sleep. I woke him after twenty minutes, and we talked about what he had said. He still remembered most of it. I congratulated him on having the courage to go through with the interview, and told him that I thought things would start getting better for him now. We agreed to talk more at the next interview, scheduled for the following day.

Over the next few sessions, John was able to recall much of his childhood between the ages of four and eight. The amytal interview had been the breakthrough needed and, once begun, the flow of memories continued. Many of the memories were painful, especially those surrounding the stabbing of his mother. Margaret had been rushed to hospital, where she had needed emergency surgery for a bleeding liver. Fortunately, there were no complications, and she came home after ten days. During this time, John had been fostered with a neighbourhood family.

John's father was initially charged with assault, but Margaret explained that the injury was accidental and refused to take legal action against him. However, it was agreed that he would live elsewhere, and shortly afterwards Margaret initiated divorce proceedings. John saw his father again only twice, both times in court. He moved to another state about a year after the stabbing, and neither Margaret nor John had heard from him since then.

Over the next few months of therapy, John began to realize that he had blamed himself for his mother's stabbing. He had thought to himself, 'If I hadn't started to cry when Dad came home, this would never have happened, Mum would be well, and I would still have a mother and a father.' So painful were these thoughts that he suppressed them, and, in a few months, he had developed a profound amnesia for the whole traumatic episode. As part of this, he had also suppressed his earlier memories. Any chance of the block lifting spontaneously was destroyed by the change in Margaret's behaviour when she came out of hospital. She started to abuse alcohol and neglected herself, although she struggled to look after John as best she could. In this difficult family environment, John's defensive repression of painful memories continued.

As John began to understand the origins of his self-destructive behaviour, and come to terms with his painful memories, his feelings of guilt and self-dislike began to lessen. He cut back his drug habit, and toward the end of the first year of therapy he announced that he was 'clean'. He added that he was determined not to go back on to illicit drugs of any kind, although he still got drunk occasionally.

Over the next twelve months, during which I saw John about once every two weeks, he continued to improve. He remained off drugs, and his alcohol binges became infrequent. He got a job, and began to study part time. He still lacked confidence, but he had made friends with a young woman with whom he enjoyed a mutually supportive relationship.

During the second year of therapy we had talked about John's very stereotyped view of sex roles. He learned that this view resulted mainly from the absence of his father, who was not replaced by any other male figure that he could identify with. Instead of having an idea of masculinity based on reality, John had internalized 'macho' images of manhood, along the lines discussed in Chapter 2. His ideas of success had been very stereotyped, relying on the acquisition and symbolic display of wealth. Having a smart, good-looking and devoted woman companion was an essential part of this. John came to see how limiting was this vision of success, and how his repeated failure to achieve it was a fundamental part of his self-destructiveness. His ambitions became more realistic, and, as they did so, he became less envious of people who displayed obvious wealth.

We finished therapy after two years. John felt confident that he would be able to manage any residual self-destructive tendencies in the future. Although he had only just started part-time study, he was enjoying it and was already doing better than he had imagined. We agreed that he should contact me if he needed any more help. He did ring me, about six months later – but not for help. He wanted to tell me that he had been sixth from the top of his class at the end of the first term! I have not heard from John since, but his former probation officer, whom I still see from time to time, tells me that he has kept out of trouble with the law.

Implications of the Case

John's case illustrates many themes that are basic to men's self-destructiveness. His story is unusual only because his self-defeating behaviour could be ostensibly traced back to a specific traumatic episode. In fact, much of what had happened in his childhood *before* his mother's stabbing contributed to his self-destructiveness later in life. It is very rare for a single traumatic episode in childhood to cause major psychological problems in adulthood. But because John had suppressed the memory of his mother's stabbing, he was not consciously aware that he blamed himself for its occurrence. His sense of guilt, and its origins, were mainly unconscious. This led to self-punishing behaviour, especially making stupid mistakes or repeatedly getting caught, which John blamed mainly on other people. Because he accepted little personal responsibility for his self-destructive behaviour, he failed to learn from it. Instead, he repeated the same patterns of behaviour over and over again.

Whatever its origins, unconscious guilt is a powerful source of men's self-destructive behaviour. In Western societies especially, unconscious guilt is intimately connected with the type of relationship that boys have with their mothers. Freud was very interested in men's unconscious guilt, and in order to explain and understand it, he borrowed the Oedipus myth from the Ancient Greeks.

The Myth of Oedipus and the Oedipus Complex

The term Oedipus Complex has become a cliché in the Western world. But it is an idea that is still basic to the thinking of many psychiatrists, especially those who are trained in the Freudian tradition.

The original myth of Oedipus is well worth recalling. Ancient Greece contained warlike groups of people who believed that weak, sickly infants were a liability. Unhealthy or sickly babies and infants were taken out of town and left in the surrounding countryside to die. The Greeks called this 'Exposure'. Such a fate befell the infant Oedipus. But instead of dying, he was discovered and rescued by a wandering tribe.

Adopted by a childless couple, he grew up believing that he was their natural child. In his teens, he sought advice from an oracle, who predicted that he would kill his father and marry his mother.

Naturally, Oedipus was horrified at this notion. Rather than risk it happening, he sadly left his parents and the tribe that had nurtured him, still not realizing that he was adopted. During his travels he fought and killed a man who was chief of another tribe. Because he fought so bravely and skilfully, he was allowed to take the chief's place, and subsequently married his wife.

Some years later, Oedipus accidently discovered the awful truth. The man that he had killed was his natural father, a member of the tribe that had originally left him to die as an infant. The woman to whom he was now married was his natural mother. The prophecy that he had left his home to avoid had come true. Confronted with this, Oedipus was filled with such self-disgust that he blinded himself and became a wandering beggar.

What is the relevance of the Oedipus myth to modern Western men? The answer lies in our child-raising practices, which encourage young children to be raised exclusively and in relative isolation by their mothers. As we saw in Chapter 1, children in developing countries – which contain a great majority of the world's population – are not raised primarily by their mothers. In such societies, any fit adult woman, whether or not she has young children, is far too valuable an economic resource to be wasted on looking after young children. All fit women need to take part in the growing, gathering and marketing of foodstuffs – activities that are basic to survival. Their young children are looked after mainly by older children, and by the infirm and the elderly.

Only highly industrialized societies cloister woman away with young children, expecting them to devote their lives to a task that, as a full-time job, is often boring and frustrating, especially for women of any education and intelligence. It is in the context of this basically unhealthy way of child-rearing that the Oedipus myth comes to life.

Little boys who are raised mainly or exclusively by their mothers often develop an excessive emotional attachment to them. Freud believed that this attachment usually has a sexual or libidinal element that is, of course, discouraged, and which the little boy learns to suppress. I described in Chapter 2 how little boys identify with their mothers, and internalize their 'feminine' attributes as part of their basic identity. This process is heightened and intensified by the powerful emotional attachment of the little boy to his mother. Although the little boy has intense feelings of longing for his mother, he is compelled to suppress or bury many of them, especially as he gets older. At the same time, he begins to feel that his father is a *rival* for his mother's attention, love and affection. Because his father is so much bigger and stronger, the little boy buries his feelings of anger and resentment toward the man whom he sees as being the only obstacle to his mother's exclusive love. When feelings of anger and rivalry toward his father do emerge, they are very frightening because they lead to the assumption that father will retaliate. Such a retaliation, believes the little boy, is likely to be very dangerous, because Father is so much bigger and stronger. Fear of retaliation from the father often has a specifically genital focus. This has come to be called 'castration anxiety', a term that should generally be used symbolically rather than literally.

Little boys who do not resolve this dilemma are said to suffer from an Oedipus complex when they grow older. The Oedipus myth reflects the unconscious components of this dilemma: first, the wish to destroy the rival father, and the fear and self-disgust about this wish, which is driven into the unconscious mind;

second, the desire to exclusively possess the mother, and the guilt and self-loathing evoked by the libidinal, physical or sexual aspects of the desire. Rather than experience such guilt and self-disgust, the little boy suppresses and buries his desire for his mother, together with his sense of identification with her 'feminine' attributes. At the same time, he cuts himself off from those maternal attributes that he has internalized, creating the beginnings of inner emptiness in later life.

Resolving the Oedipus dilemma is not easy. It requires the little boy to develop a close, caring relationship with his father. Only in this way can he work through and resolve the feelings of anger and hatred toward the man who, as part of his earliest attempts to make sense of the world, was seen as a dangerous rival. As we have noted, modern Western fathers spend only a tiny fraction of their time actively relating to their young children. In most nuclear families, the opportunity does not exist for boys to fully resolve the Oedipal dilemma. The implications of this are profound.

Oedipus and Sexual Competition

It will be recalled that after the accidental stabbing of John's mother, John's father left the family. In Oedipal terms, the feared rival was vanquished. At last, John had his mother to himself. He struggled to please her – to be a successful substitute for his father – until she rejected him after his first brush with the law. John then buried within him his longing for his mother, and transferred his emotions on to his delinquent peers. Subsequently, he began in earnest a career of self-destruction. Unconsciously, he still feared retaliation from his banished father and punishment for his wish to replace him. If, before he left, John's father had been a better parent, John might have resolved his Oedipal problems instead of developing strong self-destructive tendencies. But John's father had abused alcohol and other drugs, and was erratic and unpredictable in his behaviour. The little time that he spend with John was characterized by irritability and anger toward the boy rather than by affection and concern. This prepared the ground for the major Oedipal problems that occurred later.

Similar Oedipal dilemmas affect many men, perhaps most, in Western society. Such men, as adults, must struggle to repress and

93

deny residual thoughts and feelings of libidinal or quasi-sexual attachment to their mothers – or to any woman who may *represent* their mother.

In the nineteenth century, men coped with this dilemma by *splitting* their image of womanhood. Woman became either mothers and wives, who were 'good' and asexual, or whores, who were 'bad' and sexual. In mid-nineteenth century London, it has been reliably estimated that one in every sixty houses was a brothel, and that one in every fifteen women was a full-time prostitute. The situation was similar in big American cities. In 1856, the Chief of Police in New York City estimated that the metropolis contained over 5,000 prostitutes and nearly 500 brothels. By the 1890s the number of prostitutes had risen to over 40,000. Through the use of prostitutes on such a huge scale, men were able to maintain their split between the 'good', 'nonsexual' women they married – and who represented their mothers – and the 'bad' women of the streets, who met their sexual needs.

It is no longer possible for men to split woman into 'good' or 'bad' through the widespread use of prostitutes. In relating to women, Western men now have to manage in different ways those thoughts, feelings and impulses that derive from the unresolved Oedipal dilemma. A major way of doing this is to *avoid feeling dependent* on a woman. As children, men were almost totally dependent on their mothers. As adults, any feelings of being dependent on a woman threaten to evoke Oedipal stirrings. To a man with unresolved Oedipal issues, a woman on whom he feels emotionally dependent represents his mother. To protect himself from the confusion, anxiety and guilt attached to this dilemma, he must preserve emotional distance between the woman and himself. Even more important, he must feel that it is he, and not she, who is in control of the relationship.

It is clear from this that stereotyped ideas about male-female relationships, with men dominating essentially submissive women, are very appealing to men with unresolved Oedipal problems. This is one reason why sex-role stereotyping remains such a powerful and vigorous theme in Western society: men need those stereotypes to help protect them from conflicts that have been unresolved since early childhood. Of course, the stereotypes make it more difficult for these conflicts to be resolved, and

94

actually increase the likelihood that they will arise in the first place. Thus, sex-role stereotypes and unresolved Oedipal conflicts reinforce each other in a destructive vicious circle.

Sex-role stereotyping powerfully reinforces sexual competition, which is also directly encouraged by unresolved Oedipal problems. Men who deal with Oedipal guilt and anxiety by dominating and controlling women are also required to compete for those women with other men. Competing and fighting with other men over women is often a displacement of the basic Oedipal theme. But instead of competing with their fathers for their mothers' exclusive love and affection, these men are fighting with other men for a woman to control and dominate. Of course, the compulsive need to control a woman obscures the paradox that the man is at the same time completely *dependent* on this woman to make him feel like a 'real man'.

Sexual Competition and the Media

It is fashionable to blame the popular media, and especially advertising, for a whole range of social ills. But advertising agencies survive only by being almost superhumanly sensitive to what people want. Men still have most of the power in Western society, both financially and politically. Anyone who seriously doubts this needs only to look at the number of women in the legislative or parliamentary bodies of Western countries. Not only is their number tiny, but it has not significantly increased in recent years, in spite of the efforts of feminists. Because men's influence is still dominant at almost every level of society, the popular media reflect mainly men's needs. This is true of advertising also. Men need to feel comfortable about their roles and about their social and personal identity. That is why advertising so powerfully reinforces sex-role stereotypes: this is what men want.

How Can Useful Changes be Made?

In any society, the way in which children are socialized depends partly on what is fashionable at the time. In Western society, debate about child-raising has focused mainly on the question of discipline versus permissiveness. This has led to a situation whereby children in some families are exposed to no discipline at all, so that they find it difficult to internalize a sense of responsibility toward others. Fortunately, extremes of permissiveness are no longer fashionable. Even more important, this is true of extremes of discipline. It is now widely accepted that beating or hitting children is not a healthy or useful aspect of child-raising. In more enlightened Western countries, it has become unfashionable. In a few, it is now against the law for parents to beat their children.

This debate over discipline versus permissiveness has helped to obscure the real issues in Western child-raising. These issues revolve around the question of who should be responsible for the task of raising children. This enormously difficult and important task – a task that is often boring and frustrating – is still left overwhelmingly to women. While raising children, especially their own, women are still made to feel guilty if they do not make the role a full-time one, or at least a role that takes precedence over others that might be more personally rewarding for them. As long as this pressure exists for women to take primary or exclusive responsibility for child-raising, little boys will experience profound conflicts in their emotional and sexual development. They will grow into men who have feelings and attitudes toward women that hinder their chances of relating to them as equal human beings. Instead, they will continue to see women as objects for their convenience; as objects to enhance their status in the eyes of other men, and to make them feel truly 'masculine'. Competing for women as objects, rather than relating to them as fully qualified human beings with equal rights and responsibilities, will continue to be a fundamental aspect of manhood. Sexual competition, with its inherent wastefulness and self-destructiveness, will continue to be a lynchpin of social cohesion.

This can be changed only if men become more willing and able to take an active part in child-raising. Men who genuinely and equally share this and other tasks with the mothers of their children are becoming more common. But they remain unusual. Men who 'reverse roles' and become the main providers of care to their children are even more unusual. So rare are they that several popular movies have recently been based on the theme of role reversal. If the practice was anything other than very rare, no one would be interested in making movies about it. Statistics confirm that men with main or exclusive responsibility for child-raising are very unusual indeed.

Sex-role stereotyping discourages men from being anything other than traditional in their sex-role behaviours and attitudes. It is a major obstacle to change. In reality, many men would like to be more involved in child-raising. But the influence of sex-role stereotyping makes them feel that these desires are in some way unhealthy or improper. 'Real men' are not interested in spending a lot of time with young children. Men also tend to believe that they lack the necessary skills and attributes to be good at raising young children. They are also often very frightened of the feelings of warmth and tenderness evoked in them by the closeness of young children. Most important, commitment to the role of main or exclusive breadwinner physically prevents most men from spending regular time raising their children, let alone sharing the task equally with their partners.

To change this situation will not be easy. In fact, there is no real impetus for change. There is little understanding of the way in which child-rearing practices affect adult lives. Few people are aware of the connection between Western child-rearing practices, sex-role stereotyping, and sexual competition. Fewer still have made the link between these elements of society and men's self-destructive behaviour. It appears that men themselves are not really concerned about their self-destructiveness. They are certainly remarkably complacent about the fact that this self-destructiveness reduces their life span by an average of nearly seven years. But a few men are beginning to grapple with the issues. Some of the problems that they must face in order to do so will be discussed later.

5

Women's Dependency on Men

The last three chapters have dealt mainly with men's issues. Important themes have concerned the intimate connection between social and sexual competition, and their complex interactions with sex-role stereotypes. These interactions serve to increase the overall level of men's competitiveness. Underlying themes include the Oedipal dilemma and men's need to deny their dependency on women, a denial that depends in large part on their ability to control them. Since the Industrial Revolution, men's control of women has been made relatively easy by women's economic dependence. But in today's world, most women can choose whether or not to be economically dependent on men. Given the choice, many married women still choose economic dependency. Often, this increases emotional dependency, so that a married woman comes to believe that she cannot survive without 'her man'. For almost all women, this belief is false. But many women are convinced that it is true. Why so many women believe the myth of their dependency on men is explored in this chapter.

Women's dependency on men has a simple origin: men are bigger and stronger than women. When an argument cannot be resolved verbally, physical violence becomes an option. If this option is used to resolve an argument between a man and a woman, the man will usually win. The woman risks serious injury, or worse.

Since the dawn of human history, women have had to protect themselves against men's physical aggression. How they have done this, and the way that this relates to women's dependency on men, is the subject of what follows.

Protection Against Men's Aggression

I outlined in Chapter 3 how survival as a male in the harsh environment of our early ancestors required enormous drive and aggression. Men's aggression to each other was also essential for maintaining social structure and cohesion within the clan. It helped to create a fairly stable social hierarcy or 'pecking order' among the males. The use of ritual *submission gestures* prevented violence between men from becoming too destructive.

Submission gestures evolved as a way of preventing the destructive escalation of fights between *males*. Females of most mammalian species have not evolved submission gestures. They protect themselves from male aggression mainly by *avoidance*. For example, studies of lions in the wild have shown that females are good hunters. They are at least as fast as the males. Working as part of a team that includes both males and females, it is often the female that will single out a herd animal such as a deer, and kill it. But once the animal is dead, the female immediately retreats from it, even if she has not eaten for days. Only when the males of the pride have eaten their fill will the females approach. When they are sated, the young lions approach and eat what is left. If the female does not retreat immediately, she is at high risk of an attack from a male lion – an attack that will not be stopped by ritual submission gestures, and which may well result in serious injury.

Studies of monkeys and apes in the wild have yielded a similar picture. If a female monkey intrudes uninvited into the social space of a senior male, she is at high risk of being attacked and injured. But there are many occasions when this territorial intrusion is essential: searching for food, or reclaiming a wandering infant. Confronted with an angry male bearing down on her, the smaller, lighter female has three options. First, she can run away; this will work as long as the male chooses not to pursue her, which is usually the case. Second, she can physically confront the male, which verges on the suicidal. Third, she can present herself sexually to him, thereby distracting him from his aggressive behaviour. When flight is impossible, the third alternative is commonly used in the wild, and this introduces an important theme: the link between female sexuality and protection against male aggression.

Female Sexuality and Male Aggression

Let us return again to our early human ancestors, whom we shall call hominids. We know from fossil studies that the male-female size difference among hominids was at least as great as it is among modern humans, and probably greater. This fact is important, because it provides evidence for the historical and evolutionary necessity of women protecting themselves against male aggression.

It seems inevitable that levels of aggression were very high among early hominid groups or clans. Not only were women at high risk for injury from male aggression, but so were young children. Women therefore had to protect not only themselves, but their infants and young children also. Early hominid groups were, of necessity, very socially cohesive and compact. Especially in cold weather, they would huddle together or occupy small areas such as cliff overhangs, caves or other sheltered sites. Those groups who had discovered how to light fires would cluster around them for warmth and protection. This need for social cohesion meant that fights had to be settled, or avoided, in ways that allowed the combatants to remain in fairly close proximity. *The best way for women to achieve this was to redirect male aggression into sexual activity.* It is highly probable that, when retreat or avoidance was impossible or ineffective, hominid women presented themselves sexually to male aggressors. In this way, the male aggressive drive was transformed into a positive force that often had the effect of creating a bond between particular males and females.

The human female is unique among primates and other higher mammals in that she is sexually attractive and responsive at almost all times, and can become pregnant during most of her menstrual cycle. The females of all other higher mammalian species can be successfully impregnated only during estrus, which culminates in ovulation. Estrus occupies only a minority of the sexual cycle. Colloquially, female domestic animals during estrus are said to be 'on heat' or 'in rut', and their extraordinary capacity to attract males in this phase is well known. When not in estrus, higher mammals are relatively unattractive and unresponsive sexually.

The evolutionary basis for the unique sexual responsiveness of the human female is still a matter of scientific debate. But sexual responsiveness throughout the menstrual cycle conferred undoubted survival advantages, because it facilitated sexual intercourse as an alternative to destructive male aggression. As hominid societies became more complex, the male-female bonding aspect of sexual intercourse became more valuable than its capacity to transform physical aggression. Being the regular sexual partner of a male who was a senior member of the clan hierarchy was vital for the survival of females and their offspring. This sexual partnership conferred social status on the female, and increased the chances of her getting enough food for herself and any dependent children. It also decreased the chances of attacks from other males. Inevitably, hominid women were not passive partners in this vitally important matter of mate selection. They would use sexual presentation in order to evoke the sexual interest of a high-ranking male. By repeatedly doing this, a measure of bonding might occur, and the female would achieve increased social status. In these early times, women were often the sexual initiators, because being sexually active and aggressive increased their chances of survival.

Hominid women formed sexual partnerships on a strictly practical basis. If their current mate was displaced by a rival, or killed, they would quickly seek a new partner, as high up in the social hierarchy as possible. Failure to do so placed them and their offspring at grave risk. Finding a new partner usually meant repeated sexual pairings, often with several males. *This urge toward a range of different sexual partners was fundamental to the personal survival of hominid women*. For this reason the urge was probably stronger in women than in men, although it obviously depended on a matching male responsiveness that was reliable and rapid.

Although we have fossil evidence for the physical similarity between ourselves and our immediate hominid ancestors, we have no such evidence with regard to brain structures and mechanisms. But the evolution of the brain is characterized by its economy. Pre-existing structures are generally preserved, with evolution proceeding through the addition of new ones. On such a basis, we can assume that the basic neuropsychological mechanisms that underlie sexual behaviour have changed little. From this perspective, modern women can still be regarded as the sexual initiators. If men are biologically unsuited to monogamy, and there is little disagreement about this, then it is probably even more true of women. But, as we shall see from what follows, men have long struggled to impose monogamy on women. This struggle is one of humankind's most extraordinary sagas. It is fundamental not only to the development of patriarchy, but to many of the problems that exist between men and women, including the tyranny of compulsory relationships.

Controlling Women's Fertility

We have, from about 30,000 BC, direct evidence of the social relationships that prevailed between the sexes. Cave drawings from this era suggest that our late Ice Age and early Stone Age ancestors worshipped deities, and that these deities were exclusively female. Other evidence for the predominance of female deities comes from stone or clay figurines and statuettes, some of which are over 20,000 years old. These early figurines are always female. It is not until 7,000–8,000 BC that men, or male deities, are significantly represented in cave paintings or other symbolic forms.

Why did our Ice Age and early Stone Age ancestors worship female deities? This is a complex issue that is not yet fully understood, and which perhaps never will be. But a number of themes are fairly clear.

As the human race evolved, it developed greater mastery of its environment, through tools, weapons, clothing and control of fire. The struggle to survive became less harsh, and aggression between and within human groups became less fierce. The size of individual clans increased, and some developed into tribes containing a number of separate clans. The worship of deities emerged as part of our ancestors' attempts to explain and control the natural world. Women were the first deities because they brought forth babies: this was considered a magical act. Not only was childbirth considered magical, but it was thought to be an entirely female event. *The relationship between sexual intercourse and pregnancy was not understood*, at least by men.

It is difficult for us to comprehend this. But, in an early Stone

Age context, it is easy to appreciate that men had little chance to observe a relationship between a specific sexual encounter and the birth, nine months later, of a child. Nine months was a very long time in the Stone Age. And there was the confusing element of unpredictability: some sexual encounters did not lead to pregnancy. If sexual intercourse could occur without pregnancy, then why could not pregnancy occur without intercourse? Women had a better chance of observing men's role in pregnancy because, as we have seen, they were probably the main initiators of sexual intercourse (see also *When God was a Woman*, by Merlin Stone). They often had a rational, socio-economic basis for their choice of sexual partner. This invested meaning into the act of intercourse, meaning which was largely absent for the man. Women were more likely to remember a specific sexual act and its context; and they noticed the first signs of pregnancy well before men did, making an association with intercourse easier to establish. When women first learned of the relationship between intercourse and pregnancy, they kept this knowledge secret, and used it to increase their power and status. They were remarkably successful in this regard: men came to believe that women had exclusive control of fertility. Given this awesome magical power, it is not surprising that early deities were female. The social status of women reflected this. It was certainly equal to that of men and perhaps higher. It seems very likely that once they had achieved their elevated status, women used it to try and control their own fertility. Cave paintings and the earliest written accounts of history suggest that women achieved considerable success in this regard. They often chose their own sexual partners, and had much control over the timing and frequency of sexual intercourse.

Eventually, of course, men learned the truth. They learned that they played a fundamental part in the creation of babies. At this point began the long struggle by men to gain control of the fertility process.

The Resurrection of Patriarchy

For tens of thousands of years, humankind survived through hunting and gathering food from the natural environment. Around 7,000 BC, agriculture was established. This allowed a huge increase in population, and with it the flourishing of the first human civilizations. The early civilizations of the Middle East are those most relevant to our discussion. For a period of over 3,000 years, the agricultural peoples of the Middle East lived in reasonable harmony. They continued to worship mainly female deities, although male gods were becoming steadily more prominent. But population growth brought an end to this long era of relative peace and harmony. Increased numbers led to competition for territory, and this led in turn to increased emphasis on armed force. More and more resources were put into training men to fight territorial battles.

Over the next 4,000 years, the influence of men in the tribes and nations of the Middle East grew stronger and stronger. As more and more emphasis was placed on defence or conquest of territory, so did the structure of Middle Eastern societies become more militaristic. Territory also became vital *within* the various nations, since the amount of land held by a family or clan determined its wealth and social status. Survival of a group or clan often depended on both the physical strength and the wisdom of its leaders, just as it had in much earlier times. Strong men sought to maintain leadership and ownership of territory through their sons. Once the idea of maintaining power and influence *through male children* became established, it became necessary to *control female fertility*. How could a man be sure that the children borne by his official wife or wives were his own? How could he be sure that it was *his* eldest son who would inherit his power and status? How could the followers of a powerful chief be sure that it was truly *his* son who would succeed him as their leader? Unless all this could be guaranteed, the whole patriarchal social system would fall apart.

The only way to guarantee paternity was to exercise total control over women's fertility. This meant controlling female sexuality. As Middle Eastern societies became more warlike and patriarchal, they evolved ways of controlling the sexual activities of women. In reality, it is impossible to control a women's sexuality without locking her up. The Crusaders of the early Middle Ages attempted this through the use of the so-called chastity belt – an uncomfortable device that their wives were locked into while these men went off on prolonged Crusades.

104

Needless to say, what was locked could be unlocked, and the devices worked more for psychological than for physical reasons.

It eventually became clear that the only way to achieve control over women's sexuality was through a *psychological* approach. Women had to be indoctrinated so that they themselves believed that sexual fidelity to one man was absolutely necessary and proper. The indoctrination of women meant first achieving fuller control over them. To achieve this, it was necessary to reduce their social status, and especially to destroy the worship of female deities and replace them with male ones.

Christianity and the Confinement of Sexuality

One of the main themes of the Old Testament is the prohibition of worshipping 'false idols'. Instead, the one true God – a male God – was to be the sole object of prayer, devotion and supplication. The attempts by the Old Testament Jews to stamp out the worship of idols were largely aimed at destroying the then prevalent worship of female dieties, and hence reducing the power and status of women in Jewish society.

The early Christians continued this process with great vigour and enthusiasm. The New Testament contains many references to the inferior status of women. For example, from St Paul's First Corinthians: 'For a man ought not to cover his head, since he is the image and glory of God; but woman is the glory of man. For man was not made from woman, but woman from man. Neither was man created for woman, but woman for man' (11:7–9). And: 'The women should keep silence in the Churches. For they are not permitted to speak, but should be subordinate, as even the law says. If there is anything they desire to know, let them ask their husbands at home' (14:34–35).

Of course, it is easy to select passages from the Bible to justify a particular viewpoint. There are passages that propose equality for women, and it is likely that St Paul had this view, even though some of his utterances suggest otherwise. But references in the Bible to the inferior and subordinate status of women are much more common than proposals for their equal status. It was not until 1992 that the Church of England and the Anglian Church in Australia agreed to allow women to be ordained as priests.

Christianity not only helped to suppress women's power and influence generally, but it managed specifically to suppress women's sexuality. In the biblical story of Adam and Eve, it is Eve who is the sexual temptress, and who gets the blame for introducing Adam to the corrupt world of the flesh. Although the early Christian church sought mainly to control and diminish female sexuality, it was highly ambivalent to male sexuality also. For example, in First Corinthians St Paul says: 'To the unmarried, I say that it is well for them to remain single as I do. But if they cannot exercise self-control, they should marry. For it is better to marry than to be aflame with passion' (7:8–9).

This early tradition of suppressing sexuality continued. For example, from the fourteenth century on, the Church of England issued detailed guidelines about sexual intercourse within marriage. If these were strictly adhered to, there were very few occasions when sexual intercourse was permissable. Although this effectively controlled the sexual activities of most married women, who were largely confined to the home, it had less effect on married men, who had greater access to sex outside of marriage.

The Inquisition and Witch-hunts

The most obvious example of the Christian Church's attempts to subjugate women and their sexuality is the Inquisition. Started by the Pope in the 1320s, it developed over the next 150 years into a huge programme for the systematic extermination of women who refused to conform. In 1486 the Dominican monks Kramer and Sprenger published a book called *Malleus Malleficarum*, or 'The Hammer of the Witches'. This became the witch-hunter's handbook. It was basically a manual for the persecution of women, since Kramer and Sprenger believed that witches were nearly all female. Of an estimated 9 million witches executed throughout Europe, over 80 per cent were women. In England, women accounted for over 90 per cent of victims. This attack on witches and witchcraft was basically yet another attempt to destroy surviving remnants of the worship of female deities, around which witchcraft usually revolved. It included also a direct attack on female sexuality: according to *Malleus Malleficarum*, 'All witchcraft stems from carnal lust, which is in women insatiable.'

106

The terror of the Inquisition was indescribable. Anyone could denounce a witch, from a spiteful neighbour to a malicious child. Witches were considered guilty until proven innocent. They were often stripped naked and completely shaven in order to show up any 'Devil's marks', usually moles or large freckles. Hideous machines of torture were used to extract confessions and the names of accomplices. Those who maintained their innocence were burned at the stake. Few women burned as witches actually practised any form of witchcraft or goddess religion. The witch trials were mainly a chance to get rid of women who refused to submit to the power of patriarchy. Persecution focused on women who were rebellious or eccentric, or women who refused to obey the rules of Church and Society, and even beautiful women who had aroused unacceptable lust in priests or married men. Lesbian women, freethinkers, and women who refused to be submissive were also victims. Sometimes, whole communities of women were destroyed, with hundreds put to the stake within a few days. For example, in Germany in 1585 two villages were each left with only a single female inhabitant.

The relentlessness of the Inquisition owed much to the nature of the 'old religion' that involved worshipping female deities. In this religion, female sexuality was celebrated and revered. The priestesses were the embodiment of a goddess who was the bringer of sexual joy and passion. This celebration of female sexuality was feared and hated by the Christian Church of the fifteenth and sixteenth centuries. It was a direct challenge to their attempt to suppress and control women's fertility, a control upon which the structure of patriarchal society depended.

The Collective Power of Women

The activities of the Christian Church in Europe during the Middle Ages and later coincided with the desires of the State. The feudal system prevailed, especially in Germany and England. As we saw in Chapter 1, the feudal system was an all-embracing patriarchy that vested absolute power in the Lord of the Manor. Within this system, women and children had virtually no legal rights. The Church and the State combined in preserving the social order. In fact it was almost impossible to disentangle the interests of Church and State. They coincided in most areas, and especially in the area of controlling women and their fertility.

If women were legally powerless in the England of the Middle Ages, why did the Church, with the support of the State, invest so much time and energy in subjugating them? The answer lies in the social structure that then prevailed. Nearly everyone lived in small villages with populations of 50–200, or in small towns occupied by no more than about 1,200–1,500 people. In the villages, everyone knew everyone else. Although women had few legal rights, they had considerable power and influence at a practical level.

Women's power was partly a reflection of the way people earned a living. Most families survived through the right of the male head of family to lease some land from the Lord of the Manor. Families, and especially husbands and wives, had to create an efficient division of labour in order to produce enough both for their own survival and for payment of rent and taxes. The contribution of women to this process was fundamental. Although women had few legal rights, they had a great deal of economic power.

Allied to women's economic power was their collective power. If a particular issue concerned women, they were able to freely discuss it among themselves. Since the size of the local community was rarely more than 200, it was not difficult to achieve consensus about the rights and wrongs of the matter at hand. Women then had a whole range of options, including the right to assemble and protest in the village square. Strong local spokeswomen often emerged, and were a force to be reckoned with. They spoke out not only on matters that affected mainly women, but on more general issues also. Because they were not subordinate to the Lord of the Manor directly, but through the male heads of their families (who swore personal oaths of loyalty), they were in some ways freer than the men to voice their opinions.

The economic and collective power of women was a continual threat to the patriarchal feudal State, because it implied the loss of male control over fertility. Women's power and influence probably peaked in England between about 1550 and 1700, and this period coincides with the greatest level of witch-hunts, trials and executions. A similar upsurge occurred in the United States between about 1580 and 1700, including the infamous Salem witch trials of 1692, now part of American folklore.

Witch-hunts and executions of women were highly successful in destroying women's collective power and influence. They eliminated individuals who either by example or by acting as local spokeswomen and leaders urged other women to struggle to retain their basic human rights. Witch-hunts also encouraged and played on women's fear of the Devil and of eternal damnation. Many women, perhaps most, genuinely feared the existence among them of evil witches. Women often took the most active part in the denunciation and persecution of other women as witches, even though these so-called witches were among those most likely to speak out against women's oppression. Once the solidarity of women was broken, their collective power was largely destroyed.

The Industrial Revolution and Women's Psychological Subjugation

From about 1750, the Industrial Revolution began in England, large parts of the rest of Europe, and much of North America. At the start of the nineteenth century, nearly 80 per cent of the working population of England and North America were employed directly on the land. By the end of that century, less than 10 per cent were employed in this way. Instead, they worked in the mines, factories, mills and offices that led to the creation of the towns and cities in which nearly all Westerners live today.

The effect of this sudden change on people's daily lives was profound. They found themselves living in urban communities that lacked a geographical focus. The new industries required people to work away from home. Men left the house each day to labour in mines, factories and offices. Women continued to work at those activities that had taken up much of their time when they lived collective lives in small villages. But, increasingly, these tasks were done at home. Women became more isolated from each other. They lost their ability to plan and act collectively, and with it a major source of their residual power and influence in society. In addition, they lost most of their *economic* power. Married men now brought home a wage. Although they often handed part or all of this to their wives, these women were now almost totally economically dependent on their husbands.

Before the Industrial Revolution, this had rarely been true.

Family income had come from the co-operative endeavours of husbands and wives working closely together. For example, a common family practice in the seventeenth and eighteenth centuries was the manufacture of woollen cloth. Children carded the wool, the wife spun it into yarn, and the husband did the weaving and finishing. No single person was the breadwinner. The family worked together as an economic unit.

The Industrial Revolution, then, dealt two major blows to women. It finally destroyed their collective power, a process that had been largely achieved by the witch-hunts; and it destroyed their economic power. The effects of this on women was devastating. In fact, the Industrial Revolution did unintentionally what the combined efforts of Church and State had failed to achieve for over 2,000 years: it permitted the *psychological* subjugation of women.

To understand how this occurred it is necessary to be familiar with a basic psychological mechanism termed 'identification with the aggressor'. Situations in which a person has little or no power are often profoundly distressing, especially if physical or psychological abuse occurs at the same time. The sense of fear, anger, resentment and injustice that people experience in such situations can be transformed into mainly positive feelings by 'identifying with the aggressor'. In essence, this means the oppressed person abandoning his or her own sense of identity, and identifying instead with the oppressing person. The capacity to achieve what seems a very difficult manoeuvre has been programmed into the human species over many thousands of years of evolution. It was necessary for social cohesion in very harsh environments, and it is still used widely today.

Women in the nineteenth century were forced to identify with men in order to protect themselves from feelings of unbearable rage and frustration about their powerlessness. Not only had they been stripped of their collective and economic power, but they still had few legal rights. This was especially true of married women. As late as 1869, John Stuart Mill stated in his famous work *The Subjection of Women* that 'the wife is the actual bond-servant of her husband, no less so, as far as legal obligation goes than slaves commonly so called . . . However brutal a tyrant she may unfortunately be chained to . . . he can claim from her and enforce the lowest degradation of a human being, that of being the instrument of an animal function contrary to her inclinations.'

Women living in nineteenth-century England were, on marriage, legally obliged to hand over all their economic assets to their husbands. Any assets wives obtained after marriage were also to be transferred to the husband. The assumption was that only husbands were competent to manage financial and economic affairs. This idea was a logical aspect of the extreme patriarchy that prevailed at the time. On the death of the husband all the family's assets passed automatically to the oldest son. This was known as the rule of primogeniture. Naturally, married women experienced a great deal of pressure to have at least one boy. If they had daughters only, the family assets would eventually be transferred to the daughters' husbands. Since this meant the end of the family's status and power it was to be avoided at all costs – even if it meant the wife having daughter after daughter until finally a son was born.

It was not until the Married Women's Property Act of 1882 that a married women was given full ownership of the assets that she had before marriage or that she obtained afterwards.

Women, and especially married women, coped with this oppression by making a virtue of necessity. By identifying with their husbands, they achieved a measure of psychological well-being. This is well illustrated by the following quote attributed to a nineteenth-century 'lady of distinction': 'The most perfect and implicit faith in the superiority of a husband's judgement, and the most absolute obedience to his desire, is not only the conduct that will ensure the greatest success, but will give the most entire satisfaction.'

Women as Objects

Once women began to abandon their own personal identity as part of coping with powerlessness, they became extensions of the male psyche. In particular, they began to function as *status symbols* for men.

Before the Industrial Revolution, social status was largely fixed at birth. Most communities were small enough for everyone to know everyone else's social rank. There was little need for status symbols, although clothing served this purpose among the wealthier people. After the Industrial Revolution, most people lived in urban settings where their social origins were not necessarily well known, or could be obscured. Visible symbols of wealth and success became important.

One of the best status symbols was a well-dressed wife and children. In the second half of the nineteenth century, only about 60 per cent of men married, because marriage required significant assets. The mere possession of a wife indicated modest wealth. If she was also beautiful, charming and well dressed, this reflected greater wealth and social status. Wives were also encouraged to develop musical and artistic skills so that they could entertain and impress their husband's friends and colleagues. Thoughtful, sensible conversation from married women was, however, frowned upon by men. After dinner parties, the men retreated to the drawing-room for port, cigars and 'intelligent conversation'. The women were left alone, supposedly to chatter about domestic matters and to gossip.

I examined in Chapter 4 how the child-raising practices that became widespread in the early nineteenth century were psychologically unhealthy, especially for boys. Raised exclusively by their mothers or other women, boys commonly grew up with major psychological conflicts about women that Freud referred to as the Oedipus complex. As we saw, one way of managing these conflicts in adulthood was to split women into 'good' and 'bad'. The powerlessness of women made them very susceptible to this splitting process, with which they themselves came to identify.

For nineteenth-century women, the choice was to be married, 'good' and mainly asexual; or to be unmarried, 'bad' and the object of men's sexual desire. Unmarried women had very limited job opportunities. Most were domestic servants, easily exploited by their employers. Many were forced to be prostitutes. We know that about 1 in 15 women in mid-nineteenth-century London was a full-time prostitute. However, this was a role for younger unmarried women, who were only about 20 per cent of the total adult female population. This means that about one-third of young unmarried women were full-time prostitutes! What started off as a psychological device by men to cope with emotional conflict over women – namely, splitting them artificially into

112

'good' and 'bad' –actually became part of social reality. This is a reminder of just how much power men had over women in the nineteenth century: they were able to turn women, on a huge scale, into objects that confirmed a grossly distorted view of womanhood. Women were no longer real people. They were extensions of the male psyche.

Confronted with a choice between getting married or becoming a prostitute or a domestic servant, it is not surprising that most women craved marriage. Once married, they were grateful for being rescued by their husbands from lives of poverty and degradation. Divorce was virtually impossible. Married women who were well treated by their husbands tried to please them by being perfect wives and mothers – which meant identifying with and carrying out their husbands' ideas about this. Wives who were brutalized by their husbands had little choice but to endure it.

New Ways of Creating the Ideal Woman

During the twentieth century, Western women have largely escaped from the tyranny that they experienced during most of the nineteenth century. But the social forces that degraded women in the nineteenth century were enormously powerful and pervasive. Their influence is still strongly present in English-speaking countries.

Women living in the nineteenth century identified with men's unrealistic views of them because it was better than feeling constantly oppressed, diminished and dehumanized. Once 'identification with the aggressor' had taken place, married women no longer felt oppressed. On the contrary, they felt valued, safe and secure. But the price that they paid for that was a tragic one: they had to abandon their rights as human beings. They had to live by proxy, through their husbands and male offspring. Forbidden to take part in affairs beyond the domestic, they could experience the outside world – the world of men – only at second hand.

Many married women in today's Western world have a similar view. We know that a majority of women do not yet want to be equal with men. For example, it was women themselves who rejected recent attempts to modify the Constitution of the United

States so that it confirmed true equality for women. Women who reject the chance to become first-class citizens, preferring instead to remain subordinate to men, obviously do not feel oppressed. If they did, they would join their sisters who are struggling to achieve true equality.

I suggested in Chapter 1 that the impact of feminism, important though it is, has been secondary to *economic* changes that have created vast numbers of jobs for women. Women have undoubtedly become more liberated *economically*, and are much freer than ever before to take control of their own lives. But surveys have repeatedly shown that the Women's Movement has had a measurable impact on sex-role attitudes only in well-educated middle- and upper-middle-class women. Even in this group the effects have been modest. For example, a 1990 survey of American female university students showed that their views about the relationship between the sexes had changed very little since a previous survey in 1972 (*Sex Roles*, 24:1991: 413–23). It is clear that a majority of women consider themselves to be traditional rather than feminist. Many still actively reject feminist ideas.

Women's rejection of feminism – or at least their apathy toward it – is partly a natural consequence of the feminist movement itself. Early on, radical feminism got a bad press, and was linked in the popular mind with lesbianism. Much of this was an attempt by the male-dominated popular media to trivialize and marginalize feminism. If they could achieve this, it was unlikely to be taken seriously by women on a large scale, and men would be under no real threat. For these and other reasons, a majority of women were unable to identify with the early feminist movement. In the face of continuing opposition from the popular media, and women's persisting conservatism, the movement has lost impetus. It no longer struggles to reach ordinary women. As a result, they have little chance of hearing about feminist ideas in a way that allows them to respond.

Women, and especially working-class women, are still subjected to powerful forces that seek to turn them into objects for the gratification of men. These forces are exerted mainly through the popular media, which are almost entirely owned and controlled by men. But there are other forces, rooted in financial independence, encouraging them to take control of their own identities and destinies, and to live life at first hand, not just through their men.

Women's identities are, of course, closely connected to the images that they have of themselves. Modern woman is experiencing an identity crisis. This makes her unusually susceptible to media images. Ideal women are portrayed physically as tall and slim. This shape is a reflection of the male desire to create women as objects. The taller and thinner women appear, the more they are shaped like men. Men's desire for women to look more like them represents in part an attempt to manage their psychological conflicts over women. The more women look like men, the less men are challenged to resolve their problems in relating to them.

Women still struggle to turn themselves into objects – objects that represent men's attempts to create the Ideal Woman. But the Ideal Woman is not real. She is an invention of the male psyche, designed to make men feel better about themselves. Women torture themselves on a vast scale to conform to an unreal image created mainly by men. Instead of accepting their natural shapes, they devote enormous time and energy to losing weight. They spend small fortunes on plastic surgery – carried out mainly by men – aimed at achieving a trimmer, slimmer, shape. Women in the nineteenth century were tyrannized by unrealistic ideas that required them to be perfect models of tact, charm, morality and general 'goodness'. Modern women are tyrannized almost as much by ideas concerning their physical appearance.

When women abandon their own identity and struggle to replace it with an unrealistic, ideal image created by men, they abandon also their independence. Such women feel incomplete without a man. Their lives are devoted mainly to finding and keeping a man. Once they have found him they are fearful of losing him. They go to great lengths to keep him happy, usually at the expense of their own well-being. Women like this are still very common in Western society. There has been a recent spate of books about this problem, such as Robin Norwood's *Women who Love Too Much*. These books are exciting and challenging, and are undoubtedly helping women grapple with important issues of self-determination. But they often neglect the historical background to women's dependency on men. Without an understanding of history, it is impossible to realize just how difficult for women is the task of achieving independence and self-determination. The following case history illustrates, among other things, just how much courage and determination women need to free themselves from the idea that, without a man, they are incomplete.

Case 5: The Abandoned Wife

Julia, age thirty-two, was referred to me by her family physician because of persisting depression that had recently got worse. A petite, attractive woman, she started to speak almost before she sat down on the chair in my office: 'The real problem is that I still love my husband. And he left me just over two years ago.'

Julia explained that she and her husband Chris had what she believed was a perfect marriage. 'Everyone thought that we were the perfect couple. We were always going around arm in arm, hand in hand. He brought me breakfast in bed every morning for the twelve wonderful years we had together. We shared everything. I had no idea that he was going to leave. There was no warning. He just went, while I was at work. I found a note when I got home. It said that he didn't love me any more and that he'd gone to live with someone else. He didn't even leave an address or contact number. I was shattered, I couldn't believe it, I was numb. I felt my whole world had gone. The only thing that's kept me going since then is hoping that he'll come back.'

I said to Julia that I was beginning to understand a little of what she had been through. Then I asked her to tell me about her family background. First, Julia spoke about her mother: 'She was a very caring person, but at the same time very domineering. She was always telling me what to do, putting me down, telling me that I was too timid, that I didn't have enough confidence. She was very much a home body. She lived for us kids and Dad. Since Chris left me, her nerves have been really bad.'

Julia spoke very differently of her father: 'To the outside world he was a gentle, caring man. But at home he was different. It was almost as if he was two people in one. He would get drunk regularly at weekends, and he just became totally unpredictable. He would shout and yell at me for nothing. Often when he was in one of his moods he would hit one or the other of my brothers, although he never hit my sister or me. Most of the time, when he wasn't drinking, he was quiet and withdrawn. I used to feel a bit sorry for him. I really wanted to be close to him, but when I tried, he would always push me away. He took no part in family life. Mother did everything for him, she waited on him hand and foot, I guess. He really didn't seem at all interested in us girls. The boys got a bit more attention from him, but I suppose they got more ill-treatment, too.'

As Julia told me more about her family origin, a number of themes became clear. Most obviously, there was one set of rules for the men and boys in the family, and another for the women and girls. Julia had three older brothers and a younger sister. Although the boys took the main brunt of their father's drunken rage, they were expected to do very little housework. This was done entirely by Julia, her sister, and their mother. Julia's mother had married at eighteen and had not worked outside the home since then. Although domineering toward her daughters, she was anxious and uncomfortable in social situations, which she tended to avoid. As a result, her life had become largely confined to the domestic. As part of this, she put much thought, time and energy into looking after her husband and three sons. She expected her two daughters to help her in this, and they both became 'little mothers' from an early age.

The Little Mother

Julia was initially angry and frustrated about the 'double standards' that operated in the family. She resented being a 'little mother'. But she buried her anger deeply within her, and struggled to share her mother's view of the world – a world in which women depended on men and looked after them, even if the men that they depended on seemed rather weak, unreliable, unpredictable and sometimes brutal creatures.

Eventually, this became Julia's view also.

To survive in her family, Julia began to day-dream about escaping from it. But, to her, escape meant being rescued by a man. A man who was the complete opposite of her father. A man who was strong and reliable, and who could look after her and protect her from having to struggle alone in the world.

117

As Julia got older, this day-dream became a fundamental part of her personality. It was reinforced by television and by the magazines that she read, from which she absorbed only one message: to survive and to be fulfilled, a woman must have a man. Without a man, a woman is incomplete.

Julia's parents taught her the same thing. Neither encouraged her to study or to aim for economic or emotional independence. In fact, her mother systematically undermined Julia's self-confidence, increasing the likelihood that she would feel unable to manage life on her own. Julia's father never took enough interest in her to counteract her mother's influence.

A Perfect Marriage

At eighteen, while working at a boring job in a small factory, Julia met Chris. There was a strong mutual attraction. To Julia, Chris seemed the perfect husband: tall, strong, silent, reliable and caring. They married when Julia was nineteen and Chris twenty-three.

Julia was a regular church-goer and had strong Christian beliefs. The couple waited for their wedding night before having sex. Julia was surprised at Chris's sexual inexperience and ineptness, which led to them abandoning their attempts at lovemaking. Julia was sensible enough to arrange some counselling, and matters improved. To her surprise, Julia discovered that she had a strong sexual appetite. She enjoyed lovemaking with Chris, became interested in experimenting with different positions, and had little trouble reaching a climax. But Chris remained reserved and inhibited sexually, and refused to try anything new.

Their daughter Sharon was born eleven months after the marriage. Julia was happy to take exclusive responsibility for her care. This suited Chris as he was working very hard at his job with an advertising agency.

Julia considered their marriage to be perfect. She idolized Chris, and wanted nothing more out of life than to please him. Although Julia did not work outside the home, she had a passionate interest in ballroom dancing. Chris shared this interest, and they usually went dancing together at least once a week. They entered competitions, and won several prizes. Babysitting was rarely a problem, because Julia's mother, who lived fairly close, was always delighted to look after Sharon.

Julia emphasized, in our second session, that she had no idea why Chris should want to leave a marriage that she thought was perfect. I proposed that a major task of therapy might be to try and work out if the *reality* of the marriage was different from her image of it. Perhaps, I suggested, she might then begin to let go of the hope that Chris would come back. Julia started to weep at this point. She believed that she could never abandon hope of Chris's return: 'I don't want to become a loner. But I wish I could lose this constant aching inside that I've got for him. I could scream sometimes to get rid of it.' However, she agreed to talk about how she had coped without Chris so far, and about how she might cope in the future.

Waiting for Sir Galahad

About a week after Chris left, Julia had got a letter from him saying that he was living with another woman about eight miles away. He then rang to speak to Sharon, and Julia insisted on talking to him. It emerged that he had been having an affair with 'the other woman' for nearly eighteen months before he left Julia. Chris said that he had never loved anyone as much as this woman, and that he could not live without her.

Instead of getting angry, Julia got depressed. She blamed herself for Chris leaving, although she was unable to identify how she may have failed to meet his needs. Over the two years that followed, she never experienced any anger toward Chris, even though he seemed to take pleasure in humiliating her. He insisted that there was no chance of a reconciliation. If Julia wanted to discuss why he had left, he simply said that he had stopped loving her a long time ago, but had stayed in the marriage out of duty. When he fell passionately in love with another woman, he decided that he had to leave. He expressed no regret or remorse, and never apologized for the misery that he was causing Julia. Although he took Sharon out fairly regularly, he showed little overt interest in her well-being.

Julia talked compulsively about Chris with her friends – until she had no friends left. Although she stopped talking about him, she fantasized almost constantly about how wonderful their marriage had been. She hoped and prayed that Chris would return to make her feel happy and complete again.

Because Julia was depressed and preoccupied with Chris, she lost interest in ballroom dancing, and with it the remnants of her social network. She managed to get a part-time job, but lost it after ten weeks because she was so inefficient and erratic. She explained to me that there were only two things that had stopped her from killing herself: her daughter Sharon, and the hope of Chris coming home again.

About a month before Julia first came to see me, Chris had moved to live in a different state – alone. He had left behind the woman for whom he had abandoned Julia. This sharply increased Julia's depression because Chris seemed free to come back to her. But instead he had moved further away.

It took several sessions for Julia to describe all this. At the end of the fourth session, I suggested that Chris had been her 'knight in shining armour' – her Sir Galahad. I added that I thought that her task was to learn to cope without him, since it was clear that he had no intention of returning to her. She wept, but was able to laugh a little at the idea of Chris as Sir Galahad. For the first time, she agreed to entertain the idea that he was a wandering knight. It is well known that wandering knights often failed to come home.

Exploring the Real Marriage

I asked Julia what it might feel like to be placed on a pedestal. She reflected for a moment and replied that it would probably get pretty boring after a while. I asked her how Chris might have coped with being idealized: 'I supposed he might have thought that he had to live up to this image and try and be perfect,' she replied. Julia then recalled that Chris would never talk about his feelings. She talked freely about hers, but he always clammed up tight when she asked him to talk about his feelings and emotions. She remembered that Chris had once said that he didn't like to talk about his feelings because it made him feel vulnerable and weak. Julia had a flash of insight: 'But I didn't *want* him to seem weak. I needed to feel he was strong, reliable, solid as a rock. And rocks don't have feelings.'

Once we had started to look at the reality of the marriage, rather than the magical image that Julia had constructed, new insights emerged. Julia realized, for example, that she had never fully accepted her sexuality. Her parents never talked about sex; it was a taboo subject. When Julia had her first period at eleven, younger than most of the other girls in her class, she had no idea what it was. She was petrified. She thought that she was bleeding from some sinister internal injury. On the only occasion that Julia's mother had discussed sex with her, she told Julia that she herself had never enjoyed it: it was something rather unpleasant that had to be endured. Julia realized that she still felt that sex was rather dirty, and felt guilty about enjoying it. In order to cope with her bad feelings about sex she had idealized her relationship with Chris. We discussed other reasons, rooted in her upbringing, why she needed to idealize her husband.

Letting Go

After a total of fourteen sessions, held about once a week, Julia said that she was ready to begin the task of mourning the loss of her marriage. She had finally accepted that Chris would not return. The next few weeks were very difficult for her. She needed great courage to carry on with the grief work. Most difficult of all was learning to express *anger*. It was literally an alien experience for her. So deeply, and for so long, had she buried her anger within her, that she had forgotten how to feel it. Instead, she had transformed it into positive feelings. But once she started to get in touch with her rage, it erupted like a volcano. She became so agitated by her new feelings that she took tranquillizing medication for ten days – the first time that she had taken drugs of any kind during therapy.

In addition to confronting her anger, Julia had to confront her fears of being alone. This was a task that was just as difficult for her. She had no picture of herself as a separate person. Her only self-image was that of a half-person, waiting to be completed by a man. But these and other tasks Julia courageously grappled with.

She finally succeeded in letting go after another fifteen sessions spread over nearly six months. She started to feel more confident. She began a job that was quite interesting, and planned to study and improve her employment prospects. As a final step, she filed for a divorce and completion of the property settlement. She believed this would leave her with enough money to buy a small house of her own. She rang me eight months after we finished therapy to say that she was happily living with Sharon in her own home, and enjoying life more than she had for years. She had finally abandoned the wish to be rescued by a knight in shining armour. However difficult and challenging, she wanted to manage her own life from now on.

Implications of the Case

It is not unusual for mental-health workers to see women like Julia. Although her case is an extreme example of women's dependency on men, it illustrates themes that are very common in the lives of Western women today. Julia's family of origin was an obvious example of the 'double standard'. But many families discriminate against women in more subtle ways. The message is always the same: women are not as capable as men at managing alone in the world. They need men to protect them and to support them economically. But they are more suited than men to managing domestic matters and raising children, and they must take more responsibility for these. Research has shown repeatedly that married women who work outside the house have two jobs. One is paid. The other, to do with being a mother and housewife, is not. Most married men have only one job. Even if their wives work full time, husbands do much less housework and child-care than they do.

The extraordinary thing about this inequality is that women continue to endure it, just as they do the many other inequalities that they suffer. But an understanding of the historical pressures on women to forego their basic human rights helps to explain why this is so. Western women have been exposed for over 2,000 years to powerful, pervasive social forces aimed at making them dependent on men. Reversing the effects of over 2,000 years of oppressive propaganda cannot be done quickly. It will take many more years, and the process will not be a smooth or steady one.

6

Myths and Stereotypes of Motherhood

Chapter 5 focused on Western women's dependency on men and the powerful social forces that have shaped this dependency over the past 2,000 years. In nineteenth-century England and America, marriage became one of the very few ways in which women could achieve a measure of social status, respectability, and financial security. Hence, the pressure to marry was very great. Once married, divorce was virtually impossible, and so most marriages were truly compulsory. In the twentieth century, the pressure on women to marry remains very strong. But the economic and social basis of this pressure has become intimately connected with the *desire to have children*. For most women, this desire is very powerful. It fuels their wish to marry as much as, or more than, their need for social status, companionship and financial security.

The realities of childbirth are daunting. Until quite recently, it carried a high risk of maternal death from bleeding, infection or other complications. Now, in Western countries at least, the risk of maternal death is very low. But the price that women have paid for this is to lose control of the birthing process. In the name of safety, childbirth has been moved from home to hospital. Pregnancy and childbirth have become medical conditions rather than natural, family-centred events. Of course, medicalization has also meant that labour can be made less painful, or can be avoided wholly or in part by Caesarean section. But Caesarean section carries with it the risk of an anaesthetic. It also damages the muscles of the abdominal wall, prolonging the task of regaining full physical fitness and attractiveness. Perhaps most important, it denies the mother a chance to experience naturally the moment of birth.

However safe and painless pregnancy and childbirth can be made, they are still a profound mental and physical challenge for women. The physical challenge has been made more difficult by the modern view that women must be slim and trim to be attractive. A woman cannot be pregnant and slim. Breasts and stomach swell: after childbirth, they can never be fully restored by nature to their former state. For some women, the loss of firm breasts and a flat abdomen is a major assault on their self-image. Although plastic surgery can largely repair the ravages of nature, it is a procedure that is by no means free of risk, and one which can be painful and uncomfortable.

Sometimes for such physical reasons but more often because they wish to preserve an unencumbered lifestyle, Western women are increasingly postponing childbirth. In several Western countries, the birth rate now closely matches the death rate. This means that population growth – a traditional desire of nearly all Western nations – can be achieved only through immigration. If present trends continue, the birth rate will fall progressively below the death rate in many Western countries, and their populations will begin to fall. Whether such an assault on national pride and status will be permitted remains to be seen.

The prospect of declining populations raises the whole issue of why women choose to have children. From a purely materialistic viewpoint, it is an amazingly generous thing to do. Pregnancy and childbirth are risky and painful. Child-raising is a demanding and often frustrating task that is largely unpaid and which is incompatible with a full, active role in the work-force or the community at large. Children are very expensive to raise. When they grow up, they may not appreciate or respect their parents. They often move well away from them – to a new suburb, a new city, or even to a different state or country. Where then are the rewards to parents of years of physical, emotional and financial sacrifice?

More and more people – especially women – are asking this question. From a purely materialistic point of view, the answer is clear: the risks and sacrifices of traditional motherhood are far greater than its benefits. But the materialistic response disregards all those benefits of motherhood that cannot easily be measured. These benefits include emotional and spiritual fulfilment, and the sense of creating a new life – an experience that is unique to women.

Value systems based on purely materialistic considerations are becoming stronger and more widespread in Western society. As this happens, more and more people will make judgements about childbirth and parenthood that are based on a materialistic view of the world. It will be interesting to see how the various Western nations react to the population reduction that will be a natural consequence of this.

Historically, Western women have had little control over whether or not they become pregnant. The number of children that they raised was determined not by the number of their pregnancies, but by the number of children that survived childbirth and infancy: until very recently, the average child mortality rate was greater than 50 per cent. Parents had a substantial influence on the number of their children that achieved adulthood. Efforts by the State to increase the rate of population growth acknowledged this, and created incentives that enhanced the survival rate of infants and children. These incentives also included attempts to *idealize* motherhood, a process that, as we shall see shortly, was ultimately very successful.

The idealization of motherhood remains necessary today. In fact, it is more necessary today than it has ever been, because, for the first time in history, most Western women are now free to choose the number of children that they have. Increasingly powerful incentives are required to encourage women to have enough children to maintain population stability.

One of the most powerful incentives is the idea of the *maternal instinct*, a notion that is almost universally accepted. According to this idea, all women have a natural instinct to bring forth and raise children. Unless they do so, they will feel unhappy, frustrated and unfulfilled. Therefore, it is in the best interests of *women themselves* to have children. The idea of a universal maternal instinct is a myth. It is not based on reality. But it has been systematically perpetuated as part of Western nations' obsession with preserving power and status through population growth.

In today's Western world, the myth of a universal maternal instinct is unhelpful to women. It puts pressure on them to have children, and to then experience childbirth and child-raising as exclusively pleasant and fulfilling events. The reality for most women is different. But, because they cannot readily acknowledge the negative aspects of child-raising, they feel guilty or ashamed when they experience these. The effects of this guilt and shame on mothers and their children can be very destructive, and this is just one reason why the idealization of motherhood and the myth of a universal maternal instinct are such important issues – issues that I will now explore from a clinical perspective.

Case 6: A Damsel in Distress

Roxanne, an attractive woman of thirty-one, was referred to me by her family physician at her own request. She explained to me that she was anxious and depressed because an intruder had recently broken into her home and caused a great deal of damage, although nothing had been stolen. She was fearful that it would happen again. I expressed my sympathy and asked how I could help her, given that she seemed to have good reasons to be anxious. Perhaps, I suggested, the police might be more helpful than I could be. Roxanne then added that there had been some marital problems that she would like to discuss. I suggested that she start by telling me a little about her family background.

Roxanne described her mother, Sarah, as 'caring and loving on the outside but cold and rejecting underneath.' Sarah had married at nineteen, and by twenty-five she had four daughters. Roxanne was the youngest. Sarah never worked outside the home; she devoted herself to caring for her daughters and her husband. Roxanne believed that her mother was always more concerned about *appearing* to be a good mother than actually being one. She never enjoyed a good relationship with her, experiencing her as emotionally cold and rejecting. Quite often, Sarah was very harsh and critical toward Roxanne, more so than toward her older sisters, and often unfairly – or so Roxanne believed.

Roxanne saw little of her father, whose job took him frequently away from home for a few days at a time. When he was at home, he either ignored Roxanne or was rejecting and critical of her, and she gradually withdrew from him emotionally, although she continued to crave his love and affection. His involvement in domestic chores and child-rearing was negligible: both he and Sarah believed this to be 'women's work'. Sarah was deferential and submissive to her husband, believing that this was an essential part of being a good wife.

In private, Sarah often told Roxanne that she was a burden to her, a nuisance and a disappointment. But in public, she talked about what a good child she was and what a pleasure it was to be her mother. When with other adults, she often talked about the rewards of motherhood and said frequently that she could never understand how a mother could abandon her children to go out to work. Constantly emphasizing the rewards of motherhood appears to have been Sarah's way of coping with her ambivalence toward it.

Roxanne strongly identified with her mother, an identification that helped her to obscure the painful feelings of anger, guilt and resentment that she felt toward her. From her early adolescence, Roxanne had only one ambition: to get married and have children. She had internalized her mother's obsessive preoccupation with the maternal role, failing to recognize that this was Sarah's way of disguising her own negative feelings toward it. In spite of these purely domestic ambitions, Roxanne was very intelligent, and did well at school. On leaving, she got a job as a secretary in a large insurance firm. Although she viewed her job simply as a brief interlude before marriage, she was well-organized, conscientious and generally effective at her work, which she greatly enjoyed. She gained promotion, and within a few years was in a position of modest responsibility. But she had difficulties in relating to male colleagues, tending to be excessively submissive. This placed some limitations on her performance.

The Marriage

Roxanne married Damion, aged twenty-six, when she was twenty-three. Damion's mother was a chronic invalid. She had, for as long as Damion could remember, suffered from giddy spells, fainting attacks, migraines and severe palpitations that had often kept her in bed. During these times, she could not bear noise, and Damion and his younger sister had to creep about the house like mice; no friends were allowed to visit; and Damion had to look after both his mother and sister.

Damion's father had devoted himself to a career in the police force, achieving high rank. He spent very little time at home except when his wife was particularly ill. On such occasions he was torn between a sense of duty to look after her and a strong desire to pursue his career. This conflict left him tense and irritable, and he tended to abuse Damion, although the boy continued to idolize him.

Because of his domestic situation, Damion was a shy and withdrawn adolescent. But he was determined to prove that he was at least as good as his father, and he worked very hard at school, getting good grades. After graduation he applied to join the police force, but was rejected because of a heart murmur. He instead decided to become a private investigator. His father's police contacts were very helpful, and Damion already had his own successful business when he married Roxanne, by which time he had largely overcome his shyness. Much of Roxanne's strong attraction to Damion derived from the fact that, unconsciously, he reminded her of her father. Because Damion was affectionate towards her, she believed that he would give her the warmth, care and support that she had craved from her father but never received. Sadly, her expectations were not met. So determined was Damion to be as successful as his father that he became obsessed with his work. He attended endless courses and conferences, and was out most nights and weekends cultivating contacts, meeting clients, or pursuing investigations. Like his father, he believed that Roxanne should be happy doing all the domestic work and child-raising on her own. During the little time that he spent at home he was usually tired and preoccupied, and expected Roxanne to look after him. He was entirely unable to meet Roxanne's needs for practical help and emotional support and affection.

The Realities of Motherhood

Roxanne stopped working about a month before her first child, a daughter, was born fifteen months after the marriage. She had three more children – two girls and a boy – over the next four years. She expected the motherhood that she had craved for so long to be a blissfully rewarding experience, and was shocked by the reality of it. To her horror and extreme guilt, instead of feeling pure love and affection for her first baby, she experienced many strongly negative feelings, as well as thoughts about splashing the child with boiling water and bashing her head with a large wooden spoon. Roxanne did not realize that strongly negative thoughts and feelings, especially towards a first baby, are experienced by at least a third of Western women.

Because she told no one about these feelings, she did not learn that they were fairly common and generally reflected a natural ambivalence rather than a real desire to harm the baby. Believing that she was unique in her hateful feelings, she came to feel guilty and inadequate about her mothering, and tried to compensate by being a perfect mother. To her, this meant being a full-time mother who should, on her own, be able to meet all her children's needs. Of course, for one person to fully meet all the needs of four young children is impossible.

As Roxanne struggled to carry out a task that could not be done, she always fell short of her expectations. This reinforced her feelings of guilt and inadequacy. She became increasingly depressed and anxious. Some of her anxiety symptoms were similar to those that had incapacitated Damion's mother. Instead of reacting with sympathy to these, Damion became enraged, shouting 'I spent half my childhood looking after a bloody invalid, and I'm certainly not going to do it any more.' This rejection added to Roxanne's depression and anxiety. She sought help from her family physician, who gave her medication. Although this relieved some of her symptoms, it added to her sense of guilt and inadequacy.

One day, when the eldest daughter was six, Damion was contacted by the police and asked to return home immediately. On arrival, he found four policemen in the house, which was in a state of utter chaos. The contents of drawers were spilled throughout, much of the furniture was broken, the television and video were smashed, and many of Roxanne's clothes ripped or slashed. Roxanne explained that two men had entered through the unlocked back door, seized and bound her to a chair, and then searched the house for money and jewellery. Unable to find anything of value, they had wrecked the house in frustration. Although they had threatened her, they had not done her any physical harm.

Therapy

At the start of our second therapy session, Roxanne explained that the police had found inconsistencies between her story and the forensic evidence. After some stressful confrontations, she admitted that she had invented the entire story, and that she herself had done the damage in a fit of rage. Because of Damion's good relationship with the local police, Roxanne was not prosecuted on condition that she underwent psychiatric evaluation and, if recommended, treatment. I agreed to continue seeing her under these new circumstances.

During subsequent sessions, held about twice a week, it emerged that over the previous two years or so, Roxanne had often had elaborate fantasies about being assaulted and raped by men who broke into her home. All these fantasies ended with Damion rescuing her and beating up the criminals, who were then imprisoned. Roxanne was the classical damsel in distress, rescued by her good knight. On several occasions, these fantasies had become so powerful that Roxanne had enacted parts of them in real life. She had slashed or torn her underwear, knocked chairs over, and in other ways created a scenario of violent rape by an intruder. But on each occasion except the last she had removed the 'evidence' and tidied up before Damion returned home. On the last occasion, she had taken some tranquillizers and had several drinks, causing her to loose control and create damage that could not be repaired or hidden before Damion's return. When she sobered up and realized the extent of the mess, she chose to ring the police rather than admit to Damion the truth of what had happened.

It became clear that Roxanne's destructive behaviour was a desperate attempt, mainly unconscious, to get Damion's attention by creating a mystery and becoming one of his clients herself. If she could not get his personal support and interest, perhaps she could get it on a professional basis. Because of her sex-role conditioning, she had felt unable to confront Damion directly about his failure to meet her needs. Just as her mother had behaved toward her own husband, Roxanne had been generally submissive and subservient to Damion.

Once Roxanne understood some of the reasons for her 'bizarre' behaviour, she wanted to invite Damion to join her in therapy. After initially protesting that he was too busy, he agreed to attend. It soon emerged that much of his anger towards Roxanne came from a fear that she would become a chronic invalid like his mother, and that he might have to compromise his career to look after her. Once he learned that Roxanne's behaviour could be logically understood, and was not a reflection of a serious mental illness, he became warmer and more supportive toward her.

After the intensive phase of therapy ended, I saw the couple once every 4–6 weeks for about a year. During this time, Roxanne let go of her obsessive preoccupation with motherhood. She accepted that her refusal to let anyone else look after her children was unrealistic, and came to understand that it was based on fears that reflected her own deeply buried anger and resentment about a full-time motherhood role. She began to contemplate going back to work, initially part time. Damion reduced his work load, mainly by delegating it to a new employee whom the business was now large enough to sustain. He became more responsive to Roxanne's need for affection and support, and she in turn became more loving towards him. At the end of therapy, their relationship was greatly improved, and Roxanne's anxiety and depression were much reduced in severity.

Implications of the Case

As a child, Roxanne's rejection by her father meant that she was unable to identify with him in a way that allowed her to internalize the 'masculine' attributes of assertiveness and independence. She retained largely unmodified her early identification with her mother, who modelled submissiveness and subservience towards men. As a result, Roxanne had not developed the capacity to be assertive, behaviour which she regarded as aggressive and un-feminine.

Unconsciously, she encouraged Damion to express for her by proxy the 'masculine' aspects of her personality that she denied or buried. Although she resented his absence from the home, she achieved a vicarious sense of achievement and recognition from his success in the world, which required him to demonstrate the 'masculine' qualities of assertiveness, aggression and competitive-

131

ness. Trapped by her early social conditioning and her idealized, stereotyped views of motherhood and marriage, Roxanne denied herself any direct expression of these attributes. The more trapped and frustrated she felt, the more she relied on Damion to express her denied, split-off masculinity. Her rape fantasies were part of this, allowing her to experience Damion as a super-masculine 'warrior' who rescued her and punished her assailants. But matters got out of control when, in an explosion of intoxicated rage, she finally expressed *for herself* her view of masculinity. This view equated assertiveness with aggression, and resulted in much damage to the contents of her home. The attack also expressed her mainly unconscious resentment about the way that her domestic role had come to limit and imprison her. During therapy, both she and Damion became aware of how limiting and destructive were their stereotyped views of sex roles. They saw the need to change these and to develop more role-sharing and communication between them.

The Development of Motherhood Myths

As Roxanne's story shows, the pressures on Western women to have children, and to marry before doing so, remain overwhelming. What follows is an attempt to outline the origin and nature of these pressures. Increased understanding of them should make them easier to resist.

Child Mortality Through the Ages

Research into the fossilized remains of adult skeletons dated between 5,000–8,000 BC has revealed a remarkable fact: the sex ratio is about 3:2 in favour of males. In other words, males in the early Stone Age were 50 per cent more likely to reach adulthood than were females. A fraction of this superior male survival rate results from the built-in bias that the human race has toward the male sex: about 6–7 per cent more male babies are conceived than female babies. This is because sperms containing the Y chromosome, which determines male sex, are slightly lighter than sperms containing the X chromosome, which determines the female sex. Sperms containing the Y chromosome therefore travel slightly faster, and are more likely to reach the female egg first, and to fertilize it. Once conceived, the survival rate of male embryos is a little lower than that of females. This means that the actual ratio of male to female births is about 105:100. After birth, female infants continue to have a slightly better natural survival rate, suggesting a superior general robustness.

Obviously, the greatly increased chance of male survival to adulthood in the Stone Age was due to social rather than biological factors. As we have seen, life was extraordinarily harsh for our Stone Age ancestors, especially for the males, who were responsible for hunting often dangerous animals, and also for fighting males from other clans or tribes in order to preserve territorial integrity. Those males who reached adulthood were unlikely to live for more than a further 10–15 years. A Stone Age man was old at thirty. Survival rates among adult women were higher, because their lives were less hazardous.

It was therefore necessary to replace adult men more often than adult women. Men became a more valuable resource. More effort was put into raising male children. When food was scarce, male children were more likely to be fed than their sisters, although this was often because they were more aggressive and demanding. Death from childbirth before physical maturity probably contributed to the excess mortality of girls. But whatever the precise reasons, 50 per cent more males reached maturity than did females.

Infanticide

The excess of male adult skeletons dating from the Stone Age has been a consistent finding of research into later epochs. For example, studies of European burial sites dated between AD 100–700 showed an average male-female ratio of about 160:100. In the fourteenth century, the ratio was slightly higher at around 170:100.

These figures raise the ugly spectre of infanticide, a historical reality that we must face in order to fully understand modern motherhood. The practice of infanticide has always been directed mainly at females. We saw in Chapter 4, while discussing the myth of Oedipus, that infanticide was a common practice among the

133

Ancient Greeks. Among the more warlike communities especially, it was thought unwise to waste scarce resources on raising children who seemed unlikely to contribute usefully to society as adults, or who might be a burden. Sickly or deformed babies and infants were generally killed, often by exposure – the practice of abandoning them in the open countryside. That exposure was also commonly extended to healthy female babies we know from statements such as that of Hilarion, a prominent Greek of the first century BC. He issued the following instructions to his pregnant wife: 'If, as may well happen, you give birth to a boy, let it live. If it is a girl, expose it.'

To modern Westerners, infanticide is a hideous crime. Anyone found guilty of killing a baby will be severely punished, unless it can be proven that they were insane at the time. But to Ancient Greeks, and to people living in the harsh environment of pre-industrial Western Europe, infanticide was regarded as a necessary practice. Even today, the killing of female babies is common in some parts of the developing world, in spite of Government efforts to stop it.

Historically, infanticide was regarded as necessary because the alternatives seemed even worse. Consider, for example, the circumstances of life for most English speaking people in the three to four centuries before the Industrial Revolution of the seventeenth and eighteenth centuries. Contrary to popular belief, it is well established that the nuclear family was the basic social unit throughout this time. The idea that extended families were common in pre-industrial England is a myth: less than 10 per cent of the population lived in extended or multiple family households. Average household size in the fifteenth and sixteenth centuries was about five (excluding servants), which is not very different from the average of about 3.5 people per household in modern England. Households were small because most couples could not afford to support more than two or three children.

For over 50 per cent of the population, life was a constant struggle to secure sufficient food, clothing, warmth and shelter to keep themselves and any dependents alive. Even for that minority of the population which had a home of its own and rights to share-farm a small area of land, life was very harsh and unpredictable. This was especially so in times of war, when huge areas of land were deliberately laid waste. Malnutrition was endemic. Personal hygiene was virtually non-existent: water had to be carried from wells or streams, and was too precious to be used for washing. Soap had not been invented. Most people were infested with lice, and unpleasant skin diseases were very common. Body odours were accepted as inevitable, except by those few who could afford expensive perfume to disguise them. Infectious diseases such as smallpox and tuberculosis were rampant, and there were periodic epidemics such as the Great Plague of 1665 – also known as the Black Death.

Formal marriage was restricted to less than half the population. Only men with demonstrable assets or financial prospects could marry. Children born to married women had a much better chance of survival than children born out of wedlock. For most unmarried mothers, the birth of a child was a prospect to be dreaded. Such babies were commonly abandoned in ditches or woods, drowned, or smothered at birth. Even if they were allowed to live, the chances of them surviving infancy were small unless they were fostered or adopted by a family of some means.

Even for the children of married women living in established homes, the prospects of achieving maturity were not high: less than 50 per cent of babies survived to adulthood. Infectious diseases were the main cause of death, aided by malnutrition and poor hygiene. Accidents and other forms of violent death were also common. Often, a clear distinction between infanticide and natural death could not be made. Simply to keep a child alive required a great effort on the part of most parents. Absence of that effort, rather than deliberate infanticide, accounted for many deaths of infants and children.

For many reasons, male children were more highly valued than female children. As adults, men's greater physical strength meant that they could do more physical work. Men had access to a wider range of occupations, especially the armed forces. For most poor families, the only chance of acquiring any wealth lay in one or more of their sons joining the army. Good soldiers were well rewarded, often with booty from successful armed forays into neighbouring countries or overseas. Even more important, only male offspring had rights of inheritance within the patriarchal Feudal System that arose after the Norman Conquest of the eleventh century. It was therefore essential for a family to have a male heir if its assets were to be preserved after the death of the head of the household.

Given all this, it was logical to favour male children, and to make greater efforts to ensure their survival than in the case of female offspring. A family that had two girl children, and was struggling to survive, would not have welcomed the arrival of another daughter. It is very likely that such a child would have died early in infancy, probably as a result of infanticide, although often this would have been difficult to establish. Parents expected to lose at least a third of their children before the age of five, so that the deaths of infants were rarely questioned. Parents who presided over the death of a baby or infant knew that the alternative was in many ways harsher. An extra child to feed might mean starvation for a family that was already below subsistence level. The quality of life for that extra child, if it survived, might well have been so poor as to verge on the unendurable. The were prospects of a better life in adulthood were extremely remote. Given such expectations of life, it is not surprising that death was often seen as an acceptable alternative – perhaps even a welcome one.

Motherhood in Times of High Child Mortality

Today, the death of a young child is a comparatively rare event. Parents who lose a young child are devastated by the tragedy. Many take years to recover from it, and some never do.

How did parents, and especially mothers, cope in those times when the death of half or more of a couple's children was a regular happening? Historical literature gives us considerable insight into this. The heads of many households carefully recorded in diaries all significant family events. The death of a child is most often recorded without comment: it was generally seen as a routine event which apparently evoked little emotion in either parent. Mothers could not allow themselves to become greatly attached to their children when they knew that less than half of them were likely to survive.

In the sixteenth and seventeenth centuries, mothers who could afford to do so generally employed wet nurses. Among the wealthier classes, breast feeding and nurturing infants was widely considered to be a messy and tedious task to be avoided if at all possible. Babies were often sent away soon after birth to be wet nursed – that is, to be breastfed by another woman. Without breast feeding, a child would die, because alternatives had not been invented. The practice of giving babies cow's milk had not been introduced, and milk substitutes did not exist. The average stay with a wet nurse was over three years, although breastfeeding generally ceased at twelve to eighteen months. Many parents made only rare visits during this time. Although the use of wet nurses was initially restricted to the wealthy, it spread widely in the seventeenth and eighteenth centuries, especially in France. The Lieutenant General of police in Paris documented the use of wet nurses in that city in 1780. Out of a total of 21,000 children whose births were registered in 1780, fewer than 1000 were nursed by their mothers. A further 1000 were nursed by live-in wet nurses. The others – some 19,000 – were sent away to wet nurses, often as far as 70 or 80 miles away, a distance that was very great in the days of horse and carriage.

Parisian women were so desperate to farm out their children to wet nurses that they often took little care to check on the suitability of these women. Many wet nurses took good care of their charges, but others neglected them badly. The mortality rate among nursed children was high, even by eighteenth-century standards. Such was the poverty among wet nurses that many abandoned their own babies so that they could earn money by nursing the children of wealthier women.

Although the use of wet nurses was probably greater in France than in other European countries, it was a relatively common practice throughout Europe, and certainly in England, during the seventeenth and eighteenth centuries. Women who could afford wet nurses were expected to use them. These women were not viewed as being bad, uncaring mothers. In fact, wealthy women who nursed their own children were considered to be eccentric. Women who had the choice of employing a wet nurse usually believed that raising children was an obstacle to doing more enjoyable and interesting things. Generally, only those women who could not afford to employ a wet nurse actually nursed their own children.

This widespread and well-documented use of wet nurses has

important implications. It suggests that if women are not expected to raise their own children, and are given the opportunity to hand them over to others, then they will do so quite freely. This undermines the notion of a basic, universal maternal instinct. It suggests that, given the right circumstances, women do not experience a great desire to nurture their own children. Instead, they prefer to get on with more interesting and enjoyable activities. If this is true, then a basic, universal maternal instinct does not exist. Rather, maternal instinct is the product of social conditioning. It varies according to the social climate. More evidence in support of this view is contained in what follows.

The Low Status of Children and Childhood

If motherhood had low status in pre-industrial England and Europe, then this was in part a reflection of the low status of children. In today's Western world, children have relatively high status. They are generally valued not only in themselves, but for what they may contribute to society in the future. Because we value our children so highly, it is difficult for us to comprehend that historical attitudes to children have been very different.

Under Roman law, the child was regarded as the property of the father, to be disposed of as he wished. This view is typified in the following statement by a prominent Roman writing in the first century AD and referring to his legal rights over his offspring: 'Do we not cast away our spittle, lice and suchlike things as unprofitable, which nevertheless are engendered and bred even out of ourselves?'

Roman law formed the basis for legislation in modern England and France, and in several other European countries and their colonies. Roman attitudes to children in these countries persisted until very recently. Not only were children viewed as the property of the father, but they were considered as essentially 'bad'. This view arose in part from the concept of original sin, a concept that was fundamental to the early Christian theologians. St Augustine, a theologian who had a profound influence on the early Christian Church in Europe, had this view of infants: 'Is it not a sin to lust after the breast and wail? For if I now lust with similar ardour . . . people would ridicule me . . . It is therefore an evil desire, since in

138

growing up we tear it up and cast it aside.' Of older children, St Augustine added: 'If left to do what he wants, there is no crime he will not plunge into.'

Until quite recently, the concept of childhood barely existed. Children were seen as miniature adults with negative attributes that had to be rooted out of them, with regular beatings and threats of hellfire and eternal damnation. As part of this, maternal affection was actually discouraged. This is clearly shown in the writings of Juan Luis Vives, a famous sixteenth-century Spanish preacher and educator: 'Bodies are as much delights as weaknesses; and so mothers damn their children when they nurse them voluptuously.' He recommends 'instilling them with fear by mild verberations, castigations, and tears, so that the body and the understanding are made better, by the strictness of sobriety and food.' As a final warning he adds: 'Take heed of the well-known fable of the youth sentenced to be hanged, who asked to speak to his mother and then tore off her ear because she had poorly punished him in his youth.' This fable blames the mother for not punishing her son harshly enough, thereby causing his wrong-doings as an adult!

Similar views were expressed in a sermon given in 1783 by John Wesley, the principal founder of the Methodist Church:

It is hard to say, whether self-will or pride be the more fatal distemper. It was chiefly pride that threw down so many of the stars of Heaven, and turned angels into devils. But what can parents do, in order to check this until it can be radically cured? First . . . check everyone at the first word, that would praise children before their face. Is not this spreading a net for their feet? Is this not a grevious incentive to pride, even if they are praised for what is truly praiseworthy? . . . If, on the contrary, you desire, without loss of time, to strike at the root of their pride, teach your children, as soon as possibly you can, that they are fallen spirits; that they are fallen short of that glorious image of God . . . more ignorant, more foolish, and more wicked than they can possibly conceive. Show them that, in pride, passion and revenge, they are now like the devil. And that in foolish desires and grovelling appetites, they are like the beasts of the field.

Amazing as it may seem to us today, such attitudes to children and motherhood were very widespread throughout Europe and North America. In some parts of Europe, they persisted until very recently. This is well illustrated in Morton Schatzmann's book *Soul Murder*, about Dr Daniel Schreber, and his son, Judge Schreber. Dr Schreber, a German, wrote numerous books and pamphlets between 1840 and 1870 about raising children. His recommendations included the total suppression of the child's personality and individuality through harsh routines and severe punishment. Today, we would call this brainwashing. Schreber also invented a number of physical devices to keep children in fixed, rigid postures. These devices were in fact designed to torture children into total submission. Surprising though it may seem, Dr Schreber's views were regarded as praiseworthy in much of Germany, and some of his teachings are actively followed there today.

The low status of children and negative attitudes toward them meant that they were widely exploited. Because life in pre-industrial England and similar parts of Europe was such a struggle, children in most families were expected to work from a very early age. In one family, a five-year-old girl was kept upright by pinning her dress to her mother's knee, and slapped on the head to keep her awake, so that she could continue stitching clothes late into the night. This little girl had been sewing for long hours since she was three. Such practices were not uncommon in poor families, where the extra income obtained from the efforts of small children might make the difference between eating and starving.

This ruthless exploitation of children continued into the early stages of the Industrial Revolution. Children as young as seven or eight worked in factories for long hours. Little boys were employed as chimney-sweeps because their small size allowed them to gain access where adults could not. An eighteenth-century Nottingham sweep stated: 'No one knows what cruelty a boy has to undergo. The flesh must be hardened. This is done by rubbing elbows and knees with strongest brine close by a hot fire. You must stand over him with a cane.' Tragically, these boys often died at a young age of cancers caused by constant exposure to soot from chimneys.

It was not until 1833 that laws were passed in England affording children some protection against the ruthless exploitation that was still widely prevalent. Those laws limited to less than 48 hours a week the working hours of children 9–13; children age 13–18 were not legally permitted to work more than 68 hours a week. These laws were, at the time, considered to be very enlightened. They reflected a fundamental change in attitudes to children and motherhood that had begun to emerge in the eighteenth century.

Raising the Status of Children and Motherhood

The Industrial Revolution that began in the mid-eighteenth century was the origin of profound changes in social attitudes to children and motherhood. It coincided with, and fuelled, attempts at territorial expansion by the major European nations. Battles and wars became far more destructive than ever before, because of the invention and automated production of new weapons. Soldiers were needed to fight these battles. Men and women were needed to work in the mines and factories that turned raw materials into weapons of mass destruction. The emerging industrial nations began to experience a shortage of fit men and women that was more obvious and more acute than ever before. A state was only as powerful as the number of people available to work in its factories and fight in its armies.

The emperor Napoleon was very concerned about this problem, and took measures to remedy it: 'The fewer children who die at an early age, the more soldiers at twenty . . . The emperor, by the decree of May 5, 1810, has ordered the creation of the Mother's Society for Childhood, intended to give aid to expectant mothers and to young children.' In addition, Napoleon promised every family with at least seven boys payment for the costs of maintaining one child. It is not difficult to guess what this did for the status and well-being of girls.

Those thousands of children who were traditionally abandoned each year suddenly became potentially valuable resources rather than troublesome nuisances. This was recognized by the famous philanthropist Claude de Chamousset, whose writings were popular in the second half of the eighteenth century. He noted

141

that each year, in Paris alone, over 4,000 children were abandoned:

> It is distressing to see that the considerable outlays the hospitals are obliged to make for abandoned children produce so few advantages for the State ... Most of them perish before reaching an age at which some utility could be drawn from them. Only one-tenth of them will live to be twenty. And what becomes of this expensive tenth? Very few learn a trade; the others leave only to become beggars and tramps.

De Chamousset calculated that about 12,000 babies were abandoned each year throughout France. He advocated feeding these children with cow's milk – a new idea at the time – in the hope of keeping more than 10 per cent of them alive. He planned to export these children to help set up colonies abroad, and to use them at home for various military and industrial purposes. Even though De Chamousset was a philanthropist, widely respected for his humanitarian and enlightened views, he still regarded abandoned children as commodities. This is a reminder of the *economic* basis of the new social forces that were trying to change attitudes to children and motherhood. This social concern was not altruistic; it was not truly concerned with the well-being of children and their mothers. It was aimed purely and simply at increasing the survival rate of children so that their numbers would add to the power and influence of the State. Of course, mothers became the initial focus of this ultimately cynical exercise in social engineering.

The Idealization of Motherhood

It will be recalled from the previous chapter that the patriarchal countries and states of Europe expended for centuries much energy on controlling women's sexuality. The main object of this was to ensure that the paternity of children, and especially male children, was not in doubt. Without this assurance, the basic structure of these patriarchal feudal societies would have been undermined, since maintaining a strong, vigorous, fertile and clearly identified male line was fundamental to them.

The State was never entirely successful at controlling women's sexuality since this required exercising control over many other aspects of women's lives. Attempts to subjugate women never fully succeeded because of their collective and economic power. It was not until the Industrial Revolution that real control over women was achieved. This occurred because industrialization destroyed both the collective and the economic power of women.

Up until the Industrial Revolution, women had largely escaped propaganda about their child-raising activities. As we have seen, children had little value or status in pre-industrial Western Europe, and women were not expected to nurture them if they could afford to pay someone else to do it. But this changed when the Industrial Revolution and the associated warfare of the eighteenth and nineteenth centuries gained momentum, and an endless supply of men and women was needed for factories and 'cannon fodder'. Children became valuable commodities, and mothers became subject to propaganda urging them to take direct personal responsibility for their upbringing. Elisabeth Badinter, in her brilliant book *The Myth of Motherhood*, has described the efforts of the French state to persuade women to give more priority to the care of their children. Similar efforts were made in England and other European countries. The first phase of their propaganda exercise was to invoke the example of Roman women. The decline and fall of the Roman Empire was linked to the failure of Roman women to care for their own children. When the Roman Emperor Julius Caesar returned from a lengthy overseas military campaign, he was reported to have said, 'Do Roman women no longer have children to nurse and carry in their arms as in former days?' He made this observation because so many Roman women sent their children away to be cared for by wet nurses. This practice later became so common that laws were introduced to regulate it.

Of course, the other side of this story about Ancient Rome was not lost on nineteenth-century women. It showed clearly that when women could afford to do so, and were not actively discouraged from the practice, they often preferred to hand over to others the responsibility for nurturing their young children. French women had little trouble in resisting this, the first phase of the propaganda exercise aimed at idealizing motherhood.

The second phase involved trying to make women feel guilty by comparing them with animals and primitive tribes, who were said to put the needs of their offspring before their own, even sacrificing their lives to protect them. This phase was strikingly unsuccessful, mainly because women resented being compared unfavourably with animals and 'savages'.

The third phase was more successful. It worked not because it was intrinsically more effective (in this view I differ from Elisabeth Badinter). It succeeded because the Industrial Revolution was by now well advanced. Women had become powerless, and were coping with this through the process of 'identifying with the aggressor', the mechanisms of which I have described in Chapter 5. The third phase involved persuading women that great *personal* benefits would result if they breast fed and nurtured their own young children.

The era of the Idealized Mother had begun. Initially, men created the images. Images of women who were endlessly patient and caring; women who put their own needs second to those of their children; women who willingly retreated from the world and abandoned their own pleasures and interests to devote themselves wholeheartedly and exclusively to the welfare of their children. The beauty, happiness and contentment of nursing mothers was emphasized repeatedly in the literature and media of the day.

Powerless to do otherwise, women began to identify with the unrealistic, idealized male view of them. By the middle of the nineteenth century, women were almost as active as men in extolling the virtues of motherhood. Not much later, most women had partly or fully internalized men's idealized image of motherhood. Women themselves believed that to be good mothers, they had to be full-time mothers, endlessly and uncomplainingly self-sacrificing, striving constantly to meet as fully as possible the needs of their offspring. Of course, this was and is an impossible goal. But even today, many women struggle to achieve it, often at the expense of their own health and well-being.

Modern Mothers

In the Western world, and especially in English-speaking countries, women are only just beginning to resist the efforts of the State to persuade them to identify with an idealized, unrealistic view of motherhood. The feminist movement has repeatedly drawn attention to the oppressive nature of the expectations that Western society continues to have regarding motherhood. However, women have been slow to respond to the messages of feminism. This is partly because the radical elements of the early feminist movement alienated many traditional women, an alienation powerfully encouraged by the popular media, which still refuse to take feminism seriously. As a result, most women are not exposed to feminist ideas in a way that allows them to identify the real issues.

In my clinical work, I have been repeatedly astonished at the complete lack of awareness of feminist ideas shown by many of my female clients. It is almost as if they – or the suburbs in which they live – are surrounded by an invisible wall that prevents feminist ideas from diffusing in. Many of these women are highly intelligent. They generally read a range of books (mainly novels), several women's magazines, and at least one daily newspaper. Of course, they watch television. But in spite of this extensive reading and exposure to the media, they are rarely presented with feminist ideas. It is as if such ideas are censored from their lives.

Not only are modern women largely denied access to feminist ideas, but they are inundated instead with traditional ideas of womanhood, and especially of motherhood. Women's magazines are a powerful force in the reinforcement of traditional values of women. A glance through the most popular of these magazines reveals a relentless focus on stereotypic aspects of womanhood, and especially the joys of motherhood. The negative aspects of this role are rarely mentioned.

Of course, reinforcing sex-role stereotypes is vital for the success of women's magazines. The whole concept of women's magazines relies on women defining themselves as different from men: having different interests (such as babies and cooking) and different needs (such as perfume, skin-care preparations and cosmetics). Most of these differences are artificial in the sense that they are socially determined. Without these mainly artificial differences between men and women, most of the huge market for women's services, products and activities would vanish. Because of this, women's magazines – and the advertisements that are vital to their profitability – must work relentlessly at emphasizing the differences between men and women. This means portraying men and women in a stereotyped way, a portrayal that occurs throughout the popular media.

The extent to which television advertising reinforces sex-role stereotypes has been objectively researched. For example, P. Mamay and R. Simpson, writing in the journal *Sex Roles* (7:1981: 1223–32), reported their analysis of over two hundred television commercials depicting female roles. They concluded:

> The black civil rights movement led to rapid racial desegregation of television commercials, but the women's movement has not had a comparable effect. Women are less liberated, and sex roles more differentiated, in the commercials than in real life . . . Commercials blend two images that lower the woman's status to that of menial labourer and servant: (1) housekeeping as a complex technological process with men as the experts, and (2) children as self-centered consumers . . . These television commercials are intended to sell products, not describe social life. But it is likely that they help to perpetuate stereotypes of 'woman's place'.

Also writing in *Sex Roles* (14:1986: 141–8), S. Brabant and L. Mooney studied the question of sex-role stereotyping in the written media. They examined the comic strips in Sunday newspapers over a six-month period in 1984, and compared their findings with those of an identical study in 1974. They concluded:

> With the exception of a substantial increase in the percentage of appearances by males and females in leisure activities, change in portrayal of males and females in the Sunday comics was minimal for the decade studied . . . Given that a cultural analysis of sex roles focuses on the shared meanings individuals use in their interactions, and that development of these meanings are, in part, dependent on the mass media, it is especially disappointing to empirically document the continued depiction of a male-dominated society and the devaluation of women in everyday life. How far have women come? If Blondie, Gladys and Alice are indicators, not very far at all.

Western women are still being subjected to a massive amount of propaganda aimed at maintaining them in unrealistic roles that were originally created nearly two centuries ago. So pervasive is this propaganda that it has become part of the fabric of women's lives. It is not even recognized as propaganda. However, not all women are vulnerable to these social myths, and I will now discuss some reasons for this.

Women's Identity Formation and Some of its Problems

Chapters 2 and 4 examined the ways in which psychological problems for men arose out of the Western emphasis on mothers taking exclusive responsibility for raising young children. Women also experience problems because of this unrealistic expectation. Unlike boys, girls are not required to suppress in early childhood their basic identification with their mothers. This makes the task of identity formation easier for them in some ways, although, as we shall see, they have their own difficulties. Once they are toddlers, girls have the opportunity of identifying with their fathers, or with the men in their lives who represent a father. Such a father figure can be an entirely satisfactory replacement as long as he is a caring, warm, flesh-and-blood person rather than an image from the media or pop culture. Ideally, the father's 'masculine' attributes are internalized and blend harmoniously with the 'feminine' attributes of the mother that were internalized previously. When this happens, the girl is likely to mature into a reasonably well-adjusted young adult with a healthy balance of masculine and feminine characteristics. She will be relatively invulnerable to stereotypic pressures, and will be able to make decisions about her life based on her own reality rather than a reality based on myths of womanhood and motherhood.

Unfortunately, the process of identity formation rarely unfolds smoothly. Two problems are particularly important. One, which is very common, concerns the problem of *acknowledging and expressing* the internalized masculine attributes. This has major social repercussions that are considered during discussion of the Electra complex in Chapter 9. The other problem is less common but is psychologically more disabling. It involves the *failure* to identify with a father or father figure, which arrests the process of internalizing 'masculine' attributes. This failure of identification has many causes. The most common is the presence of a father who is abusive, hostile, critical or pathologically withdrawn. The absence of a father or father figure is also fairly common. In families where the mother takes exclusive responsibility for the upbringing of the children, the father is often emotionally absent, even though he may be present physically. Some mothers actively exclude their husbands from taking a significant role in the upbringing of their daughters. Not uncommonly, such mothers are fearful that if their husbands are left alone with their young daughters, some form of sexual activity is likely to take place. These fears, although rarely spoken of, add to the daughter's difficulty in identifying with her father.

Whatever its precise origins, *failure to identify with a father or father figure often means that girls internalize idealized, stereotyped images of men and manhood*. Because the male sex-role stereotype demands a reciprocal female stereotype, such girls acquire an image of themselves which is based primarily on the *female* sex-role stereotype. This image is both created and reinforced largely by media pressure, to which these girls are especially vulnerable.

Often, girls who have been unable to identify with their father or with a father figure have difficult relationships with their mothers, with whom they may identify very strongly. This strong identification leads to problems for the daughter in *separating* from the mother, on whom she is often very emotionally dependent. Classically, such mother-daughter relationships are fraught with tension, ambivalence and suppressed anger. The sex-role stereotyped views that the daughter usually has are generally shared by the mother, who, because of her powerful influence on the daughter, consolidates her stereotyped view of the world. When stereotyped ideas that originate in this way are reinforced by media and social pressures, they may become extremely rigid and fixed. Women whose psychological development is distorted in this way often become obsessed with aspects of the female role as they perceive it. A common obsession concerns fertility and the need to have a child at all costs.

There is, of course, a big difference between an obsession about having children and a balanced wish to do so. In my clinical work with women obsessed about giving birth to a child, I have been struck by how often this desire is a fundamental aspect of their personality structure. From early adolescence, or even before,

148

these women think of themselves only in terms of wives and mothers. Usually, the obsession with having a baby is linked with an obsessive desire to get married. The stereotyped world view that traps these women demands that they marry before having children. Until they achieve these goals, they are restless and dissatisfied. Women obsessed with having a baby often get married young, not uncommonly to the first man who asks them. They get pregnant as soon as possible, and dream fondly of the birth of their child. These dreams are mainly about the perfect happiness and fulfilment that their baby will bring them.

The reality of motherhood is nearly always profoundly different for such women, who are generally ill-prepared for the huge demands that their baby makes on them. The image that they have of motherhood does not include the messy, exhausting and frustrating aspects of looking after a baby. The reality sometimes overwhelms them, and they become depressed or incapacitated by fears and anxieties. Most worrying of all to them are their feelings of anger and hostility toward their babies. Although these feelings are in fact entirely natural, these women believe them to be dangerous and unhealthy. According to their stereotyped view of motherhood, a mother must experience only warm, loving feelings to her baby. The absence of such feelings, or the presence of negative feelings, is, to them, a sign that something has gone very seriously wrong: it means that they are bad mothers. Because their whole lives up to that point have revolved around the idea of becoming good mothers, even perfect mothers, they panic. They often fear that they will act upon their negative feelings toward their babies and physically harm them. This adds to their sense of panic.

Not uncommonly, such a sequence of events leads to a failure to cope and the development of a recognizable psychiatric disorder. Even if women in such circumstances manage to adjust without becoming ill, their attitudes to themselves and their children may be permanently affected in a negative way.

A distressing early experience of motherhood is by no means confined to women who are vulnerable to myths and stereotypes. Research has shown clearly that at least a third of mothers experience strongly negative feelings toward their first baby in the first few months after its birth. Although some women accept these feelings as normal, many others view them with alarm and self-disgust. Such experiences contribute to and worsen the post-natal depression that afflicts at least a third of women after the birth of their first baby. They undermine the mother's sense of competence as a care-giver to her child, and make the process of mother-infant bonding a more difficult process than it might otherwise be.

As long as motherhood is portrayed in idealized terms that ignore just how difficult and challenging it really is, many women will react to their first babies in this negative way. But, if motherhood was portrayed as it truly is, women might become less willing to have children. This idea threatens the whole basis of family life and population maintenance that is fundamental to the modern State. As such, it is especially threatening to traditional men. For these reasons, women continue to be exposed to relentless propaganda about motherhood through the media and popular culture.

Fertility Clinics and False Pregnancy

Women with an obsession about having babies are vulnerable not only to the realities of motherhood. They are vulnerable also to infertility and to fertility clinics. Before the invention of fertility drugs and fertility clinics, women who were infertile generally resigned themselves to this. They were then able to adopt a child, or could plan to do so. Alternatively, they could abandon the idea of motherhood – however difficult and painful this task – and divert their time and energy into new channels.

Fertility clinics are fairly new. Few existed thirty years ago. They are undoubtedly beneficial for most of the women – and their partners – who attend them. By insisting on fully testing the fertility of *both* partners they protect women from being unfairly blamed for infertility that originates in the husband. This was not uncommon even in the recent past.

The new fertility technologies are often successful, but they are not always so. They often involve women in repeated and time-consuming clinic attendances that may persist for several years. For women desperate to have a baby, this process, when unduly prolonged, can by psychologically devastating. This is especially so if repeated miscarriages occur, or if the much desired baby is never born. During the months or years of fertility treatment, women often put their lives on hold. If the programme is ultimately not successful, they often become depressed. Failure of a prolonged programme may leave them feeling that their lives are doubly useless and wasted: firstly because the motherhood role is denied them; and secondly because they feel that it is too late for them to pursue alternative goals. Many fertility clinics pursue the purely technological side of their role without paying enough attention to the psychological needs of their clients. Women considering approaching a fertility clinic should beware of this, and choose carefully.

False pregnancy – or pseudocyesis as it is technically known – illustrates very clearly how some women are remarkably vulnerable to social pressures urging them to become mothers. False pregnancy can be clinically indistinguishable from true pregnancy. The abdomen swells and the breasts become engorged, sometimes producing the kind of secretions seen in true pregnancy. The monthly periods cease, and morning sickness occurs. At the appropriate time, movements of the foetus are subjectively experienced, and labour pains occur at the expected date of confinement. Sometimes, the womb itself enlarges and shows other signs of foetal implantation.

Research into false pregnancy has shown that it almost always occurs in women who are obsessed with having a baby. In a typical case reported recently, the response of the woman to the news of her false pregnancy was: 'But what point is there to being married if you can't have babies? They have been my whole life.' In most cases, women who develop false pregnancies have a history of infertility. Often, they are actively involved in strict or fundamentalist religious groups of a kind that reinforce traditional sex roles.

False pregnancy is usually accompanied by some of the hormonal changes seen in true pregnancy, although it can persist even if hormone levels return to normal. We understand very little about how the mind alone can produce physical changes in the body like those occuring in false pregnancy. But a major factor appears to concern the reduction of profound psychological stress or conflict. It seems that women who experience false pregnancy

151

have such a strong desire to give birth to a child that they can unconsciously create all the usual bodily signs of pregnancy without actually being pregnant. That they are able to achieve this remarkable feat is in large part a reflection of their obsession with motherhood, and the great distress that they experience if their wishes are unfulfilled. Such women are very obvious casualties of the myths of motherhood. But, as we have seen, many other women are less obvious victims of these myths – myths that are still very potent in today's Western world.

Creating the Perfect Child

Those powerful and influential men of the nineteenth century who began creating new myths of motherhood had one aim: to increase the chances of children, and especially boys, reaching maturity. Because of improvements in the technology of destruction, warfare had become more costly of human life than ever before. Wars in the eighteenth and nineteenth centuries created a demand for young soldiers that was unprecedented. The supply of young men for the battlefields was not keeping up with demand. Since the mortality rate among children was at least 50 per cent, the logical solution was to increase the chances of children reaching adulthood.

Persuading mothers to put child care at the top of their list of priorities was the most obvious way of reducing child mortality. As we have seen, the nineteenth-century propagandists were strikingly successful in this goal: by the start of the twentieth century, the myths of motherhood that they created had been accepted by most women.

The widespread acceptance of motherhood myths dramatically increased the status of motherhood. But the price that mothers paid for this increased status was confinement to the home and the expectation that they would put their own needs second to those of their children and husbands. In sum, they were expected to live their lives by proxy, at second hand, through the endeavours and exploits of the men in their lives. Only men had free access to the world beyond the domestic; only men could actively and directly seek success, power, status and recognition.

Raising the status of motherhood appeared to have had its

152

desired effect. The mortality rate of children fell progressively from more than 50 per cent in the eighteenth century to the very low levels that have prevailed throughout the second half of the twentieth century. Although some of the reduction in child mortality that occurred in the second half of the nineteenth century was caused by changes in the attitudes of mothers to their children, most was in fact attributable to improvements in hygiene and nutrition. Infectious diseases were greatly curtailed, and knowledge about appropriate nutrition became more widespread. In the twentieth century, continuing rapid decreases in child mortality were attributable mainly to medical advances, especially the introduction of antibiotics.

Through a combination of these and other processes, child mortality in today's Western world has become very low indeed. For the first time in human history, the death of a child has become a rare event. This has contributed to a dramatic change in the status of children, who can now be cared for almost free of the fear that they will not survive to adulthood. Parents can invest each of their children with love, care and affection, knowing that they are very unlikely to experience the pain and grief of losing the objects of their devotion.

Loving children in this unqualified way is largely new to the Western world, and its effects on children and their parents, especially their mothers, are still unfolding. But already a number of themes have clearly emerged. One of the most obvious of these is the 'perfect child', created in the following way.

Many mothers still believe that they must strive to meet all the needs of their children in a total and comprehensive way. Such mothers generally become tyrannized by this idea, first because it is impossible, and second because it requires them always to put their children's needs before their own. Failure is inevitable, and this breeds guilt, especially when mothers finally reach unbearable levels of frustration and yell at their children or smack them. Guilty mothers increase their efforts to be 'perfect', and repeated failure to be so perpetuates a vicious cycle of 'failed perfection'. Mothers who try to be perfect expect their children to be perfect also: perfect in dress, in behaviour, in ability and in aspiration. Dressing children to perfection is powerfully reinforced by advertising, to the extent that expensive designer clothing has become the norm for children of affluent parents. Such parents invest a great deal of time and money in their efforts to create perfect offspring. Competition for the best pre-schools is fierce in many affluent suburbs: children who do not manage to get in to these prestigious educational hot-houses often experience a deep sense of failure – at the age of three. Their parents, nonetheless often persist in their attempts to create a perfect child, and this highly competitive process may continue throughout the remainder of childhood and adolescence. Children who do not meet the expectation to be 'perfect' often grow up with a deep sense of inadequacy, guilt and inferiority.

Girls are especially vulnerable to such pressures because of the strong mutual identification that usually occurs between mothers and daughters. Mothers who are confined to the domestic sphere often rely heavily on their daughters to achieve and experience those things that they cannot achieve for themselves – an achievement denied them because they have sacrificed their own aspirations to meet the needs of their husbands and children.

Many mothers invest almost endless time and energy in taking their daughters to a whole range of activities outside of school. These include dance, drama, singing, music and sports. Where these activities represent the mother's own wish to have her needs met through her daughter's achievements, they can have a very destructive effect – especially if the daughter fails to live up to her mother's often unrealistic expectations.

The female sex-role stereotype firmly discourages women from competing against men. This limits women's outlets for their natural competitiveness, and encourages extremes of competition *between* women, either directly or by proxy through their daughters. But vicarious gratification of women's competitive and aggressive drives is often achieved through their sons and husbands also. This means that these men carry a double burden: they are driven to succeed both by their own competitive and aggressive instincts and by those same instincts expressed and experienced vicariously, first in their mothers and later in their wives. The more time that such men spend struggling to be successful, the more time are they away from home. This emphasizes the confinement to the domestic sphere of their wives, and increases further the need of these women to compete and be successful by proxy.

In this way, a vicious cycle is established, the end result of which is often a home full of the symbols of affluence and success, but empty of those human elements that might make it a home. The house has become a shrine for the worship of status symbols. Once the children have left, its original purpose, to shelter and support a growing family, has been forgotten. The wife is there most of the time because it is her world. The husband is there as infrequently as possible, because the world of work and business is his natural environment. He feels more comfortable in that world – however demanding and stressful – than in a house which has become a shrine. Because husband and wife lead such different lives, and because the husband has so much more economic power and wordly status, it is impossible for them to achieve any real intimacy or emotional harmony. Their marriage has become an empty shell. They have become martyrs to the tyranny of coupledom.

7

The Third Sex

The last two chapters have focused mainly on women's issues. They examined ways in which patriarchal Western nations have sought to diminish women's power and status, with the ultimate aim of controlling their fertility. As we have seen, patriarchal societies relied on a male heir for the preservation of family lineage and the transmission of inheritance. This required accurate and reliable knowledge of paternity, which could be guaranteed only by ensuring that wives had no male sexual partners other than their husbands. Achieving absolute control over women, and hence over their fertility, has long been a goal of strongly patriarchal societies. Achieving it by purely physical means proved impossible: witness the futility of the chastity belt! Even the combination of physical and psychological intimidation manifested on a huge scale in the witch-hunts of the Middle Ages failed to create an adequate degree of control. It was only after the Industrial Revolution destroyed both the collective and the economic power of women that their lives could be almost totally controlled by men. This control reached a peak during the nineteenth century: the Victorian era.

In oppressing women so absolutely, Victorian men distorted women's experience and expression of femininity. What men created instead was a corrupted, split-off extension of the masculine. The new femininity was idealized and unrealistic, and it required a new masculinity which was equally unattainable; a masculinity that was harsh and absolute, without the tempering influence of a feminine element. It represented man as a ruthless warrior. Men identified as strongly as did women with these distorted images of masculinity and femininity, which became consolidated as sex-role stereotypes.

Because men had created the new femininity as an extension of

156

their masculinity, their identity came to depend on it. As women learned to behave towards men in the stereotyped way that men expected, men became increasingly dependent on women to preserve their sense of manhood. This dependency of men on women has persisted, reinforced by sex-role stereotypes. But, as we have seen, men are encouraged to deny this dependency. In men who rely on a sex-role stereotyped self-image, this denial must be absolute. As we saw in Chapter 2, when total denial is threatened by the wish of the woman who sustains it to do so no longer, murder-suicide may be the final outcome.

Patriarchal men created the new image of femininity to control women, and in this they have been remarkably successfull. But they have paid a heavy price for this success. The idealized, stereotyped images of masculinity and femininity that men created represent for them a tyranny which is as great as that which is imposed on women. The main objects of this chapter are to illustrate the full force and extent of this tyranny, and to clarify further its nature and origins. I examine these issues from both a personal-psychological and social-cultural perspective. In doing so I develop the themes introduced at the end of Chapters 2 and 3. These themes concern the relationship between sex-role stereotyping and the overall social structure of English-speaking nations, especially the maintainence of high levels of aggression and competitiveness.

The Desire to Change Sex

Many people in Western society are uncomfortable with the gender allocated to them by nature. Some are so uncomfortable with it that they seek to become a member of the opposite sex through surgical means. For both men and women, sex-change surgery, otherwise called gender reassignment, is an extensive and mutilating procedure. In men, it includes amputation of the penis and testicles, followed by construction of a vagina. In women, it includes amputation of the breasts and removal of the womb, followed by construction of a penis and, usually, a scrotum, out of skin flaps from the abdomen and thighs. In spite of the physical and mental trauma involved, at least 300 people have sex-change surgery each year in the United States of America, together with a similar number in Europe.

Although sex-change surgery is comparably extensive and mutilating for both sexes, it is requested most often by men who wish to become women. Ratios vary somewhat from country to country, but the overall average is about 4:1. That is, out of every 100 people seeking gender reassignment, at least 75 are men. The main social influence on the sex ratio appears to be the rigidity of attitudes to sex roles. Sweden and Denmark, for example, are countries that have a fairly flexible attitude to sex roles; in them, the male:female ratio of transsexuals requesting surgery is about 3:1. In Australia, a country with very rigid sex roles, the ratio is about 8:1. In the USA it is about 5:1, and in the UK about 4:1.

The more rigid are sex roles the greater is the excess of men who seek sex change by surgical means. The reasons for this are not fully understood, but a major factor is the *restrictive nature* of the male sex role. This starts in early childhood. For example, there is far more tolerance of 'tomboys' than of 'sissies'. Girls with interests, attitudes and behaviour traditionally associated with boys are generally not stigmatized, and may even be encouraged. But boys who show female traits and interests are invariably the victims of prejudice. The very term 'sissy' is a strongly negative one, and has strong links, in the popular mind, with effeminacy and adult homosexuality.

The restrictive process continues in adulthood. Men have far less opportunity than women to deviate from traditional sex-role behaviours. For example, women are free to wear conventional male clothing, such as long pants and business suits. But men are totally prohibited from wearing female clothes such as dresses and skirts. Women can cut their hair very short without comment. If a man has long, flowing hair, even today, he is unusual, and may be regarded as deviant. A man who has long hair which is styled, waved or curled in women's fashion would undoubtedly give rise to comment, mainly of a negative kind.

Women are also much freer than men to be openly affectionate and loving, and to express a whole range of emotions. They are able to admit feelings of fear, anxiety and vulnerability without the risk of being stigmatized as weak or 'unmanly'. Women also have much more flexibility about work and careers. They are not generally criticized for withdrawing from the work-force, or for working part time, especially if they are caring for young children. Men, however, are expected to remain full time in the work-force until they retire at sixty or sixty-five. If they work only part time, especially when they are fairly young, they are often viewed with suspicion or resentment. If they choose to withdraw entirely from the work-force to look after young children at home, then they find themselves one of a tiny minority of men who are often viewed with suspicion by both sexes.

These role restrictions on men are to a large extent compensated by men's higher socio-economic status and greater power at all levels of society. But for those men who seek to become women, the disadvantages of the male sex role far outweigh its advantages: being a man is a tyranny so oppressive that they will endure extensive and mutilating surgery in an attempt to escape it.

Of course, the restrictive nature of the male sex role is not the only factor that contributes to the excess of male transsexuals. Equally important is the difficulty that men have in letting go of their primary maternal identification, an issue that has been discussed in previous chapters. This is a challenge that women do not generally have, making the task of achieving a normal gender identity a less difficult one.

The desire to change sex through surgery seems to be a characteristic of Western societies, with their Graeco-Roman origins and influences. Most other societies have less radical alternatives, usually involving what is best termed a *third sex*. In these societies, members of the third sex are generally highly valued: they rarely experience the prejudice and hostility suffered by those Westerners who deviate in an obvious way from traditional sex-role behaviour. Much can be learned by examining the ways in which different societies allow deviation from sex-role norms. I will start by looking more closely at Western attitudes to this, paying particular attention to transsexualism.

Transsexualism

One of the earliest accounts of sex change occurs in Greek mythology. It concerns the renowned seer Teiresias. There are several versions of the legend, and I have chosen the one described by Robert Graves in his famous work *The Greek Myths* (Vol 2: 11). While walking on Mount Cyllene, Teiresias came upon two snakes in the act of coupling. They both attacked him, and he killed the female. The gods chose to punish him for this by turning him into a woman. To their surprise, Teiresias took to his female form with enthusiasm, and became a celebrated prostitute. Some years later, the chief god Zeus and his wife Hera were arguing about Zeus's compulsive womanizing. Defending himself, Zeus said that on those occasions that he and Hera did make love, she had far more pleasure than he did: 'Women, of course, derive infinitely greater pleasure from the sexual act than men.' Hera became enraged at this suggestion, insisting that the opposite was true. The couple agreed to find someone to settle the argument, and Teiresias was chosen because of his unusual experience as both a man and a woman. At this stage of his life, Teiresias seems not to have acquired a great deal of wisdom, because he rather tactlessly judged in favour of Zeus:

> If the parts of love-pleasure be counted as ten,
> thrice three go to women, one only to men.

On hearing Teiresias judge that women's sexual pleasure was nine times greater than men's, Hera flew into a rage and punished him – by turning him back into a man! Other versions of the legend tell that she punished Teiresias by blinding him, and that Zeus compensated him with the inward sight that allowed him to become a great seer. But whatever version is chosen, the basic message is the same: men believe that it is far more enjoyable to be a woman than to be a man.

Greek mythology also includes what may be the earliest account of gender reassignment surgery. Followers of the Phrygian goddess Cybele castrated themselves and dressed like women (*The Greek Myths*, Vol 1: 117). The object of this was to achieve ecstatic unity with the goddess. It is said that many of the priests went beyond castration and completely removed their genitals. This behaviour has striking parallels with modern male-female transsexualism. It is referred to rather cynically by the Ancient Roman poet Juvenal in describing male transvestites (men whose wish to become women is limited mainly to cross-dressing and the adoption of female mannerisms):

But why are they waiting? Isn't it now high
time for them to try
The Phrygian fashion to make
the job complete . . .
Take a knife and lop off that
superfluous piece of meat?
              (Translated by Creekmore, 1963)

This poem reflects the negative attitudes that ancient Romans generally had to those who deviated from traditional gender roles. Rigid attitudes to sex roles in ancient Rome make it very likely that most transsexuals were male-female. There is one well-known account of gender reassignment in ancient Rome. The emperor Nero, in a fit of rage, kicked his pregnant wife in the stomach, killing her. He tried to find a woman who resembled her, but the closest match was in fact a young man, Sporum. Nero ordered his surgeons to change Sporum into a woman, after which the couple were formally married.

Another Roman emperor, Heliogabalus, is said to have been formally married to a strongly built male slave. Heliogabalus rejoiced in the female role and took up all the traditional tasks of the wife. Apparently, he offered half the Roman Empire to the physician who could equip him with female genitalia!

I could find no accounts of female-male transsexualism in Greek or Roman history. The Amazons come to mind as female warriors who were said to amputate their right breasts so that they could use a bow and arrow more effectively. But the Amazons were not Greeks. In fact, the Greeks became very hostile to the Amazons, launching repeated military campaigns against them. Ultimately, Amazonia was destroyed and the few surviving Amazons forced to flee to other parts of the world.

The Western world has inherited the Graeco-Roman tradition of rigid sex roles and negative attitudes to those who depart from them in an obvious way. Western accounts of transsexualism in the years between the Roman era and modern times almost all describe the desire of men to become women, or men who actually experience themselves as women. Accounts of women who wish to become men, or who successfully pass as men, are rare. This trend persists today.

Attitudes to sex-change surgery vary widely. Some believe that bodily mutilation on such a scale can never be justified. Others say that sex-change surgery should be much more freely available than it is. But one thing is unarguable: many men who desire sex-change surgery go to extraordinary lengths in order to achieve this goal. Some devote their entire lives to saving enough money to have an operation. If it is not available locally, they travel to centres – sometimes overseas – where it can be done. Where local programmes are available, some male-female transsexuals take desperate measures to achieve surgery. These include threatening to mutilate their sex organs so that surgery is inevitable, and occasionally carrying out these threats by damaging or entirely severing the genitals.

Insight into the desperation of these people is best gained through detailed case histories such as those written so well by Ira Pauly in *Transsexualism and Sex Reassignment*. One case is that of A.B., a young man who had wanted to become a girl ever since he could remember. This is true of at least two-thirds of male transsexuals. His parents had shown unusual flexibility, allowing him to dress as a girl at home, but understandably insisting that he wore boy's clothes to school.

Eventually, the strain of coping with his female identity caused A.B. to drop out of school. He moved to San Francisco, where he experimented with homosexuality. However, he found that he could not tolerate homosexual men. This is true of nearly all male transsexuals: most studies show a rate of homosexuality that is less than 15 per cent, which is only a little above the rate among non-transsexual men. Of course, in describing nearly all male trans-sexuals as heterosexual, I am fully accepting their view of themselves as female.

Although A.B. could not tolerate homosexual men, he was strongly attached to *heterosexual men who would accept him as female*. This is a characteristic of nearly all male transsexuals, and it is a very important one that they share with members of the 'third sex' in non-Western societies. I will elaborate this further on.

Although A.B. was strongly attracted to heterosexual men, he was fearful of any physical contact with them, because this meant the embarrassment and humiliation of being exposed as a man. Again, this fear and avoidance is reported by most male transsexuals. A.B. became increasingly socially isolated, moving frequently from job to job and place to place. Eventually he became suicidal, and at that point he was psychiatrically assessed. It was noted that A.B.'s feminine appearance 'is so convincing that she passes without question. In others, however, there is the need to overdo and exaggerate the feminine characteristics and thus their behavior becomes a caricature of women's behavior . . . male transsexuals as a group score higher on femininity scales than a control group of normal women.' Eventually plans were made for gender reassignment surgery, but the outcome of this is not reported.

The other cases described by Pauly poignantly reveal the profound distress experienced by those men who experience themselves as women but who cannot publicly reveal this. Despair about their situation had brought them to the point of suicide. However, sensible and caring psychological evaluation helped to create other options for them, although in every case the desire for sex-change surgery was very strong.

Although female transsexuals are much less common, their desire to become men is no less intense than is the desire of male transsexuals to become women. Research has shown that almost all female transsexuals have experienced themselves as males for as long as they can remember. Virtually all are disgusted by their female sexual characteristics, and crave surgical transformation to the opposite sex. The main object of this transformation is to allow them to enjoy social and sexual relationships with heterosexual women. On balance, female transsexuals tend to be better adjusted socially and psychologically than male transsexuals, and they are even less likely to be homosexual. Most studies report that female transsexuals, when defined as males, have a rate of homosexuality that is less than 5 per cent.

The Results of Sex-change Surgery

The results of sex-change surgery are difficult to evaluate because methods of assessing social and psychological adjustment vary

163

between different centres, as do surgical techniques and the willingness to perform surgery. Because male-female reassignment occurs with much greater frequency than the female-male procedure, we know more about the results of the former.

Virtually all men who seek to become anatomical women do so mainly in order to achieve satisfying relationships with 'normal' men. They desperately want to be like 'normal' women, which to them means being in a relationship with a heterosexual man, ideally in the married state. Transsexual men generally have a much more rigid, stereotyped view of sex roles than other men. They tend to see the female role in highly idealized terms. They have a reciprocally negative view of the male sex role, which they also see in a highly stereotyped way. Because of these rigid, stereotyped attitudes to sex roles, the idea of being a woman *psychologically*, while remaining a man *physically*, is totally unacceptable to them. The only way that they can accept the experience of being female is through surgical transformation.

Not surprisingly, the success of male-female gender reassignment is determined mainly by how well the new 'woman' is accepted by heterosexual men. This depends on two main factors: first, how convincingly female the transsexual is before surgery; and second, how effectively surgery creates apparently female genitalia. Where both these criteria are successfully achieved, outcome is often very good. The new 'woman' is usually able to settle into a reasonably happy and stable relationship with a heterosexual man. But if neither of the two main criteria are achieved, outcome is likely to be poor, and sometimes the transsexual is worse off than before the surgery. Recent research suggests that, overall, at least 80 per cent of male transsexuals are better adjusted and happier after surgery than they were before. As far as we know, the outcome of female-male surgery is determined by factors similar to those applying to male-female transformations. Generally, it is easier for female transsexuals to pass as men than for male transsexuals to pass as women. But surgery is more technically challenging in women, and it is especially difficult to create a functional penis-equivalent. These two factors, one positive and one negative, tend to balance out, so that the overall results of surgery in women are probably comparable to those in men.

164

Can Transsexuals Escape Sex-role Tyranny?

Transsexuals are among the worst casualties of sex-role tyranny. They are socialized in such a way that they acquire a fixed, highly stereotyped view of sex roles. From early childhood they experience themselves as members of the opposite sex. For them, gender is an all or nothing thing: one is either all woman or all man. There are no shades of in between. Because of these unrealistic views, transsexuals believe that only physical transformation will free them from the torment of feeling like a woman in a man's body, or a man in a woman's body. They feel incomplete and unhappy unless they are in a relationship with the opposite sex – true victims of the tyranny of togetherness.

If gender reassignment is successful, they believe that their psychological gender now coincides with their physical gender. As a result, they are generally much happier than before surgery, especially if they are able to keep a satisfactory relationship with a member of the opposite sex. In reality, of course, a surgically created 'woman' is not a true woman. And she is no longer a man. Equally, a surgically created 'man' is neither a man nor a woman. In reality, the surgeons have fashioned a person who belongs to neither sex: *they have created a third sex*. We shall see from what follows that creating a third sex is one way of avoiding the tyranny of a rigid sex-role system.

Alternatives to Transsexualism

The Berdache

Many societies, spread throughout the world, have created a third sex without resort to sex-change surgery. Particularly well documented is the third sex among many North American Indian tribes. For much of my basic information about this I am indebted to W. L. Williams's brilliant book *The Spirit and the Flesh: Sexual Diversity in American Indian Culture*. I must emphasize that at no stage does Williams refer to a 'third sex'. Neither does he make any comparisons with transsexualism. These concepts are my own.

In describing members of what I call the third sex in North American Indian culture, anthropologists employ the term 'berdache', and I shall use it here. The berdache in many tribes appears directly comparable with the male transsexual in Western society. Berdaches are, by anatomical definition, men. Although there is probably a female equivalent to the berdache, this role is undoubtedly much rarer, and is very poorly documented, so I have been unable to include it in what follows. In discussing berdaches, I use the present tense, because they still exist, although their roles have been less clear cut and valued since the decline of traditional North American Indian culture.

Most berdaches experience themselves as female from a very early age. As boys they show an interest in girls' activities. Often, they are attractive physically. As adults, they almost invariably dress in women's clothes. Sexually, they overwhelmingly prefer relationships with heterosexual men. During sex they are usually the passive partner, encouraging and enjoying anal penetration. It is clear that they enjoy sex only if it validates their experience of themselves as female rather than male. For example, most berdaches dislike it intensely if their penis is touched by their sex partner. This draws attention to the fact that they are anatomically male, which conflicts with their experience of themselves as women. It seems that many berdaches prefer to view their penis as a clitoris, a view that is an entirely logical aspect of their female self-image.

Berdaches are not usually stigmatized for dressing and behaving as women. The reverse is generally true. In particular, berdaches are valued for their combination of physical strength and skill at tasks traditionally performed by women. Many tribes emphasize that the skill of berdaches at tasks such as beadwork, pottery, weaving, sewing, crocheting, saddle-making, tanning and cooking, is often greater than that of women. This skill is combined not only with superior physical strength, but also an unusual willingness to work long and hard. Given these attributes, it is not surprising that berdaches are highly regarded in traditional Indian societies.

Berdaches are valued not only for their domestic skills and physical strength. They are considered to be highly developed spiritually, and to have special powers in that regard. For example: 'These people had the natural desire to become women, and as they grew up, gradually became women. They gave up the desires of men. They were married to men. They had miraculous powers and could do supernatural things' (p. 22).

The Indian emphasis on spiritual values helps to explain the acceptance and status of berdaches. From the Indian perspective, a person's spirit can be male, female, or anywhere between the two sexes. If a male child happens to be born with a female spirit, this is regarded as an unusual but natural occurrence that has special significance. The growth of the boy toward female interests and activities is acknowledged and supported as a natural development, rather than suppressed as deviant or abnormal. In fact, because berdaches have high status in many Indian tribes, and frequently acquire considerable wealth, parents will often strongly encourage a son to become a berdache if he shows a natural inclination toward the role.

Social roles similar to that of the berdache have been well-documented in South America, Indonesia, Southeast Asia, Siberia, Polynesia, India, Madagascar and Africa. From the available data it seems that the berdache role is so widespread that its absence from a particular society should be considered unusual. In Western culture, the lack of a role equivalent to that of a berdache is clearly a deficiency. But because we value our own cultural traditions so highly, we cannot readily acknowledge this.

A Third Sex or Transsexualism?

I have argued that transsexuals in Western society are directly comparable to the berdaches in North American Indian society, and to those berdache equivalents that are commonly found in other non-Western countries.

The main point of my argument is this. In the West, our attitudes to sex roles are so rigid that we cannot easily tolerate any deviance from the norm. This compels many of those who experience themselves as being of the wrong sex to seek surgical transformation to the opposite sex. The end result of surgery is not men and women of the opposite gender, but the creation of a third sex. The surgically altered transsexual denies that he or she has become a member of a third sex, clinging instead to a belief in their

167

true transformation to the opposite sex. The existence of a third sex is denied also by the surgeons, whose aim is to create as perfectly as possible a woman from a man, or a man from a woman. Society at large denies a third sex, accepting instead the idea of transformation from male to female, or female to male. All this helps to perpetuate the rigid and constricting nature of existing sex roles.

The Liberating Influence of Berdaches

Societies that include berdaches generally have a much more flexible attitude to sex roles than Western societies. Obviously, the berdaches alone are not responsible for this greater flexibility. Rather, the nature of society has allowed the development of the berdache role which, once established, helps to avoid rigidity in the area of sex roles generally. As Williams points out in *The Spirit and the Flesh*, societies that value the berdache role also have a remarkable *equality* between the sexes. North American Indian men, for example, have great respect and trust for women, and vice versa. None the less, sex roles in these societies are highly differentiated. Men and women lead very different lives. In some tribes, the sexes are so separate that women have acquired different patterns of speech and language.

These circumstances would appear ideal for the development of rigid attitudes to sex roles, but the reverse is true. Just as the anatomically male berdaches are free to live as females, women, if they wish, may adopt the male role and identity. For example, men are happy to accept a woman on a hunting party, as long as she has demonstrated sufficient skill and strength. But because women who wish to live as men are much less common than men who wish to live as women, only the latter transformation has been institutionalized as the berdache tradition.

If men value, trust and respect women as equals, they will not look down on men who display female traits. Similarly, if women feel that they are truly equal to men, they will not feel threatened by a male who adopts the role and identity of a female. This mutual respect and trust between the sexes seems to be the key to understanding the berdache role. Once the role is established, it helps to preserve equality between the sexes and to remind people

168

that gender is a flexible social construction which, if permitted to do so, can transcend the constraints of biology.

Men's Envy of Women

As psychoanalysis has emerged from its patriarchal origins, it has begun to develop non-sexist views of the human psyche. One aspect of this has been the recognition that *envy of women* is a powerful and pervasive aspect of the psychological structure of Western man. This envy is primarily based on the fact that only women can bring forth children, which is the fundamental creative act. Sometimes called *womb envy*, it may extend to women's capacity to nurture, as symbolized by their production of breast milk. Envy of women's creative and nurturing attributes undoubtedly contributes to the excess of male transsexualism. The way in which men deal with their envy of women's fundamental creative and nurturing abilities is crucial to male-female relations, both at an individual and a broad cultural level.

In Western society, men have managed their envy of women primarily by devaluing, confining and controlling them. If an object of envy is devalued, the level of envy is reduced and the pain of the emotion lessened. As we have seen in previous chapters, Western men have spent enormous energy in subjugating and controlling women. Although the main object of this has been to control women's sexuality, a secondary, mainly unconscious objective has been to reduce men's painful sense of envy concerning women's fundamental creative and nurturing attributes. This envy is a major obstacle to women achieving true equality in today's Western world: as long as Western men need to devalue women in order to protect themselves from painful envy, they will resist women's efforts to achieve equality.

I mentioned earlier the remarkable equality of the sexes in societies that value the berdache role. These societies are characterized by a mutual trust and respect between men and women. The berdaches undoubtedly contribute to this equality. If men are freely permitted to adopt the female role and identity, then their envy of women is greatly reduced. It is not necessary to envy attributes that can be freely acquired. Just as important is the view in berdache-oriented societies that male and female are

169

spiritual attributes that exist independently of anatomical sex, and occur in varying proportions in both men and women. This flexible idea of gender makes envy less likely.

To illustrate the power of men's womb envy to shape social structures, I will now describe a culture that is very different from both Western society and berdache-oriented cultures.

The Tribes of Papua New Guinea

Much has been written by anthropologists about the various tribes of Papua New Guinea, an island nearly 1,500 miles long in the Pacific Ocean just north of Australia. The most famous of these writers is undoubtedly Margaret Mead. Her books about New Guinea have been enormously popular, although anthropologists have challenged many of her assumptions. What follows owes much to a remarkable book about Papua New Guinea by two psychoanalysts, T. and R. Lidz. They aptly titled it *Oepidus in the Stone Age*, which reflects the fact that several tribes in Papua New Guinea have remained isolated enough from the mainstream of civilization to preserve, even today, Stone Age tribal traditions largely unchanged. Even for those tribes that have changed, there is a rich source of data available from studies by anthropologists over the past ninety years or so.

Although the spirit world is profoundly important to most tribes in Papua New Guinea, it is a world quite different from that of the North American Indians and other societies that value the berdache role. In the Papua New Guinea spirit world, the sexes are strictly and totally separated, occuring as independent qualities that cannot mix, and which cannot coexist within the same spiritual entity. This is in marked contrast to the spirit world of berdache-oriented societies, where male and female are fluid, flexible attributes that occur in different proportions within all spiritual (and human) entities.

This strict separation of male and female occurs at all levels of Papua New Guinea tribal society, and is fundamental to the people's world view. This is well described by Lidz and Lidz: 'The dichotomy between men and women is among the most striking aspect of New Guinea societies, particularly in the highlands. The women are derogated and despised. They are forbidden to enter

170

the cult houses on pain of death; and may, to the outsider, seem to be treated as little more than beasts of burden' (p. 31).

In spite of these strongly negative attitudes that men have to women, women's status in tribal Papua New Guinea is protected to a large extent by the economic contribution that they make. Because men rely on women to gather and prepare food, and to perform a whole range of domestic tasks, they are dependent on them. Historically, women were dependent on men to protect them from the frequent attacks by war parties from neighbouring tribes that were characteristic of Papua New Guinea until recently. The economic and social co-dependence of men and women helped to ensure that the lives of women were not degraded too far. Women were further protected by the fact that they lived and worked together in a very cohesive and mutually supportive way, giving each other the affection and positive regard that they did not get from men.

Men in many Papua New Guinea tribes put a great deal of energy into vilifying, disparaging and humiliating women. This devaluation is unconsciously aimed at protecting them from their envy of women. So strong is their dislike of women that Papua New Guinea men sometimes collectively attack them. But when the women flee, the men do not pursue them, and little harm is done. Although tribal Papua New Guinea men put much effort into denigrating and devaluing women, women's collective and economic power enables them to steadfastly reject these negative attributions. Because of this, men must find additional ways of managing their envy of women. How they attempt this makes a fascinating story.

Managing Envy in Papua New Guinea

In many Papua New Guinea tribes, the almost total separation of the sexes in adulthood is reinforced by men's *fear* of women's sexual fluids and odours, which are widely believed by both sexes to be poisonous and even lethal to men. Because of this, men are able to feel safe during sexual intercourse only after chanting to themselves protective spells and incantations.

Boys are raised exclusively by their mothers, with whom they live until they are about ten. They see little of their fathers until

171

the crucial *prepubertal initiation rites*, which, because of their great expense, are carried out only every 3–4 years. A central aspect of the initiation rites, which are often prolonged, brutal and degrading, is *nasal bleeding*. The young initiate is dragged into a shallow river, where two rolls of razor-sharp leaves are pushed up and down his nostrils, causing profuse bleeding. The adult men do this to themselves also.

An important function of nasal bleeding, which is commonly referred to as *male menstruation*, is to help manage envy of women. Men regard women's menstruation as a vital means of ridding the body of toxic wastes; it is also symbolic of their fertility. As such, it is envied; by mimicking women's menstruation, men protect themselves from painful feelings of envy.

There are other examples of male menstruation. In several tribes, boys are taught at age eighteen or nineteen to wade into the ocean and cut the head of their penis with a sharp crab claw. The cut must be deep enough to produce a gush of blood that is supposed to mimic menstruation. In other tribes, bleeding is caused by cutting or scraping the tongue. This is repeated whenever men feel the need to be cleansed and strengthened, and especially before going on a raid or hunting expedition. In some tribes, bleeding during initiation ceremonies is produced by perforating the nasal septum using a boar's tusk, which is subsequently reinserted on ceremonial occasions.

Obligatory Homosexuality

A striking feature of Papua New Guinea's culture is the presence in several tribes of what is best termed obligatory homosexuality. After the prepubertal initiation ceremony, the boys, usually aged 11–14, are paired with young bachelors aged about 17–21. The bachelors become the boys' guardians, guides and tutors, and they live together with them in or near the men's house. Regular sexual activity takes place between the boy and his bachelor guardian. Most commonly it is oro-genital, with the boy performing oral sex on the older male. Alternatively, the older male performs anal sex on the younger. This process continues for 4–5 years, at the end of which time a second initiation ceremony is performed. It mimics aspects of the natural childbirth process, and allows the adolescent

172

boy to be reborn as an adult. He will then take on a young boy of his own for the next 4–5 years.

Although this homosexual activity is generally erotic and enjoyable for both partners, it has a purpose beyond this, namely to protect men from their envy of women's child-bearing and nurturing abilities. Although men are forced to accept the fact that only women can actually bring forth babies, they firmly believe that only men can give birth to men, through repeated impregnation with semen. Without this impregnation, boys cannot mature into men. The main function of obligatory homosexuality is to ensure that the boy receives enough of the male essence to grow into a man. To the men who donate the semen, the penis represents the mother's breast, and the semen is analagous to nurturing breast milk. In this way, the men are able to convince themselves that they have women's creative and nurturing abilities.

These ideas are linked with a ritual of central importance, namely the playing of ceremonial flutes, the sight of which is forbidden to women on pain of death. Playing the flutes allows men to control the spirits that govern women's fertility, and this helps to protect them from envy of women's capacity to bring forth new life.

Surprisingly, it is very rare for men to continue to be homosexual. Nearly all of them naturally make the transition from homosexuality to heterosexual marriage. Most men appear to enjoy sexual relations with their wives, subject to the various spells and incantations that protect them from the dangerous effects of wives' sexual fluids and odours.

The Making of a Warrior

The rituals, ceremonies and other events that are or were part of boys' traditional upbringing in many Papua New Guinea tribes have one overriding purpose: to create fierce and fearless warriors and hunters. Girls are largely spared the rigours of boys' initiation ceremonies, having their own much less violent and intimidating procedures.

Because of the almost total separation of the sexes in adulthood, boys are raised exclusively by their mothers until puberty or a year or two before. As a result, their maternal identification is unusually strong. This powerfully reinforces the envy of female attributes that they experience, mainly unconsciously, as adults. These internalized female attributes must be ruthlessly repressed. After brutal, frightening and degrading initiation ceremonies, boys live exclusively with men. Male attributes are constantly praised and encouraged, whereas female attributes are denigrated and disparaged.

By the time they achieve adulthood, the boys have acquired the ability to totally suppress any internalized 'female' attributes, including feelings of compassion and mercy as well as feelings of fear and timidity. They have learned also to totally dehumanize their enemies, a process helped by the dehumanization that they themselves experienced during initiation rites.

Because of years of close proximity to other males, they have bonded strongly, and have very positive feelings for each other. This process of bonding is doubtless aided by obligatory homosexuality. Toward outsiders, however, and especially toward warriors from other tribes, their feelings are strongly hostile. This hostility, combined with the ability to suppress fear and to dehumanize their enemies, turns them into extremely dangerous fighters.

Are there other ways of creating fearless, ruthless and aggressive warriors? To answer this question, we must look at a range of cultures, and examine the relationship between their aggressiveness and their child-rearing practices.

First, let us return to the Indian tribes of North America. There is no doubt that many of these tribes were very aggressive toward other tribes. But there appear to be some crucial differences between warfare among Indian tribes of North America and the tribes of Papua New Guinea. In Papua New Guinea, the object of raiding parties for many tribes (although certainly not all) was to kill as many enemies as possible. This allowed the maximum number of heads to be severed for later shrinking and display. The number of heads displayed was an important symbol of the status of the warriors, both individually and collectively.

Although a number of Indian tribes attached a similar value and status to scalps, this practice was much less widespread than its equivalent in Papua New Guinea. For warriors in many Indian tribes, the aim of raiding parties was not primarily to kill, but to display bravery, physical strength and agility, horsemanship and skill in the use of weapons. It is true that injury and death occurred during these displays, but such deaths were often regretted by the warriors responsible. Similar attitudes to warfare were found in many parts of Africa, where the emphasis was traditionally on rival displays of skill at spear-throwing. In these parts of Africa, men and women generally had fairly equal status, and enjoyed mutual trust and respect. The existence of a berdache-like role was not uncommon.

The most striking difference between Papua New Guinea and American Indian warriors is in their attitudes to a dead rival. Papua New Guinea warriors vigorously celebrated a successful head-hunt and showed no signs of remorse or guilt. In contrast, North American Indian warriors were generally very remorseful, often entering a period of seclusion and mourning which could be quite prolonged. This is well described by Sir James Frazer in his classic work, *The Golden Bough*:

> When a Choctaw had killed an enemy and taken his scalp, he went into mourning for a month . . . This ceremonial mourning for the enemies they had slain was not uncommon among the North American Indians . . . When the Osages have mourned over their own dead, they will mourn for the foe just as if he was a friend . . . There was no law among the Pima observed with greater strictness than that which required purification and expiation for the deed that was at the same time most lauded – the killing of an enemy. For 16 days the warrior fasted in seclusion and observed meanwhile a number of tabus' (Part II: 182–3).

At one stage, the Pima were allies of United States troops operating against the Apaches. The United States military complained that the compulsory seclusion of a Pima warrior for at least sixteen days every time he killed an Apache greatly limited the value of the Pima as fighting men! This is a perfect illustration of the different attitudes to warfare held by the Pima and the United States troops. To the Pima, the death of an Apache in fair combat represented the loss of a valued human being, who had behaved with valour and honour. It was an event to be mourned.

For the United States troops, the death of an Apache simply meant one less enemy.

We are now in a position to draw some conclusions. In the various societies that we have examined, there is a close relationship between men's attitudes to women and their attitudes to warfare. In those societies where men have strongly negative attitudes to women, men also have the capacity to kill their enemies without any apparent remorse or guilt. They are able to suppress or deny such feelings, and also to *dehumanize* their enemies, thereby turning them into objects or creatures with non-human or sub-human qualities. Killing a sub-human creature causes much less guilt than killing a fellow human being.

In contrast, in those societies where men have a positive attitude to women, and where the berdache role is often valued, men generally experience much remorse when they kill an enemy. This remorse greatly limits their capacity and willingness to inflict death on their enemies.

Why are men's attitudes to women so crucial to these different attitudes to warfare? The answer lies mainly in the process of maternal identification. Where men and women lead separate lives – and this is true of warlike tribes in both North America and Papua New Guinea – boys are raised mainly by women until puberty or a year or two before. This gives them a very strong identification with their mothers and with women in general. To be turned into men – or 'masculinized' – these boys must abandon the world of women and be exposed to male culture. Where the sexes enjoy fairly equal status, and respect and trust each other, there is little need for men to suppress the female element in boys, or in themselves. This female element is positive rather than negative. Not only can men act as women, but women can act as men, becoming hunters and even warriors. Initiation ceremonies for the boys are less brutal and degrading, and the boys develop into men who value the feminine within themselves. They have compassion and respect for women, whom they regard as equals. They extend these values to men, even those from enemy tribes.

In societies such as those once widespread in Papua New Guinea, women are despised and degraded by men, and treated as little more than beasts of burden. Feminine attributes are considered by men to be strongly negative. For boys to become men, their maternal identification must be ruthlessly and totally suppressed. With it is suppressed also their basic humanity to other men. This allows them to treat their enemies as sub-humans, to be slaughtered without restraint, regret or remorse.

Warriors and Compulsory Relationships

The English-speaking nations have a long tradition of large-scale and effective warfare. Successful warriors and fighting men have had a glorious place throughout the history of English-speaking countries. The briefest glance at this history reveals that many wars fought by the British, and later by the Americans, involved human slaughter on a grand scale. In the First World War, from 1914–18, over 7 million soldiers were killed on the battlefield. In one confrontation alone, the Battle of The Somme in 1916, 650,000 German soldiers were killed together with 420,000 British and 200,000 French troops.

In spite of the vast scale of this human slaughter, attitudes to war changed very little, and even more soldiers were killed in the Second World War, from 1939–45. It is only since television brought the realities of the Vietnam War into the homes of every American that attitudes have begun to change. War is no longer regarded as glorious, and brave soldiers are no longer universal heroes. Even so, there was strong support in England and America for the Gulf War of 1991. The fact that this involved the ruthless slaughter of many thousands of poorly armed Iraqi soldiers by overwhelmingly superior British, American and French forces has almost entirely escaped the attention of the popular media. The involvement of the French is a reminder that glorification of war is by no means unique to English-speaking nations. But they have embraced warfare, at least historically, with as much enthusiasm as any nation.

What is it about English-speaking nations that allows their troops to slaughter huge numbers of enemy soldiers without apparent remorse or regret? What allows the English-speaking people to support and justify such slaughter, and to value and celebrate it as victory? It seems that such attitudes to warfare are strikingly similar to those held by the most hostile tribes of Papua New Guinea. What does this tell us about our own society? I believe that it reveals some remarkable similarities between our own culture and that of many Papua New Guinea tribes, especially with regard to creating soldiers and warriors.

In English-speaking countries, when young men join the army, especially if conscripted, they are subject to a series of procedures that are reminiscent of the brutal and degrading initiation ceremonies of many Papua New Guinea tribes. Fresh recruits are degraded and humiliated by older recruits. These ceremonies are less harsh than they used to be, but they remain frightening and unpleasant, and include such things as holding the recruit down and blackening his genitals with boot polish. This humiliation is institutionalized by compulsory shaving of the head, removal of personal clothing, the starkness and ruthless discipline of life in the barracks, and constant humiliation by training personnel, especially non-commissioned officers.

Once sufficiently intimidated, degraded and humiliated, recruits are taught how to kill mercilessly and in a whole variety of ways. They are praised and rewarded for their skill at this. The emphasis throughout is on the enemy as an object, devoid of human attributes.

Even if a few female recruits are present, the male recruits live in their own segregated barracks. This encourages strong male-male bonding. Although not officially sanctioned, negative attitudes to women are common among young soldiers, who tend to regard them merely as objects for their sexual gratification. This attitude to women is powerfully reinforced by the large number of prostitutes that tend to accumulate near large army bases, especially those in developing countries.

Basic army training is, then, strikingly similar to the process by which boys are turned into ruthless warriors in the more hostile tribes of Papua New Guinea. As we have seen, this process is so highly effective because women in these tribes are denigrated and despised by men. How true is this of women in English-speaking countries? At this point it is helpful to recall John Stuart Mill's statement, quoted on page 110, about the position of women in England in 1869. He showed that from a legal perspective, married women had the same status as slaves. Although married women were ostensibly treated with respect in the nineteenth century, in reality they were victims of the deepest humiliation, namely the complete removal of their basic human rights. Unmarried women, as we saw in Chapter 5, were viewed mainly as objects for men's sexual gratification. Women were either patronized and confined as wives or degraded and despised as prostitutes. But the institutionalized humiliation of married women was obscured by men's idealization of them – as long as they believed precisely as their husbands wanted them to. It is only very recently that the word obey was omitted from women's marriage vows: many women alive today vowed to 'love, honour and obey' their husbands.

Boys were raised almost exclusively by their mothers or other women until they suddenly entered the world of men at puberty, or a year or two earlier. For middle- and upper-class boys, the male world was invariably a single-sex school, usually as a boarder. Treatment of boys at private boarding schools is legendary for its harshness, brutality and degradation. Although not openly discussed, it is a fact that homosexuality was rife among the boys in these large, isolated, all-male boarding schools. For the younger boys, intimidated by the older students and with little power to resist, homosexuality was often obligatory. This is yet another parallel with the lives of many adolescent boys in traditional Papua New Guinea.

For working-class boys, the world of men was often a factory or a mine, where the work-force was almost exclusively male. The work was hard, menial, and dehumanizing. Compulsory service in the armed services awaited nearly all, with the real prospect of death on the battlefield or at sea in one or other of the wars that were waged almost constantly in the nineteenth and early twentieth centuries.

To achieve adult status, boys had to ruthlessly suppress their identification with their mothers and the other women who nurtured them. In this respect they were identical to boys in traditional Papua New Guinea, with whom they also shared an experience of adolescence and early adulthood that was often brutalizing, degrading and humilating.

In the Western world, the nineteenth and early twentieth centuries saw the bloodiest and most destructive wars in the history of humankind. These wars coincided with strongly negative attitudes toward women, who, as we have seen, had become almost powerless to resist them. This coincidence is not accidental.

Envy, Guilt and the Degrading of Women

The pervasive and powerful social conditioning of nineteenth-century Western men to suppress the feminine within laid the groundwork for them to be turned into ruthless killers. In time of war, those few men who refused to join the armed forces were imprisoned and despised as cowards or 'conscies' – a corruption of the term conscientious objector. During the First World War, young men walking the streets out of uniform were likely to attract groups of women who screamed abuse at them for being cowards. Men who refused to kill on the battlefield, or who fled, were often shot as traitors by their own officers, middle- and upper-class men who achieved a level of ruthlessness even greater than that of the men they commanded.

Western governments in the nineteenth and early twentieth centuries spent large sums on propaganda campaigns aimed at depicting the enemy as sub-human. These campaigns were quite successful. But no amount of propaganda could obscure the truth. In reality, the enemy were human beings, with exactly the same qualities as the men who killed them. Because of this reality, guilt and remorse about homicide were constantly threatening to emerge in the consciousness of fighting men. In Western European countries, including England, almost every fit young man was forced to become a soldier. As a result, this problem of guilt eventually came to affect virtually the entire male population. The guilt of soldiers who survived was heightened even further: why, they asked themselves, should they have survived when so many millions of their comrades did not? These ideas generated *survivor guilt*, which was added to guilt about homicide. This guilt to some extent recapitulated the basic *Oedipal* themes that were discussed in Chapter 4, and it also interacted with pre-existing Oedipal guilt.

We have discussed how envy can be managed by *devaluing* the envied person or attribute, or by *identifying* with the envied qualities. Guilt can be managed in similar ways, although it requires viewing 'innocent' people as if they are guilty. This important psychological process is called *projection*. If the process extends to *actively treating* innocent people as if they are guilty, it is termed *projective identification*. To be more precise, guilt is first projected on to another person. Next, the person who projects the guilt identifies with the other person. Finally, the one who projects actually treats the other as if he or she were guilty. This psychological concept is crucial to an understanding of how men deal with Oedipal, survivor and homicide guilt.

In essence, men began to manage this guilt by *projecting it on to women*. By the start of the nineteenth century, women had already been devalued and disempowered to a high degree, and this was helping men to manage their envy of women's creative and nurturing powers. To use women as vehicles for the projection of guilt was a logical next step. Because nineteenth-century women were essentially powerless, they could not reject men's projection of guilt on to them. As a result, men were able to achieve the next stage in the process, namely projective identification. Men began to treat women, especially married women, who could not escape, as if they really were guilty. Powerless to resist, they internalized the guilt projected on to them, and began to feel and behave as guilty creatures.

This combination of devaluation and projective identification was irresistible. It had a devastating effect on women's self-image, an effect from which they are, collectively, only just beginning to recover. Projective identification meant that women began to *blame themselves* for problems and difficulties that were really those of men. For example, if a woman was beaten by her husband, she would blame herself for provoking him. Women who were raped were often blamed for provoking their attackers sexually – and they accepted the blame and the guilt attached to this. Such attitudes are still widespread in English-speaking countries, although they are by no means exclusive to them.

Men's need to project guilt on to women created a monstrous vicious cycle. The more that women felt and behaved as if they were guilty, the more readily did they accept men's devaluation of them. The more devalued and degraded were women, the more negative were men's views about feminine attributes, which, when internalized, had to be ruthlessly suppressed. This suppression of the feminine made it easier for men to be turned into soldiers who could kill without restraint or conscious guilt. Partly because of this, wars increased in frequency and destructiveness, and men's survivor and homicide guilt accumulated steadily. It then became even more necessary for men to project this guilt on to women, contributing to their further devaluation and humiliation.

This vicious cycle has been interrupted over the past thirty years by the economic emancipation of women. The same technology that created weapons of mass destruction created millions of new jobs. These new jobs have allowed women to re-enter the workforce on a huge scale, and to achieve economic independence from men. For the first time in history, it has become possible for nearly all women to escape from men's oppression by becoming financially independent of them; no longer do most women have to endure devaluation and projective identification within compulsory marriages. But compulsory marriages remain common; as we have seen, sex-role stereotyping is a major contributor to this.

The Persistence of Sex-Role Stereotypes

Sex-role stereotypes were a consolidation of the idealized images of masculinity and femininity that became widespread in the nineteenth century. Because stereotypes are dehumanizing, they make it possible for people to be viewed as objects. The more that people identify with stereotypes, the easier it is to dehumanize them – and for them to dehumanize others. Once established, sex-role stereotypes became central to a number of emerging social processes. As we saw in Chapter 4, they facilitated sexual competition. Because of the intimate links between sexual and social competition, they facilitated the latter also. Men's use of projection to manage guilt relied on turning women into objects. Since this was also an effect of sex-role stereotyping, the two processes were mutually reinforcing. Stereotyping also facilitated modern warfare by helping to create an image of man as warrior; as a propaganda technique, stereotyping and dehumanizing the enemy made their mass destruction possible without unmanageable guilt or remorse. Through multiple, complex interactions with psychological, social and economic processes, sex-role stereotypes eased the birth of modern industrial society.

In today's post-industrial society, sex-role stereotypes still have an important place, but it is mainly an economic one. Numerous industries have arisen that depend primarily on sexual and social competition, and on exaggerating the differences between men and women. These include the clothing, footwear, cosmetics, perfume and personal toiletry industries; much of the automobile industry; and the popular media, especially women's magazines and men's speciality magazines. Pornography might be included in the last. Sex-role stereotypes are crucial to the viability of all these major industries, and to that of many smaller ones. The advertising industry reinforces sex-role stereotypes directly, by portraying them as social norms, and indirectly by boosting turnover in the relevant industries.

Sex-role stereotypes are, then, a fundamental aspect of post-industrial society. This helps to explain their persistence. They will doubtless persist as a powerful social force, and will continue to exert negative social pressures, especially on the more vulnerable members of our society. As long as they persist, they will keep alive the tyranny of coupledom.

The remaining chapters in this book will explore how men and women can avoid or escape the negative effects of sex-role stereotyping. Also to be looked at are ways of avoiding the tyranny of coupledom, and with it the risk of compulsory relationships. Although women are the most obvious victims of this tyranny, it is clear that men suffer from it as much or more: their denial of the feminine within makes them incomplete human beings, and that is perhaps the greatest tyranny of all.

8

Independent Men

In previous chapters I have traced the origins and effects of the patriarchal desire to control women's fertility. In Western culture, this desire was most nearly fulfilled in the nineteenth century. But men paid a heavy price for this. In destroying so effectively women's economic and psychological status, they destroyed the essence of femininity. They replaced it with a corrupt version of their own, which was really an extension of the male psyche. In doing this, men corrupted their own masculinity, turning it into an ideal that was as impossible to achieve as the ideal of feminity that they had imposed on women. In trying to live up to a false ideal of masculinity, men created for themselves many of the problems that confront them today. In a fundamental sense, it is the task of contemporary Western men to allow women to reclaim their own true femininity. If men can permit this, they will have a chance of reclaiming for themselves a true masculinity.

In discussing these matters further I use the terms *feminine principle* and *masculine principle*. The feminine principle concerns that which is essentially feminine. It has a spiritual element, but most importantly it embodies female power as legitimate and beneficient. Especially over the past twenty years, many books have been written in an attempt to define and celebrate the feminine principle, and I have included several of these in the bibliography. One of the most successful is *The Laughter of Aphrodite* by Carol P. Christ, who borrows the following quote from M. Wittig's *Les Guerilleres*: 'There was a time when you were not a slave, remember that. You walked alone, full of laughter, you bathed bare-bellied. You say that you have lost all recollection of it . . . You say that there are not words to describe it, you say it does not exist. But remember. Make an effort to remember. Or, failing that, invent' (p. 89). I chose this quote not just because it was emotive but also because it suggests that the feminine principle is really a historical idea. It is beyond accurate definition, because it exists only through its relationship with the masculine. The two principles define one another, and each shifts and changes throughout history. Instead of trying to define the feminine principle, I will explore it in Chapter 9 as it relates to modern woman and her journey toward independence. I will treat the masculine principle in the same way.

Creating a new feminine principle out of the masculine left patriarchal men profoundly dependent on women to maintain their sense of identity. This dependency, and the need to deny it, is sustained by an interaction with sex-role stereotypes, and vice versa. These interactions represent a tyranny for men that has powerfully eroded their well-being and which finds its ultimate expression in their reduced life-span. This tyranny is the end-point of over 2,000 years of Western patriarchy. It will not be easy for men to escape from it and become truly independent. But what does it mean to be an independent man? I offer the following definition of my own:

> A man who is independent has learned to accept the 'feminine' part of himself. He is comfortable about owning and expressing feelings of dependency, weakness, helplessness, inadequacy, anxiety and fear. The open expression of affection to others is not a problem for him. He does not need a woman to manage the emotional side of his life, to help him deny his own feminine attributes, or to make him feel like a 'real man'. Being economically responsible for a woman is not necessary for him, and he has no need to help a woman manage her life. He is able to live contentedly without being in a relationship, but is happy to enter one if he believes it will truly enrich his life – a life that is already reasonably healthy, happy and fulfilled.

I must emphasize that this definition refers primarily to men's *emotional* independence. It is not meant to imply social or geographical independence, except as a means of achieving emotional independence. Throughout this chapter, emotional independence is viewed as a prerequisite for a man to form a harmonious, intimate, equal and fulfilling relationship with a woman. Without an adequate degree of emotional independence, a man is at grave risk of entering a relationship that becomes compulsory in the destructive sense outlined in Chapter 2.

Men who have never married are rare, making up barely 5 per cent of the adult male population. For this reason alone, discomfort about being different, and fear of being regarded as abnormal, are powerful pressures on men to marry. Single men often complain of loneliness, especially after the age of twenty-six or so, when most of their friends have already married. Relatives and friends make comments, often not very subtle ones, that challenge their single status. Because of these powerful social forces pushing them in the direction of coupledom, many men get married before they have achieved independence. For such men, the chances of achieving it while married are not high.

Marriage in the Recent Past

A brief glance at the history of marriage in the West shows that the current very high marriage rate is unique. In the early nineteenth century, only about half the adult population was formally married. At that time, and for many centuries before, marriage was essentially an *economic* institution. Men married only when they had acquired some modest wealth. The idea was to marry a woman who had some assets of her own, often in the form of a dowry given by her parents. The husband, on marriage, acquired absolute rights to his wife's financial assets, a situation that prevailed in England until almost the end of the nineteenth century. In America, married women achieved property rights somewhat earlier, although the more conservative states resisted the trend until the second half of the nineteenth century.

Surprising as it may seem to us, marriage partners in the nineteenth century and before were generally chosen by their respective parents. Since the basis of marriage was economic rather than emotional or romantic, partners were selected mainly with a view to improving their family's financial status. Financial status was not simply an aspect of social status. It was intimately related to the prospect of physical survival. The progress that we have made over the past century in improving our quality of life is so great that we cannot easily comprehend the harshness of life before the second half of the nineteenth century, when the positive economic effects of the Industrial Revolution began to spread throughout the community. Until then, life for a least half the population was a constant struggle to survive. As we saw in Chapter 6, this was especially true of children. The average child mortality rate was about 50 per cent; it was much higher in poor families struggling to survive than in wealthier families who could afford heating during harsh winters and adequate food throughout the year.

The following quotation (Harrison: *The Dark Angel*, p. 212) clearly illustrates how grim life was for many people in England as recently as the 1880s. It describes a scene in a church courtyard, one of many open-air places where homeless people gathered.

> On the benches on either side arrayed a mass of miserable and distorted humanity . . . a welter of rags, and filth, of all manner of loathsome skin diseases, open sores, bruises, grossness, indecency, leering monstrosities and bestial faces. A chill, raw wind was blowing, and these creatures huddled there in their rags, sleeping for the most part, or trying to sleep.

Being poor meant the grave risk of being reduced to the desperate circumstances of these tragic people. The thought of such a fate was not far from the minds of most people, even those who were comfortably off. There were no state welfare or medical services. When a family was reduced to poverty, this often meant orphanages for the children and, for the adults, a workhouse or a struggle to survive on the streets.

Against such a background, it is not surprising that the main object of marriage was to improve the financial status of the families of both partners. Although most people lived in dwellings that contained nuclear rather than extended families, the commonest size of rural communities before the Industrial Revolution was less than 150 people. Often, these communities were comprised of a few extended families, together with unattached men and women who worked mainly as farm labourers or domestic servants. These unattached people, especially the men, were usually highly mobile. They followed work from town to town and village to village, often on a seasonal basis. They were not considered to be eligible for marriage, even though they made up as much as half of the rural population. Informal liaisons were common among these unattached men and women but they did not usually endure, often because of the illness, injury or death of one or other partner.

For most young adults, the choice of a suitable marriage partner was limited to less than half a dozen or so. The final choice was rarely made by the husband- or wife-to-be. Parents and relatives of both parties discussed the matter and, when suitable financial arrangements had been agreed upon, the couple were told of the plan. Often, financial arrangements involved the transfer of farmland and its improvements from one family to another, usually as part of creating more easily manageable and profitable farms. This process could be facilitated by a generous dowry.

In making the choice of marriage partner, physical and psychological attributes were rarely considered to be of major importance. Homely men married beautiful women, and plain women married handsome men. It was irrelevant whether women with dominant personalities married men of a meek disposition, or whether submissive women married aggressive, dominating men. These matters of appearance and personality were overshadowed by the vital struggle to preserve or increase economic status.

Naturally, young men and women hoped for a partner who was physically and psychologically compatible. But when this could not be arranged, they almost always accepted the situation. Often, the alternative was poverty. Young adults who defied their families' wishes usually lost their economic support. Until the Industrial Revolution was well advanced, jobs outside the family's social and geographic sphere of influence were rare. Given the choice between poverty and marriage to someone who was ugly or obnoxious, nearly all young adults chose the latter.

In reality, such an arrangement was not as bad as it sounds today. Because people did not expect much emotional or sexual fulfilment from marriage, they were not greatly disappointed when these failed to eventuate. Most married couples, especially wives, regarded sex as a duty required for procreation rather than something pleasurable. This view was powerfully reinforced by the Church of England. Life was so harsh and demanding for most people that the idea of relationships providing emotional support and psychological compatibility was largely irrelevant to them.

Ordinary people could barely conceptualize such a viewpoint. Human interaction was in those days characterized mainly by mutual suspicion and mistrust. The daily struggle to survive was so exhausting that most people had little time or energy to develop emotionally supportive relationships with those around them. The concept of intimacy barely existed. Most families were tightly run economic units, within which everyone, even young children, had tasks that were closely interrelated. Members of these families were forced to work together closely and co-operatively, not out of pleasure, but because their survival depended on it. Relationships that had strong elements of affection and trust were more likely to be developed outside the family than within it. Overall, human interaction was governed not by love, affection and mutual respect, but by the need to work together in order to survive in a harsh and unpredictable world.

The Popularizing of Romantic Love

Stories and legends of romantic love go back to the dawn of Western history. The Greeks wrote about it in a heterosexual and homosexual context, and their accounts show that both these expressions of romantic love were highly valued. In England, the earliest written stories of romantic love appeared around the twelfth century. But probably before that time, and certainly afterwards, wandering minstrels and troubadors included romantic love songs and poems in their repertoires. Ideas of romantic love and chivalry were inextricably linked. This is perhaps best illustrated by the story of Lancelot and Guinevere. Set in King Arthur's time, it is also a story of adultery, reflecting the prevailing belief that romantic love arose mainly out of adulterous liaisons or relationships between unmarried people. It was rarely written about as an aspect of marriage. Moreover, it was seen as an indulgence that, in the main, was the province of the most wealthy or privileged members of society. Foremost among these were the aristocracy and their retinues, and perhaps especially members of the royal court.

Although the idea of romantic love had become somewhat less exclusive by the start of the seventeenth century, it was still regarded as something that rarely happened within marriage. It was thought to lie mainly in the realm of the unmarried or the unfaithful. It had a strongly illicit flavour. Playwrights such as William Shakespeare helped to popularize this idea of romantic love at a time when the theatre was a major means of spreading popular ideas. Access to literature was very limited. Books were extremely rare and expensive until the introduction of the printing press in 1472. Even after that, they remained rare and costly because very few people could read. This created little demand for books, and hence no impetus for the mass production of paper, which remained expensive until the early nineteenth century. The first mass-produced popular book in English was probably Charles Dickens's *Pickwick Papers*, published in 1836.

Other than through books and pamphlets, there were very few ways in which new ideas could be introduced to the community. The theatre was a potent source of information, entertainment and challenging notions, but it was limited to audiences in large towns and cities. And when the theatre threatened to become too effective as a means of introducing new ideas, creating the risk of popular unrest, it was banned: the English Parliament outlawed all public theatre in 1642. Even after the ban was revoked, censorship greatly limited the capacity of the theatre to introduce ideas that were regarded by the Establishment as a threat to social stability.

By the mid-nineteenth century, a substantial proportion (although still a minority) of the population of England could read. This created a demand for the works of authors such as Charlotte Brontë, who published *Jane Eyre* in 1847, and her sister Emily, who published *Wuthering Heights* in the same year. These books eventually sold millions of copies. They are still selling well. Their authors dealt with romantic love in a way that made it seem both precious and accessible. *For the first time, ordinary people began to think of romantic love as something that belonged to them, and not just to the rich and leisured*. Nineteenth-century love stories started a genre that came to dominate the popular fiction market, and still does: the romantic novel. This same romantic theme has now come to dominate popular cinema, is strongly represented in popular magazines and newspapers, and is the basis of much television.

Reading became increasingly popular as more people became

literate. The Education Act of 1876 made attendance at school compulsory for all children up to the age of eleven. Within a decade, a large majority of the population could read, and the written word, for the first time in history, became accessible to nearly all. Similar events occurred in America and other English-speaking countries.

The impact of this on popular thought cannot be overstated. New ideas were introduced and absorbed at an extraordinary rate. This coincided with the start of the age of leisure. From the beginning of the twentieth century, technology and mass production allowed more and more manual tasks to be done by machines, releasing people from physical toil and giving them the time and energy to enjoy leisure activities. Social conditions improved greatly, especially in the areas of public hygiene and housing. The child mortality rate dropped steadily.

The effect of all these changes on popular attitudes to sex and romantic love was dramatic. People had surplus energy that could be directed into activities other than those demanded by the daily struggle to survive. As we saw in Chapter 4, much of this surplus energy went into increased sexual interest and activity. But as people became more enlightened, and as the overall quality of human relationships improved, a greater sensitivity towards sexual matters emerged. As part of this process, attitudes to marriage were changing also.

Marriage had become an important symbol of men's status in the nineteenth century, because it indicated that the husband was a man of some means. But whereas barely 50 per cent of men could afford to marry at the start of the nineteenth century, this had increased to 75–80 per cent by the start of the twentieth century, both in England and America. Marriage was no longer a potent status symbol, because most men could afford it. But it none the less became steadily more popular, and it is now something that almost all English-speaking men and women both aspire to and achieve.

Marriage as a Psychological Institution

Marriage has become increasingly popular because its basic nature has changed. It has been transformed from an economic institution into an essentially psychological one. As we have seen, until the nineteenth century, marriages were contracted for primarily financial and economic reasons. By the mid-nineteenth century, although economic factors were still important, marriage had come to function also as a status symbol. Men could display a well-dressed and attractive wife and children as visible evidence of their ability to support them in style. For women, marriage was one of few ways of achieving any social status at all.

In the nineteenth century, men in English-speaking countries idealized married women as non-sexual guardians of the domestic, to which they were strictly confined. Men themselves were free to attend to worldly matters. Married men were able to use prostitutes for discharging surplus sexual energy, and they did so on a large scale. But women came to identify with men's unrealistic image of them. They came to share men's view that only married women were truly virtuous; unmarried women were simply objects of men's sexual desire. Increasingly, women demanded marriage as proof of society's respect and esteem for them. Hoist with their own petards, men could hardly refuse.

Increasing affluence through industrialization during the first half of the twentieth century meant that a steadily increasing proportion of men were able to afford marriage. Women were still largely confined to the domestic sphere, and achieved social status and respect mainly through marriage, which they demanded relentlessly. As a result, the proportion of people getting married steadily increased.

In the 1990s, women no longer have to marry in order to achieve social status and esteem. They are free to pursue careers and other ways of defining themselves socially and personally. But although marriage is no longer necessary for basic economic and social reasons, nearly all women believe that having children is best done in wedlock. This is an option, not a necessity. But such is the social pressure on women to marry before having children that very few do otherwise. Most men have no economic need for marriage, which generally involves a dilution rather than an increase in their disposable income. Unless they have a strong desire for children, their need for marriage is mainly psychological. But, as with women, social pressures are so strong that they overshadow individual psychological factors. Although men and women have considerable freedom to remain unmarried, they are not exercising this choice. This is especially true of men. A major reason is the emergence of an intimate connection between marriage, romantic love and sex. It is this connection that has turned marriage into a mainly psychological institution.

Romantic Love, Marriage, and the Feminine Principle

In the Victorian era, and for some time before, most men believed that married women, in their virtue, had no sexual desire. Women themselves widely shared this notion, which had arisen out of patriarchy's attempts to control married women's fertility. Removing their sexuality greatly decreased the chances of extra-marital sexual liaisons. Married men were free to seek sexual fulfilment from prostitutes, or, if they were wealthy, from mistresses or domestic servants. This arrangement, degrading and humiliating as it was, remained workable as long as only 50–60 per cent of women ever married. This left 40–50 per cent of women with little socio-economic status or protection from exploitation. As we saw in Chapter 4, almost one-third of young women in mid-nineteenth-century London were full-time prostitutes. But, by the start of the early twentieth century, nearly 80 per cent of women got married. Prostitutes became less available and less fashionable. Because the overall quality of human relationships was improving, married women expected more intimacy, openness and honesty from their husbands, who became increasingly guilty about meeting their sexual needs outside marriage. Improved public hygiene had led to the virtual disappearance of life-threatening epidemics. Having a better chance of longevity, people became more concerned about personal health and hygiene. Fears of venereal disease further increased men's reluctance to have extramarital sex. The increased reliability and availability of condoms and 'Dutch caps' meant that marital sex could be enjoyed by couples who wished to avoid pregnancy.

For the first time in Western history, both men and women had the opportunity and the motivation to seek sexual fulfilment within marriage. The newly popular idea of romantic love meant that they began to seek emotional fulfilment also. Instead of splitting women into the category of wife or prostitute, men expected married women to combine both roles.

I discussed in Chapters 4 and 7 the ways in which Western men have traditionally dealt with their maternal identification, Oedipal guilt, and envy of women's creative and nurturing attributes. These traditional mechanisms – devaluation, denigration, patronizing, confinement to the domestic and ultimately projective identification – were no longer so readily available in the twentieth century. Increasingly, women resented being devalued, denigrated and patronized by men. They became more and more reluctant to be confined to the domestic. Men, among themselves, were still able to continue talking of women as mere sex objects, and to disparage and criticize them – until they fell in love.

The idea of romantic, passionate love became necessary for men because it was the only way of preserving the traditional split between wives and mothers, who were virtuous and asexual, and other women, who were mere objects for sexual gratification. Because almost all women now expected to marry, and a large majority achieved it, women as a whole had achieved greatly elevated status and respectability. There no longer existed a huge subclass of women to be denigrated and sexually exploited. *Men dealt with this problem by creating a new class of women who had even greater status than wives; namely, the women with whom they fell in love.* Once a man fell in love, there were again two classes of women. There was the unique, glorious and perfect creature with whom he was enraptured; and there were all other women.

Men rapidly became addicted to the idea of falling in love, because it solved so many psychological problems for them. Not only did it create two classes of women, but it allowed them to continue to idealize, patronize and control women as objects. A woman who was the object of a man's passionate and undying love was strictly confined by this adoration. When a man conferred his absolute love on a woman, she was required to live up to his expectations, however unrealistic they were. These expectations included reciprocal devotion. If a woman rejected a man's undying love, he would implore her to reconsider. If she persisted in her rejection, he would say that without her, life was not worth living. Continuing refusal evoked hints or threats of suicide, which were occasionally carried out. Men died of love, and they still do.

The effect of men's behaviour toward women they fell in love with was generally to make the women feel *guilty*. In reality, it was impossible for a woman to live up to a man's idealized image of her. The more she tried, the more she failed, and the more guilty she felt. Being in love allowed men to project their Oedipal guilt on to women. Men were also able to project their denied feminine attributes, which freed them from the task of constantly suppressing them. But this use of projection meant that women had to carry men's femininity as well as their own. This was part of the corruption of the true feminine principle. For a woman, the experience of being the object of a man's passionate adoration was an unsettling and disturbing one – until she either escaped or yielded. If she yielded, the next step was marriage.

In English-speaking countries, divorce was extremely difficult until the 1950s. This meant that once married, most women stayed married. Within a few months of the wedding, the husband's sense of being in love almost inevitably waned. It was replaced, if the wife was fortunate, by affection and respect. But often, once the husband's idealized image of his wife became tarnished, he replaced it with an increasingly negative one. Adoration became indifference; indifference turned to criticism; criticism became humiliation and degradation, often reinforced by physical violence. Projection of guilt became projective identification: the husband began to treat his wife as a guilty person. If she stayed in the marriage, she would eventually come to feel and behave as if she were guilty – guilty of never being able to live up to her husband's expectations. Guilty of not being a perfect wife.

As long as the marriage endured, the husband could avoid facing up to his own feelings of envy and guilt by projecting them on to his wife. Since men die, on average, seven years younger than women, such husbands have a good chance of going to the grave while still projecting all their unwanted psychological attributes on to their wives.

Men have now become so dependent on the idea of falling in love that the search for the perfect mate dominates the life of many. Most men attach the greatest importance to finding a woman whom they can fall in love with and marry. But falling in love involves projecting aspects of oneself on to another person. Falling in love means being incomplete.

It often means, for men, denying the feminine within. The idea of romantic, passionate love as a necessary preliminary to marriage has become a tyranny for men. It makes true companionship between men and women almost impossible to achieve. But the idea is so firmly entrenched that most men change their views only when they discover for themselves that falling in love is not always the best basis for an enduring relationship. This often occurs in the context of separation or divorce.

Men and Divorce

In the 1990s, women are much less likely to remain with men who brutalize and degrade them, or treat them as objects. The men they leave often continue to project guilt on to their former partners, blaming them for the marriage problems and break-up. Since the wife most commonly initiates the divorce, the husband often gets some support for his views from friends and relatives, who rarely know the full truth of the marriage. Such men, especially if they are physically attractive, charming or wealthy, are frequently able to remarry without having to look at their own contribution to the break-up of the previous marriage. They can avoid examining their problems in relating to women. But the same difficulties usually emerge in the second marriage, and, if lack of insight persists, in subsequent ones: 45 per cent of remarriages end in divorce. Of course, women behave in comparable ways. But the figures show clearly that men are not only more likely to remarry than women, but to remarry more quickly.

Research into adjustment problems after divorce has focused on women, a focus justified by the fact that in a large majority of cases, women gain sole custody of any children of the marriage. The presence of children makes it important for society to understand what factors influence well-being in such families. This focus on women has meant that we know less about men's adjustment after divorce. But the available data show that men generally have greater emotional problems than women, usually taking longer to adjust to the unmarried state.

In spite of legislation that allows deduction of maintenance payments from the salaries of divorced men, a great majority are better off financially than they were before divorce. The opposite is true of women. This mainly reflects the fact that married women often sacrifice or compromise their employment status and prospects in order to look after their children. After divorce, it is difficult for them to get reasonably well-paid jobs. If they choose to look after their children on a full-time basis, they rely entirely on savings, maintenance or welfare payments. If they choose to resume full-time work, they have the expense of child care. A recent study showed a decrease of 73 per cent in women's average income after divorce; in contrast, men's average income rose by 42 per cent.

Although divorce for many women with young children means near-poverty, women's post-divorce emotional adjustment is superior to that of men. This underlines the extent to which marriage sustains men's emotional well-being. Men's adjustment problems after divorce are aggravated by a number of factors. Seeing less of their children is very distressing for most, and adds to the sense of loss that they experience. Many men, even today, rely on their wives to organize their domestic lives; they lack the skills and knowledge to manage on their own. But by far the most important factors are men's difficulty in talking about personal problems, and their frequent lack of an effective social support network. This makes it very difficult for them to work through their grief and other painful thoughts and feelings about the loss of the marriage; instead, they try and suppress or deny them, often using alcohol and other drugs to help. While alcohol and drugs may relieve emotional pain in the short term, they hinder the process of examining and working through the real issues.

As we saw in Chapters 2 and 3, this style of coping with psychological and interpersonal problems is a fundamental one for many men. Finding new ways of coping is a profound challenge for them, especially if projection and projective identification are used together with denial of painful thoughts and repression of painful feelings. If unacceptable thoughts and feelings are habitually projected onto others, the task of reclaiming them may be almost impossible. So difficult is this type of psychological work for many men that they are unable to attempt it even if the need for change is made urgent and obvious by major health problems.

With so many difficulties confronting them, it is not surprising that men are more likely than women to remarry early in an attempt to avoid the pain of self-examination and psychological change. Alienated from the woman in his life, the newly separated or divorced man may initially be fearful of forming fresh relationships with women. But he will probably be equally fearful of turning to other men for emotional support and understanding. Most men, while married, do not invest much time or effort into making close male relationships. For men in their thirties and older, making new, close male friendships is nearly always a major challenge. It is even more so in the aftermath of separation, when most men are lonely, anxious, confused and depressed.

Although employment looms so large in the life of men, those who are newly separated or divorced are unlikely to get emotional support from work colleagues. Most workplaces are competitive and hierarchical. Men who reveal distress about personal problems at work rarely get sympathy from their male colleagues. They are more likely to be denigrated, or at least made to feel foolish.

In their desperation for someone to talk to about their anguish, rage and despair, newly separated men may approach other males who are simply acquaintances. Often, they are rebuffed, and this adds to their sense of loneliness and despair. They remain desperate for someone who will listen sympathetically without judging them; who will be comforting as they shed tears; and who will be willing to hold them physically, even for a brief moment, when they desperately need to be held. Finding that they cannot get these things from the men that they know, it is not surprising that they turn back to women. But what a newly divorced man seeks from a woman is emotional support and nourishment. He yearns to be mothered and held, to be nurtured and cared for until his sense of loss and abandonment becomes manageable.

The woman who tries to meet his needs has her own agenda. She may be able to relate comfortably only to men who seem weak, vulnerable and dependent. Her idea of womanhood may be confused with the idea of motherhood, so that she can relate to men only by mothering them. Whatever the precise basis of her wish to nurture a vulnerable, dependent male, it serves to meet the needs of the newly divorced man. It also reinforces the stereotyped idea that men are unable to manage their own emotional lives, and need women to do it for them.

Relationships that begin like this often proceed to marriage. But the chances of the marriage being successful are not high. As the husband recovers emotionally, his need for his wife decreases. He comes to resent her attempts to nurture him; he feels suffocated by them. But he will be reluctant to state this openly, because he feels beholden to her for 'rescuing' him. He therefore suppresses his feelings of resentment, but they emerge indirectly, and his wife senses them. She may also sense an underlying anger which really belongs to his first wife, but which he has avoided resolving by early remarriage. All this increases tension in the relationship, which becomes more and more frustrating for both partners. Unable to talk openly about the real issues, and bound together by guilt, they will often live together unhappily for years; it is more difficult for many people to admit to the failure of a second or subsequent marriage than the first.

Life Crises and Growth Towards Independence

For many men, divorce is the greatest crisis that they will have to face in life. For most, it is a psychological challenge matched only by the death of a parent, brother or sister. Any personal crisis represents an opportunity for change and personal growth. Failure to recognize and grapple with the issues thrown up often means returning to a way of life that is constricted and self-defeating. For newly divorced men, early remarriage is a classical example of this.

If many men experience the crisis of divorce, even more must go through another crisis: that of mid-life. The idea of the male mid-life crisis is not as fashionable as it was ten years ago. The term has become a cliché. We have discovered that women have mid-life crises also, although female themes are different from male ones. None the less, the male mid-life crisis is still a real event, and a common one. It represents a chance – the last chance for many – to reclaim the feminine within.

The male mid-life crisis has its origins in men's socialization. In earlier chapters we have seen the numerous ways in which men are trained to deny and suppress their maternal identification and to split off or bury their feminine attributes. As part of this process, they are encouraged to be unemotional, competitive, physical, performance orientated, and to become good providers. Most men accept their socialization without demur. They strive to find good jobs and work hard at gaining promotion and business success. When they marry, they are often willing to take on an extra job, or even two, so that they can provide well for their families. For years they work long hours, often at jobs that have become boring and routine, or which make heavy physical demands on them. They may crave to spend more leisure time with their children, but they feel too drained and exhausted by the demands of work to do the things that interest children.

When men like this approach their mid to late thirties, they often start to review their lives, a process that is usually initiated by a specific event such as failure to achieve a long hoped-for promotion, or the unexpected death of a friend or relative. The first thing that they must acknowledge is the likely failure of their boyhood or early adulthood dreams to be realized. As part of their training to be competitive, most men have dreams of becoming rich, famous or powerful. Even if they know that these are just dreams, there is always the hope, however faint, that they will one day be realized. On a more mundane level, most men seek continuing promotion at work, or success in their own business. If these hopes have not been realized by the time forty approaches, a reappraisal of life goals is required.

Acknowledging that they are most unlikely to achieve their original goals in life is a profoundly painful task for most men. First, it requires the capacity to grieve. Without this capacity, it is impossible to let go of cherished hopes and dreams, and to shed tears over them. Not all men are able to grieve. If they have been conditioned too relentlessly to be 'strong', to bury their tender feelings, and to shed no tears, then they may be unable to initiate the process of grief and mourning. This is especially true if they have already suffered a major loss earlier in their lives – perhaps the death of a parent or sibling – which they failed to grieve. Unresolved grief accumulates, and the more it does so, the more difficult it is to start letting go.

But even with the capacity to grieve intact, letting go of

cherished dreams is a profoundly painful and difficult task. Often, it means that the years of hard work and struggle to achieve success seem pointless and futile. Men begin to feel that their willingness to work hard and long has been exploited. They wonder what they themselves have gained from it. It is other men – their employers or their more successful colleagues – who have become wealthy and successful. They may even start to feel used and exploited by their families, especially if they are still supporting them financially. Men who are used to working long hours often have difficulty in relating closely to their children, or even to their wives. They may feel excluded and misunderstood by their families, which adds to their sense of being exploited by them. Once a man starts feeling and thinking along these lines, he becomes angry, bitter and resentful. If he is able to start to grieve, to accept that he must let go of past ways and dreams, to forgive himself for being so naive, and to forgive others for using him, then his rage will slowly lessen. Gradually, he will cease to be preoccupied with past failures, past errors and lost opportunities. He will learn to forgive himself for not being the superman he always wished to be. He will acknowledge his ordinariness and become more accepting of himself as he is.

His job will probably become less important to him, and he may become less willing to support his dependants financially. He may encourage his wife to try and earn more, in the hope that this will reduce the burden on him of supporting the family. If the marriage is a stereotyped one with traditional sex roles, these changes will be profoundly liberating for both partners. The wife will feel free to make more of her talents and abilities in the world of paid work, and she will become less dependent on her domestic role to give meaning to her life. The husband will feel free to begin to consider his own needs and wishes, rather than thinking only of his family and how best to support them. He will stop feeling responsible for his wife's financial and social situation, and will feel less trapped in the marriage by these and other traditional commitments. Feeling less trapped, he will be able to start disentangling himself emotionally from his wife. His need to project his own denied femininity on to her will lessen, and he can begin the task of reclaiming it for himself. His wife in turn will have less need to project her denied masculinity on to him. This reduces his guilt

201

and anxiety about no longer wanting to be a traditional, stereo-typed male.

Not all men deal with their mid-life crisis in a constructive way. Some abandon their jobs completely, but later come to regret this as financial and other problems begin to erode their well-being. Others abandon their families, sometimes to pursue younger women in the vain hope of recapturing their lost youth. A few drop out of society altogether, seeking alternative lifestyles because of their total disillusionment with the conventional lives that they have led thus far. Few men who try such radical solutions to their discontent find any more happiness than they had previously. Successfully resolving the mid-life crisis requires patience, thoughtfulness and a great deal of hard work over a lengthy period. But the hard work needed is of a psychological, introspective kind. This is work that most men struggle to avoid.

Other Paths to Independence

I have emphasized the crises of divorce and mid-life as oppor-tunities for men to free themselves from the danger of compulsory relationships. But waiting until a crisis creates the opportunity for change is far from ideal. In what follows I explore other paths toward independence, paths that are open to all men, whatever their age or marital status.

Confronting Homophobia

I briefly mentioned homophobia – fear of male homosexuals and homosexuality – in Chapter 2. It is such a major obstacle to men relating to each other in an open, honest and affectionate way that it deserves further consideration. Only if men can learn to relate more freely and supportively to each other will they be able to lessen their dependency on women.

Although attitudes to male homosexuality are more relaxed now than they were twenty years ago, it is still viewed with distaste or even disgust by a majority of people in Western societies. Sex between men, even by mutual consent, is still illegal in some conservative states in Australia and America. For many North American, British and Australian parents, the thing that they fear most of all concerning their children is a son or sons becoming homosexual. Because of this fear, they are constantly vigilant for any behaviours or attitudes in their male offspring that they believe indicate a homosexual tendency. Generally, this means any interest in things that are traditionally in the domain of girls. It means any mannerisms, behaviours or attitudes that are regarded as belonging to girls. In some families, any such signs of looming homosexuality are so ruthlessly suppressed that male children are forced down a constricted path of 'macho' maleness that may result in severe emotional and behavioural inhibitions in adulthood. A common effect of such prohibitions and constraints is to generate in boys a mistrust and avoidance of girls. This makes it difficult in adulthood to relate to women as people rather than objects. In some instances avoidance of girls becomes almost phobic; so deeply ingrained can this be that it persists into adulthood. Fear of women is often a significant factor in male homosexuality. It is, then, not uncommon for parents' attempts to protect their sons from homosexuality to misfire: they make it more likely, rather than less, that they will become homosexual as adults.

Perhaps the most destructive effect of actively homophobic parenting is that it encourages boys to disclaim or suppress any attributes that they believe are girlish or feminine. These attributes include many that are essential for a balanced life, especially the capacity to freely give and receive affection, to acknowledge and discuss the full range of emotions, and to be comfortable in a position of dependency.

A married man can be fairly comfortable with his homophobia. He can avoid close, intimate relationships with men, relying on his wife for emotional support and nurturing at times when his life is not running smoothly. Only if he loses his wife, or her emotional support, will he have to look elsewhere, and perhaps to other men, for what she gave him. Homophobia is usually a major issue for a young single man. Without a wife to rely on, he needs a social network for emotional support. But if a lurking fear of homosexuality stops him from being alone in an intimate or private setting with another man, then he can turn only to women for affection, intimacy and understanding.

Most men find it very difficult to acknowledge or discuss their homophobia. When they have found the courage to discuss it with me as a psychiatrist, I have noticed several recurring themes. The most important is a man's fear that he might be homosexual himself. So strong is social prejudice against male homosexuality that most heterosexual men are highly vigilant for any signs of it within themselves. They suppress any homosexual thoughts, feelings and impulses as deviant. But this suppression serves only to create in the psyche a reservoir of forbidden material. Any impulse of physical affection toward another man is seen as evidence of possible homosexuality, so that situations that might evoke such impulses are avoided.

Although a fear of being homosexual is the core of homophobia for most men, this fear is usually disguised. Sometimes the disguise is obvious. For example, a man who fears homosexuality in other men, and hence avoids closeness with them, is really expressing fear of his own homosexuality. His deepest anxiety is that if he is approached by a homosexual, he will respond – and enjoy it. A less obvious disguise is to denigrate homosexuality or attack homosexuals, a disguise that has its most extreme expression in 'queer-bashing'. This is a classical example of projective identification: the unwanted homosexual attributes are denied and projected on to someone else who is then degraded or persecuted. This unconscious psychological mechanism is at the root of prejudice of all kinds.

Most men find that discussing their homophobia with a psychiatrist, psychologist or psychotherapist allows it to diminish or even to disappear. Of course, the initial basis for consultation is very rarely homophobia itself. But in the course of discussing other psychological problems, it sometimes becomes clear that overcoming these requires homophobia to be confronted. Clearly, the chance to resolve these issues during therapy occurs for only a small minority of men. But there is another way, open to all.

Men's Support Groups

Today, there are few cities or towns of any size without men's support groups. Often, one or more organizations exist with their own facilities where men can relate to other men about their experiences and problems. Unfortunately, strongly homophobic men tend to avoid men's support groups, often because they suspect their members of being homosexual. Even if they do not harbour these suspicions, their habitual fear of getting close to men will make them very reluctant to join such groups or organizations.

The reality is that men's support groups rarely include homosexuals. This is mainly because homosexual men have their own support groups, although they may not always describe them as such. Another important reason is the discomfort of 'straight' men about male homosexuals. Even those heterosexual men who consciously struggle to overcome their homophobia are rarely entirely successful. It is quite common for a 'straight' man to be unable to relax fully in the company of a man whom he knows is actively homosexual. As well, the issues of most concern to homosexual men are often different from those that concern heterosexuals. For these and other reasons, men's support groups generally work better if the men in them are heterosexual. Should a homosexual man join, he will often leave when he becomes aware of the group dynamics.

The truth is that no man, however homophobic he may be, has any real reason to fear men's support groups. If he finds the courage to join one, the benefits can be very great indeed. In a successful group, he will discover that men can be open and honest with each other about their feelings, however painful and distressing. He will find that men can weep in front of other men, and feel nurtured and held rather than embarrassed and humiliated. It will become clear to him that men can do anything that women can do in the area of giving and receiving emotional support. Men, he will come to realize, can be affectionate toward each other, and can hug and hold each other, without being homosexual.

For men to relate to each other with such honesty and openness, they must be fairly secure in their sexuality, and free of the fear of being regarded as deviant. Men who regularly attend a support group become progressively less homophobic and steadily more secure and confident about their own sexuality. Once this happens, it greatly increases the chances of their forming genuine friendships with other men. As part of this, they learn that male friendship does not need to revolve around doing practical things together, such a working on a car or a boat, or carrying out other shared tasks. An exclusive focus on doing things actually hinders real friendship from developing. True friendship, they discover, includes a desire to spend time together not to do things, but simply to sit and talk. True friends want to be together because they feel a deep liking for each other, even a love. This strength of feeling demands expression through open, honest and intimate talk, especially about relationships, fears, hopes and dreams. Real friendship is based on love and affection openly expressed, and not obscured by an obsessive preoccupation with shared activities.

Regularly attending a successful men's group modifies not only stereotyped ideas about other men; it modifies stereotypes about women also. In the usual settings where younger men get together socially, such as sporting events, clubs and bars, they tend to talk about women as objects. They often feel compelled to talk about their sexual exploits, or to invent them if this seems necessary to be 'one of the boys'. Sexist jokes are almost mandatory. In a men's group, such talk is rarely acceptable. It is regarded as self-defeating and in bad taste. Instead, men are required to talk about their relationships with women as they really are. From this they begin to learn that women have worthwhile attributes other than stereotypic ones such as a 'bubbly personality', a 'nice body', cooking skills, and a willingness to be patient and nurturing. Women cease to be sex objects. It becomes possible to relate to them – even very attractive ones – without sex being constantly on the agenda. The idea of platonic friendship with women emerges. This is absolutely vital. Once men become able to relate to women in an intimate but non-sexual way, they have the chance of getting to know women who do not fit sex-role stereotypes. Talking with them, they discover that such women have many 'masculine' qualities, such as a strong desire to be competitive and financially independent, to have adventures, to explore, and to seek out challenges in life. These women are obviously comfortable with their 'masculine' qualities. Talking with them, men begin to ask themselves why they as men should not be comfortable with those 'feminine' traits that they previously disowned. This is the beginning of reclaiming the feminine within. It is the start of the journey towards independence.

Of course, not all men's groups are successful, and there are many reasons for this. But there are ways other than joining a men's support group to start reclaiming the feminine within. Some men begin the task spontaneously, or as a result of a new relationship, or by developing existing relationships. For all men, there is the choice of taking a path towards greater creativity.

Developing the Creative Self

For many men, confronting and developing the creative self is a challenge that is even greater than that of confronting homophobia. This challenge is rooted in men's profound envy of women's natural creativity through childbirth. Men commonly deal with this envy by denying their own creativity and identifying instead with women's. We saw in Chapter 7 how men's envy of women can underpin and shape whole social and spiritual structures. It has not gone away, and is probably increasing: as women's status grows, men's envy of them tends to grow also. It is a challenge that must be dealt with.

The work ethic is a major practical obstacle to men's creativity. In the West, men do about 70 per cent of all paid work. Few men have jobs that allow them to express their creative selves. If their work is both routine and physically demanding, or unpleasantly stressful, it diminishes their creative energy. Single men often work hard at such jobs as a means of increasing their financial and social status. Married men with children have the additional burden of earning enough to support them and often their wives also. After a few years of such pressures, the creative self usually stagnates and withers.

Accessing the creative self can be initiated in many ways. For some men it may mean taking up or resuming hobbies of a practical kind such as woodworking or pottery. For others it may be learning or relearning a musical instrument, or how to draw or paint. A few find a talent in creative writing, whether it be poetry, fiction or non-fiction. The process may require going back to school and writing and thinking creatively about the course material. But whatever path to creativity is chosen, it is often a profoundly difficult one. Men whose creativity has been suppressed for many years often believe that they have lost it entirely, or that it never existed. The prospect of doing anything that is unstructured, has no clear agenda or goal, or is not obviously useful in a practical sense, fills them with uncertainty. For years they may have disparaged as wimps men who like to write poetry, play musical instruments, or just read a lot. Recognizing and acting upon such urges and inclinations within themselves requires a radical change in their self-image.

Perseverance is very rewarding. Men who learn to develop their creative side become less envious of women's creativity. Because managing their envy then requires less energy, they can put yet more into constructive, creative pursuits. Married men, having less need to project unwanted aspects of themselves onto their wives, become more emotionally independent of them. They have less need to try and control them. Their marital relationships are less likely to feel conflicted, constraining and constricting, and more likely to feel harmonious and companionable.

Men who develop their creative side are also developing their inner world, a world of emotion, a world that does not obey the rules of logic that seem to govern the outer world, and which represents to them much that is stereotypically feminine. Initially, the inner world may seem frightening, dangerous, and unpredictable. But once accessed, it can become a source of nourishment, of entertainment, even of excitement and challenge. Men who are comfortable with their inner world can obtain from it much of what they sought previously from their wives, or from the other women on whom they were emotionally dependent. This frees them to explore new and better ways of relating to women.

Towards Sexual Independence for Men

Most men rely heavily or totally on women to gratify them sexually. This in itself makes men dependent on women, and for most men this dependence is primarily emotional. To reduce it, men must lessen their sexual reliance on women.

A married man who seeks to have sex outside his marriage is not seeking greater sexual independence. Let us be clear about that. He is seeking simply to transfer his sexual dependency from one woman to another. For this reason, I will not discuss marital infidelity now. This important issue will be examined in Chapter 10.

Creating Realistic Expectations

I noted in Chapter 4 that books and manuals on sex tend to emphasize its technical rather than its emotional aspects. Although this emphasis often creates unrealistic expectations, it seems unavoidable: technique is the essence of sex manuals and, in order to sell, they must fully exploit it.

The marketing of sexual techniques has recently become a significant theme in women's magazines, which regularly include articles that only a few years ago would have been regarded as unacceptably frank and explicit. These articles often emphasize women's orgasmic capacity, including their ability to achieve multiple climaxes. Research suggests that only about 20–25 per cent of women experience multiple climaxes. The ability to do so appears mainly inborn, and claims that most women can regularly achieve multiple climaxes if they or their partners use the right techniques are probably false. But women's sexual pleasure is increasingly equated with the number, frequency and quality of orgasms that they experience.

Women generally manage their own sexuality, with the help of masturbation, better than men do (see Chapter 9). But popular books and articles on sex emphasize the role of the partner. This reinforces sexual dependency between men and women. It also puts great pressure on men to deliver the necessary level of sexual expertise. If a woman's sexual dissatisfaction is attributed to her partner's poor sexual technique, he will often try to become more technically proficient. This may work but frequently it does not, usually because the emphasis on technique has obscured emotional and interpersonal conflicts that are the real cause of the woman's sexual dissatisfaction. As long as the woman is sexually dissatisfied, the man will feel guilty, frustrated and sexually inadequate. Both may start to believe that the solution lies in finding a new sexual partner.

A historical perspective helps to create more realistic expectations. It is only very recently that men ceased to define women's sexuality. It is barely two generations since most English-speaking women regarded marital sex as a duty to be performed for their husband's pleasure. The idea that it is the husband's duty to give his wife sexual pleasure is new. It represents a profound revolution in Western thought about sexual matters. Implementing the idea that marital sex is fulfilling for *both* partners is a social experiment on a grand scale. If we view it as such, our expectations of sex within marriage become more realistic.

It becomes possible, for example, to accept the idea that the strong mutual sexual attraction which characterizes the start of a romantic liaison is naturally of quite brief duration. For most couples, after the first six months or so, their sexual attraction decreases over the next 2–3 years until it reaches a plateau with fairly small peaks and troughs. During this process, it frequently emerges that one partner has a greater sexual appetite than the other, either habitually or intermittently. If such changes are recognized as natural, rather than seen as a deviation from a romantic ideal, they are more likely to be managed constructively. This often involves accepting relatively infrequent sexual intercourse. It certainly means accepting that it is virtually impossible for a man to bring his partner to a climax every time they make love. If she climaxes on half those occasions, the couple are doing much better than average. Most importantly, it means understanding that many women greatly enjoy the warmth, tenderness and intimacy of lovemaking without caring if they have regular orgasms. Once a man understands this, he can free himself from the performance tyranny. He may then become more sensitive to his partner's real sexual needs, and perhaps to his own.

Men who fail to recognize that modern marriage is a social experiment with major intrinsic limitations often blame their partners when difficulties emerge. Usually, they continue to rely entirely on women for sexual fulfilment, frequently outside of marriage or through serial monogamy. These manoeuvres are usually traumatic for all concerned. Alternatives require men to take greater personal responsibility for their sexuality. This is the essence of sexual independence.

Celibacy and Sexual Independence

Many men, both married and single, lead happy and fulfilled lives in a celibate state. A few have the courage to talk openly about their celibate lives, and about the benefits, to them, of celibacy. Once a single man gives himself permission to be celibate, if only for a while, he is freed of the tyranny of trying to have regular sex with women. For a married man, willingness to be celibate for a while takes some of the tension out of the marriage; it also allows the husband to realize that his life is manageable without regular sex, and that its absence does not make him less of a man. Celibacy does not preclude masturbation. In fact, regular and enjoyable masturbation is essential for the well-being of many celibates.

But very many men, both married and single, have a dislike of masturbation. Although few refuse entirely to masturbate, many do so only in circumstances that they regard as extreme.

Men's attitudes to masturbation are well illustrated in *The Hite Report on Male Sexuality*: 'Most men . . . felt that they should not masturbate, and that masturbation was basically acceptable for a man only as a substitute for sex with another person – many adding that they felt defensive, lonely, or guilty about doing it' (p. 487).

Although the report has been criticized on grounds of scientific method, its 1,100 pages make fascinating reading and are a rich source of anecdotal material: 'Masturbation always leaves me depressed despite the good physical sensations. This state of depression lasts for about two days' (p. 489); 'I do not enjoy masturbation. It's kid's stuff. It means you just struck out' (p. 498); 'The last ten years I hate myself and my wife whenever I found it necessary to masturbate. I feel cheated psychologically. It makes me feel alienated' (p. 487).

It was clear from the anecdotes that although nearly all the men did masturbate, they would rarely admit this to others, because such a disclosure was acutely embarrassing and they risked being thought of as unmanly. Some men even had fears that masturbation might damage their health. The origins of men's strongly negative attitudes to masturbation are complex, and are not dealt with by Hite. But it seems highly likely that they are linked with rigid, stereotyped attitudes to sexuality. The refusal or reluctance to masturbate is, for many men, a major obstacle to celibacy. Only if they change their attitudes to masturbation can they become more flexible about their sexual expectations of women. Accepting masturbation as a pleasurable and acceptable alternative to sexual intercourse is profoundly liberating for many men. But such is the depth of male prejudice against masturbation that a majority are unable to accept it as a legitimate option. In such

211

circumstances, pursuit of regular sexual intercourse often remains a central, compulsive aspect of a man's life. It requires the expenditure of time and energy that could be directed more creatively. It becomes another aspect of the tyranny of couple-dom.

The Wild Man

The title of this section comes from Robert Bly's exciting book *Iron John*. Bly, a highly acclaimed poet, has come to be regarded by many as the leader of a new approach to men's liberation, called the mythopoetic movement. This name reflects a heavy use of Greek, Roman and Celtic mythology, together with mainly contemporary poetry, to illustrate men's true nature. Bly uses the Wild Man as a complex analogy for men's unconscious mind. At the same time, the Wild Man also represents what Carl Jung termed an *archetype*, a controversial concept that is difficult to define. In essence, an archetype is the *biological* representation in the psyche of a key aspect of mankind's social and cultural evolution. Just as basic instincts are biologically programmed in the brain so, Jung argues, are many of those higher sentiments that make us human.

The animus and the anima are two archetypes that broadly represent masculinity and femininity. They are close to what I have termed the masculine and feminine principles, although Jung called these Logos and Eros respectively. He emphasized that animus and anima, or Logos and Eros, always coexisted within an individual man or woman, although one was usually suppressed. (For those wishing to learn more about Jung's ideas, which are still quite fashionable, I have included two works in the bibliography.)

Although some of Bly's ideas have parallels in the work of Jung – for example, the Wild Man as the Logos or masculine principle – Bly's approach is very different. Ultimately, he relies on his poetry, and perhaps also on his personal rendition of it, to move men emotionally. Once he has reached them, he helps them to reach within themselves by using myths, parables and metaphors. Bly is easy to read. Judging by the sales of *Iron John*, and by the response of men to Bly's earlier work, he has struck a powerfully resonant chord in modern man's psyche. Although Jung's ideas are just as relevant, and in many ways richer and more comprehensive, Jung lacks Bly's immediate impact. This is partly because his writing style is dense, especially in translation. The continuing currency of Jung's ideas owes much to those who have translated them into a readable idiom.

Because Bly's ideas are expressed in a subtle, metaphorical way, it is easy for them to be misunderstood or misrepresented. Good examples of this are so-called mythopoetic weekends run by men who are charismatic leaders but who have no real understanding of Bly's ideas, much less those of Jung. At such gatherings, men may be encouraged to access their Wild Man as a literal being, related closely to a primitive warrior. This leads to an emphasis on expressing aggression, both physically and verbally. The effect may be immediately cathartic, but it has little more long-term value than a vigorous game of football.

Bly himself relies mainly on poetry, chant, music and dance to encourage men at his gatherings to access the masculine principle. There is a profound gentleness about those meetings over which Bly himself presides. I believe that the great success of these meetings lies in a paradox. Men go to them searching for the essence of masculinity. This is a powerful draw-card. But what they actually find is their femininity. In reclaiming this, or at least some of it, they find themselves closer to a true masculine principle. I shall say more about this in Chapter 10.

9

Independent Women

Radical feminists have no problems in defining an independent woman. For them, independence is simply not needing a man at all, a definition neatly summarized in the radical feminist adage, 'A woman needs a man like a fish needs a bicycle!'.

Of course, the great majority of women have no wish to live entirely without men. And the great majority of feminists seek not to live without men, but to enjoy more equal relationships with them. How successful have women actually been over the past thirty years in achieving equality with men? Most feminists claim that useful progress has been made, and that the Women's Movement has made a major contribution to this. But the improvements in women's status over the past thirty years owe as much or more to their greatly increased employment opportunities. Does this truly equate with increased independence from men? Can economic independence be directly equated with psychological independence, or with greater freedom of choice?

We saw in Chapter 1 that a very large gap still exists between the average incomes of men and women. This gap exists for two main reasons: First, far more women than men are in part-time jobs; second, women generally occupy jobs that have lower status, and are less well paid, than those of men. We saw also that married women who work outside the home still do most of the work *inside* the home. As a result, married women usually have two jobs, whereas their husbands usually have only one. If liberation for married women means two jobs instead of one, is it really worth it? Has greater economic independence actually led to more freedom for married women?

The Superwoman Syndrome

The Superwoman Syndrome became a popular term in the early 1980s, and owes much to Betty Friedan (*The Second Stage*). It is

214

used to describe women who 'want it all', which basically means that they want to combine a highly successful career with being a perfect wife and mother. Although many women have successfully combined the two roles, others struggle to do so, and many have failed. A major obstacle to success is the desire to be a perfect wife and mother. As we saw in Chapter 6, ideas of wifely and maternal perfection are essentially male notions, notions that arose from a desire in the eighteenth and nineteenth centuries to reduce child mortality. These ideas are not based on reality, but on men's fantasies of the ideal wife and mother. They represent ideals that are impossible to achieve. Married women who try to live up to them are doomed to fail, whether they work outside the home or whether they are full-time wives and mothers.

The Superwoman Syndrome is mainly a product of the generation gap. The change in women's economic status and aspirations over the past thirty years has been very great. Women born in the 1940s and adolescent in the 1950s and early 1960s had negligible exposure to feminist ideas. Their children, adolescent in the 1970s and 1980s, could not avoid exposure to them. Some got only a little, others got a lot. It is those women who absorbed feminist ideas, but whose mothers did not, who are most at risk of developing the Superwoman Syndrome.

In the 1950s and early 1960s, only 10–15 per cent of married women had regular paid employment outside the home. Nearly all women who grew up during these years had full-time mothers, and most of them became full-time mothers themselves. But by the time their children were entering adolescence in the 1970s and 1980s, the feminist movement was is full swing. Married women who did not resume work outside the home when their children started high school began to feel a little guilty about this. This was especially true of middle-class, well educated women. These women were those most likely to be exposed to feminist ideas, and they were also likely to have the intelligence and education to get jobs and careers that were interesting and worthwhile. But instead of doing so, they had mainly become full-time mothers. Raised with the expectation that they would be supported financially by their husbands, they had not done justice to their professional opportunities. The superior education received by these women had often been aimed at helping them to achieve a 'good marriage'. This meant marrying a man of high socioeconomic status, or with excellent prospects of acquiring it. The husband's status would be conferred by proxy on his wife; she was not expected or encouraged to achieve status through her own efforts.

In the 1970s, many women who had fulfilled these expectations were exposed to feminist ideas for the first time. They became dissatisfied with lives that were confined to the domestic. But they were intimidated by the prospect of re-entering the workforce. Unless they had the courage and motivation to go back to school, their chances of getting a job that was interesting and worthwhile were remote. They could not easily accept low status jobs in factories, offices and shops because of their husbands' relatively high social standing; as well, many husbands resented the idea of their wives abandoning a full-time wife-mother role, and overtly or indirectly undermined their efforts to do so. Often, husbands could not understand their wives' aspirations to work outside the home. They saw their wives as having comfortable, privileged lives of leisure. They failed entirely to perceive their wives as human beings with the right to independence, dignity and self-respect on their own terms, and not the terms imposed on them by their husbands.

Most of these women were unable to escape. Many felt trapped and betrayed. They had struggled to do what they believed was right. But now their daughters, who had been exposed to feminist ideas, looked down on them for being full-time mothers. And working women tended to despise them for being idle and boring. These women struggled, and continue to struggle, with the dilemmas that Women's Liberation introduced to their lives. Their daughters struggle even more, because they are the ones who have become superwomen. This is how it happened.

Women who grew up in the 1970s and 1980s were widely encouraged to abandon the idea of achieving status and security through marriage. Instead, they were encouraged to try and lead their own lives, and to compete directly with men for the privilege and status that their mothers could achieve only by proxy. This encouragement toward independence and self-determination was especially powerful for middle- and upper-middle-class girls, who had the best chance of actually achieving it. Surveys during the 1970s and 1980s showed repeatedly that the aspirations of female

216

college students were overwhelmingly towards successful careers; but 95 per cent of them wanted to marry and have children also.

The ideas that these young women had about marriage and motherhood were mainly those of their parents. Feminism had urged them towards careers and competing directly with men; it had neglected to explain how they might at the same time be good wives and mothers, much less perfect ones. They naturally turned to their own mothers for help with this dilemma. Their mothers were clear about the issue: good wives and mothers were full-time ones, just as they had been. It was impossible to be a good wife and mother *and* do paid work outside the home. But they urged their daughters not to make the mistake that they had made – the mistake of sacrificing their independence and allowing themselves to be confined to the domestic. They encouraged their daughters to pursue successful careers. They put their daughters in a perfect double-bind: they urged them to become financially independent, but told them that if they did, they could not be good wives and mothers.

Raised almost exclusively by their mothers, with fathers mainly peripheral, these young women had a very strong maternal identification. Their mothers loomed large in their lives, and had a powerful influence on them, even as adults. The mothers with whom they identified so strongly, and who had made so many sacrifices for their daughters' well-being, were not just good mothers; they were perfect, or struggled constantly to be so. Daughters experienced enormous guilt and conflict if they thought of their mothers differently. Deep inside, these young women felt that they, like their own mothers, should devote themselves full time to their husbands and children, sacrificing if necessary their own needs and aspirations. Young middle-class women who grew up in the 1970s and 1980s have coped with this impossible dilemma, this classical double-bind, by becoming today's super-women. They have tried not only to be perfect wives and mothers like their own mothers, but also to be successful career women. This striving for the impossible has created lives so busy and stressful that in pursuing them they have lost their sense of identity. In losing their sense of identity, they have avoided confronting the dilemma of whether they are traditional women, like their mothers, or modern women, as they consciously wish to be. In struggling to be both, they become neither.

Are the superwomen of today more independent than their mothers were? They are certainly more independent financially. They are perhaps more independent emotionally. But they are no more independent of the ideas that partriarchal men created, ideas designed to control and subjugate women. In truth, superwomen are controlled as much by these ideas as were their mothers. They struggle to achieve not only men's image of the ideal wife and mother, but men's image of the ideal man. This man is highly competitive, and aggressive and ruthless when necessary. He puts the acquisition of status, wealth and power at the top of his personal agenda. In order to compete directly with such men, women must become like them.

Superwoman in Retreat

The start of the 1990s has seen superwoman in retreat. Or rather, we have read widely in the media about sophisticated, well-organized and successful professional women who are agonizing about whether it is really worth being a superwoman after all. The media neglect working-class women, women who work long hours in menial, boring and poorly paid jobs, returning to do similar work, unpaid, in their homes.

The retreat of superwoman shows just how little feminism has really changed basic attitudes to sex roles. The modern super-woman is beginning to believe that doing two jobs is just not worth it. She is saying that trying to be a perfect wife-mother and a successful business woman is too stressful. Superwoman could insist that doing two jobs is unfair and unreasonable, and demand that men do more at home. But she does not. Instead, she abandons her professional status and aspirations so that she can devote herself to full-time motherhood. She does not abandon unrealistic nineteenth-century ideas about motherhood and arrange for others to manage the bulk of her maternal and domestic duties, even though this would free her for what she was educated to do, and what fulfils her most, namely a challenging career.

According to the media, increasing numbers of superwomen or potential superwomen are abandoning their careers and becoming full-time mothers, seeking fulfilment not in the competitive world of men, but in the domestic world of women. But it is too early to say whether we are witnessing a major, long-term trend or only a brief retreat from women's struggle toward independence. The media, still dominated by men, take every opportunity to portray women as happiest in a traditional, domestic role. Talk of superwoman in massive retreat may be largely media propaganda. But the fact that the phenomenon is being so widely discussed indicates just how precarious are the gains made by women over the past thirty years or so.

Why are women retreating from the traditional domain of men at a time when, for the first time in Western history, they have invaded it on a large scale? They are doing so because they have failed to challenge the male view of the world. Instead, they have continued to accept and internalize a world view that is profoundly patriarchal. A view based on a male world in which fierce competitiveness and constant striving for status are seen as natural and healthy. A view that regards men as naturally superior to women, who need to be both controlled and protected by men, and who find their only true fulfilment in the role of wife and mother.

Because of this failure to challenge a traditional, patriarchal view of the world, many women feel guilty about inhabiting the domain of men. They feel guilty about being assertive, aggressive and competitive, and about putting their own needs first. They feel guilty about abandoning the traditional role of mother and wife, a guilt that is commonly reinforced by their own mothers and other women who have a conservative view of sex roles. Although this guilt is mainly unconscious, it must be dealt with. One way of dealing with it is to retreat from men's domain and accept confinement to the domestic sphere once again. But this leaves women struggling with feelings of envy about men's freedom, power and status. Another way is to try and redefine the world along non-patriarchal lines. I will discuss later in this chapter the attempts of some feminists to do this. A third way is to use psychological defence mechanisms such as identification with the aggressor, denial, projection and projective identification. Although these mechanisms are employed by both sexes, some are used more often by women and others more often by men. What follows is an outline of the defensive manoeuvres that women tend to use in their management of envy and guilt.

The Electra Complex

Chapter 7 examined how men manage their envy of women and what may broadly be termed their Oedipal guilt. As adults, women use somewhat different mechanisms, although the childhood origins of their envy and guilt are similar. The Oedipus complex in men has its parallel in women's Electra complex. Freud himself was never comfortable with this term, but it has none the less become part of the psychoanalytic tradition. It derives from the work of Aeschylus, a Greek dramatist of the fifth century BC who popularized the original legend. Aeschylus himself was aware of the enormous complexity of father-daughter-mother relationships, and his original work reflects this: it is a trilogy of five-act plays. In outline, Electra's mother and her mother's lover kill Electra's father, with whom Electra is in love. Electra then feels justified in killing her mother in revenge, although it is her brother Orestes who finally carries out the matricide, which is portrayed as an act of justice.

The Electra complex refers to events in a girl's life that occur around the age of 3–4. At this time, the girl is said to develop a strong sense of affection and physical desire for her father. This desire is linked with envy of his physical attributes such as size and strength, although there is often a greater envy of his independence and freedom – attributes that the little girl realizes are much less evident in her mother. Just as the little boy's Oedipal complex revolves around his envy of, and desire for, his mother's 'feminine' attributes, so does the little girl's Electra conflict revolve around desire for her father's 'masculine' attributes. The term 'penis envy' has been widely used to describe this aspect of the Electra complex, and it is broadly equivalent to womb envy in men.

Unfortunately, the idea of penis envy has been interpreted too literally; the term evokes wrath or derision from feminists and hilarity or disbelief from others. But when construed as women's envy of men's 'masculine' attributes, it is an idea that is valid and useful. In fact, the notion of penis envy is crucial in understanding how girls learn to manage feelings of envy and guilt.

The little girl's desire for her father evokes feelings of rivalry towards her mother and a wish to displace her. In this way, the daughter believes that she can become the sole object of her father's affection. The wish to displace or destroy the rival mother evokes strong feelings of guilt in the little girl, together with fears of retribution from the mother. These feelings of guilt and fear are dealt with by repressing the desire for the father. Part of this desire represents a wish to acquire his masculine qualities, with which the little girl identifies. These qualities are then internalized. When the little girl represses her desire for the father, she also represses the envied masculine attributes that she has internalized. Subsequently, she will feel guilty and fearful about experiencing or acknowledging these buried masculine qualities. Unless the Electra complex is resolved satisfactorily, she will enter adulthood unable to express the 'masculine' aspects of her identity. This restriction parallels that of the man with an unresolved Oedipus complex which leaves him unable to acknowledge or express the 'feminine' aspects of his identity. Just as a man may attempt to deal with his denied feminine attributes by projecting them on to a woman, so a woman may project her unwanted masculine attributes on to a man. But male attributes are valued more highly than female ones, so that women's projections are likely to result in idealization of men, rather than denigration. This helps to sustain the superior status of men in patriarchal societies.

The Electra complex is resolved if the young girl is able to develop an affectionate, close relationship with her father that includes shared activities and intimate conversation. In this way she learns that it is safe to feel love and affection for her father, and that she can express these positive feelings without displacing her mother. Her mother ceases to be a feared or hated rival and becomes instead someone with whom she can identify freely and safely. As she grows up, the girl has no need to bury her internalized 'masculine' attributes because they evoke feelings of guilt and fear. In adulthood, she can acknowledge and express them freely. They have blended smoothly with the 'feminine' attributes that she internalized during the development of a fairly positive, unambivalent relationship with her mother.

In English-speaking societies, fathers traditionally have very little contact with their young daughters. If they interact much with their children, it is usually with sons in the context of sport or other 'male' pursuits. Girls are raised almost exclusively by their

221

mothers. It is very unusual for them to develop close, intimate relationships with their fathers, at least in childhood or adolescence. Some manage to achieve it as adults. This means that an unresolved Electra complex is so common as to be almost the cultural norm. The implications of this are considerable, especially concerning women's ability to compete directly with men. Competing directly with men requires women to experience and express their masculine attributes. But if this evokes the guilt and fear of being masculine that is attached to an unresolved Electra complex, women are at a great disadvantage in men's domain.

The mainstream feminist movement has encouraged women to compete directly with men as part of achieving greater equality with them. But it has not sufficiently acknowledged the difficulties that many women have in accessing their denied, masculine attributes. For women restricted in this way, competing directly with men evokes fear and guilt. Mainstream feminists have done little to help women manage these difficulties. In fact, they may have inadvertently made it *more* difficult for women to compete with men. This paradox has come about in the following way.

Feminism has given a voice to women who were previously silent. One effect of this has been the increased willingness of women to talk about childhood sexual abuse. It has become clear over the past few years that sexual abuse of young girls by men is a massive social problem. Although reliable figures are hard to obtain, it appears that at least one-fifth of adult women experienced significant sexual abuse as children. The main perpetrators of this abuse were fathers and brothers.

English-speaking societies are only just beginning to come to terms with these alarming findings. But the discovery of this widespread corruption in the heart of the family, an institution still treated with almost holy reverence, has had a significant effect on women's attitudes to men. It has made many women fearful of leaving their young daughters alone with men, even their fathers. Some women now view all men as potential child molesters, even though only a small minority have ever sexually abused young girls, or are likely to do so.

The overall effect of all this has been to increase the emotional and cultural distance between men and women. Even though attitudes to sex roles are more flexible than they were thirty years

222

ago, it is no easier today for fathers to get close to their young daughters. In fact it is probably more difficult. This means that the chances of girls resolving the Electra complex are decreased. As adults, they will find it more difficult, and not less, to compete with ease and confidence in the world of men. Superwoman in retreat is a visible casualty of this emerging trend.

Envy, Guilt and Radical Feminism

As we have seen, men have ready access to the mechanisms of projection and projective identification for managing their envy and guilt. The disempowerment of women in the nineteenth century made it impossible for them to resist men's projections. Instead, they absorbed and internalized them, ultimately feeling and behaving as men wished them to. Women had a double burden of guilt to manage: their own, and the projected guilt of men. Women's internalized guilt has been crucial to men's control of them. For traditional women, deviation from roles prescribed by men evokes strong and painful guilt feelings. Husbands do not need to keep traditional wives in line. Internalized guilt does it for them. Even women who are less traditional carry such a burden of internalized guilt that departure from men's expectations is often difficult for them. Radical feminists refuse to accept men's projected guilt. They refuse to accept men's definition of womanhood, and struggle to create their own. In refusing to accept men's projected guilt, they project it back at them. As part of this, men are often devalued and denigrated by radical feminists, mirroring the attitudes that many traditional men have toward women.

In talking with and about radical feminists, I learned that as children many had more than their fair share of negative experiences with men. Often, they had abusive fathers. The abuse that they suffered was not usually sexual. Mostly, it was of a general physical and psychological kind, frequently experienced in the context of the father's alcoholism. The father was abusive when drunk, but at other times he could be warm and affectionate, or at least fairly pleasant. Often, the daughter came to see her father as a 'Jekyll and Hyde' figure – an evil Mr Hyde when drunk, and a good Dr Jekyll when sober. Even if alcohol or other drugs were not always involved, the father's behaviour was often erratic

223

and unpredictable, encouraging the daughter's perception of duality. This split into good and bad creates special problems in managing envy and guilt.

The young girl both fears and envies her father's strength and potency when he is abusive. Paradoxically, she is likely to identify with him unusually strongly, because there is an element of 'identification with the aggressor'. When he is not abusive, she is able to feel some desire and affection for him. This evokes guilt and a fear of retribution from the mother. Because the little girl relies on her mother for protection from the abusive father, she cannot risk alienating her. She copes with this dilemma by ruthlessly repressing her desire for her father and also his internalized 'masculine' qualities. She enters adulthood with her Electra complex active and unresolved. This requires her to project her denied masculine qualities on to men. Because these qualities are mainly negative rather than positive, men must be devalued and denigrated instead of being idealized.

These negative attitudes toward men that are commonly held by radical feminists (although certainly not by all, and perhaps not even by a majority) are also common among lesbians. This helps to explain the links between radical feminism and female homo-sexuality, links that were crucial to the early development of the radical feminist movement, and which remain important. The following case history illustrates not only this relationship, but more general aspects of the Electra complex.

Case 7: The Woman Who Hated her Father

Sonya was thirty-six when she first came to see me. I thought that she was strikingly attractive, with rich auburn hair and a pale, creamy complexion. Even the dark shadows under her eyes, and her tense, worried expression, took little from her beauty.

Sonya explained why she had come to see me. She suffered from *bulimia nervosa*, or binge-vomiting. For several years, she had binged uncontrollably at least twice a week. After most binges, and sometimes after normal meals, she forced herself to vomit up the food that she had swallowed by sticking her fingers down her throat. In this way she had managed to keep her weight close to an ideal of slimness.

Recently, she told me, things had threatened to get out of control. She was bingeing 3–4 times a week. Even the addition of strong laxatives to her self-induced vomiting had failed to stop her weight from increasing. Sonya knew that she needed professional help, and her family physician had referred her to me.

An Abusive Father

I asked Sonya to tell me about herself, starting with her family background. She described her mother as a rather cold, detached woman who never seemed very interested in her. Of her father she said: 'He was a bastard, a fascist bastard, a real bully. He liked to hit people. He used to beat us up all the time. I remember he had a thick leather belt without a buckle that he kept handy to strap us with. Sometimes he'd lose control, hit us for the smallest things.'

As Sonya continued to describe how brutally she had been treated by her father, I commented on how she was able to tell me about these awful happenings without appearing distressed. At this point she gave a wry smile and explained that in order to survive as a child, she had taught herself not to cry. Although this made her father hit her more, it lessened the extent to which she felt humiliated and powerless. Ever since, she had been able to exert almost total control over her emotions.

Sonya had one sibling, a brother two years her senior. She recalled that he had been the victim of even more physical abuse than she had. They were not close as adults and saw little of each other.

I asked Sonya if her father had a drinking problem. She remembered that he was often drunk at weekends, when he was generally most violent. She recalled also that 'he always claimed to love me, but he never showed it'. Sonya acknowledged that there were times when her father tried to be affectionate toward her; but she always rebuffed him.

At this point I thought that Sonya looked sad, and I was about to mention this when she said: 'I always prayed that he'd die alone and in agony. And the bastard did! I was delighted.'

Because Sonya had talked about her father with such vehemence, as if he was still alive, I had assumed this. In fact, about five years earlier he had suffered an unusually unpleasant death from suffocation. A motor vehicle that he was working under while alone in his garage had fallen off its supporting jack and crushed his chest. It was clear that Sonya viewed this as a form of justice, a view that gave her some satisfaction. She had never grieved her father's death: rather, she claimed to celebrate it.

The Emergence of Lesbianism

Sonya's natural intelligence allowed her to do quite well academically, and she graduated from high school at seventeen. After about six months she was able to get a job as a trainee warden in a nearby women's prison. Up to that point, Sonya had not viewed herself as a lesbian. She had gone out with boys, and had sex with one of them, although reluctantly and without enjoyment. When approached sexually by another female warden, Sonya had responded. She said that her first lesbian experience was 'like a whole new world opening up for me.'

Thereafter, Sonya had sexual relationships with many women, and had lived with several for fairly brief periods. These relationships were always stormy, ending in conflict. At thirty-three Sonya entered a relationship with a younger woman that had endured, although over the few months before I saw her fierce fights had been frequent. These fights mainly concerned the couple's mutual infidelity, both real and alleged. They were close to breaking up, and anxieties about this had clearly made Sonya's bulimia worse.

Radical Feminism and its Problems

Sonya had remained in the prison service and become a senior warden. She was well respected by her colleagues, most of whom accepted her lesbianism, which she had never hidden. Early in her career, Sonya had developed an interest in women's issues as they affected female prisoners, about whose welfare she cared deeply. These concerns had brought her into contact with feminists outside the prison service, and soon she found herself in the thick of the radical feminist movement.

During the past 3–4 years, Sonya's radical feminism had brought her into increasing conflict with her superiors in the prison service. She had tried to implement prison rehabilitation programmes that taught women non-traditional skills such as carpentry and metal work. These programmes were against prison policy, and Sonya had been ordered to abandon them. Because of her feminist principles, she refused to do so, and her conflict with the prison authorities escalated.

It was clear that Sonya had been under huge stress both at home and at work for at least a year before she came to see me. Not surprisingly, her bulimia had now reached a stage where it was seriously threatening her health.

Therapy

During our second session, Sonya expressed concern that I might be hostile to her lesbianism, and that I might wish to try and change her into a heterosexual, which she did not want. She emphasized that she was comfortable with her lesbianism. I reassured her I was happy to accept her as she was, and that only she could decide what goals to pursue in therapy.

As we talked further, it became clear that Sonya's bulimia had first become a problem soon after her father's death. I had noticed a relationship between bulimia and unresolved grief in previous cases, and I mentioned this to Sonya. Her initial reaction was of amusement, and then of anger. How could I suggest, she asked venomously, that she might be grieving the death of that bastard?

Over the next few sessions (held roughly once a week for the first three months, and then less often), we talked mainly about other issues. I saw Sonya together with her partner on three occasions, with some clarification of matters and a subsequent slight improvement in their relationship. They decided to stay together and try and work things out between them. But Sonya's problems at work continued unabated. She absolutely refused to change her views, and dismissal from the prison service was a looming possibility. Because she seemed to be getting more depressed I suggested some medication, but she adamantly refused to take it. She wanted to work through her problems unaided by drugs.

I pursued as tactfully as possible the idea that Sonya had some buried grief about her father that she needed to resolve in order for her bulimia to improve further. She continued to resist this notion until she had a very vivid deam, in which she was a little girl walking hand in hand with her father through an apple orchard. Her father plucked an apple for her, but, just as she was about to bite into it, it turned black and rotten. As she told me this dream Sonya began to weep. She had recalled, she explained, that when she was a young girl, her father had often been loving and caring to her. But as she got older he changed into the brutal man who dominated her memories.

This was a major breakthrough. It allowed Sonya to recognize that, underneath the rage and hatred that she felt toward her father, there was a deep love. Once she understood this, she realized that she needed to grieve not only the father who had died, but the father she had lost when, as a child, he began to abuse her.

Sonya worked very hard at resolving her grief. It was a huge challenge, for which she needed all her courage and perseverence. But after about four months of grief work, she was able to go to her father's grave and say goodbye to him. Although unable to forgive him for his abuse of her, Sonya saw that it was probably a reflection of his own deep emotional problems. She realized also that she had habitually exaggerated the extent of his physical abuse. Although it remained unforgivable, he had actually hit her on relatively few occasions. This was confirmed in a talk with her brother, with whom she had not discussed these painful matters before. Surprisingly for Sonya, he did not regard physical abuse as the major issue in his childhood, although he recalled that the threat of violence was always there.

Within a few months, Sonya's bulimia had almost ceased. It was no longer a worry to her. Her relationship with her partner continued to improve. To her surprise, she found herself becoming more flexible at work. She negotiated a compromise whereby she was able to continue rehabilitation programmes that observed some of her feminist principles, but which were acceptable to the prison authorities.

At this point we had been working together for about nine months. Sonya decided that it was time to stop. I suggested that perhaps there was a little more work to do, but she insisted that she had gone as far as she wanted to at this stage. Jokingly, she said that if we continued to work together, 'I might get to fancy you –

and where would that lead me?' I understood what she meant, and told her so. We agreed that our next session would be the last.

Implications of the Case

It was clear that Sonya had enjoyed a warm, close relationship with her father up to the age of five or six. In terms of the Electra complex, this would have required her to suppress her identification with his 'masculine' attributes as part of avoiding conscious sexual feelings toward him. When his love turned to abuse, his masculine attributes became negative, and she coped with her internal representation of these by projecting them back on to him. As a result, he became more and more wicked and hateful in her eyes. Her sexual feelings toward him became so deeply buried that this later became a block to sexual feelings for any man.

These mainly unconscious manoeuvres had helped Sonya survive her difficult childhood. Although in adulthood they were less appropriate, she clung to them. Her hatred for her father remained powerful and relentless. Unable to have sexual feelings towards men, it is understandable that she turned to women for sexual and emotional gratification. Once established as a lesbian, becoming a radical feminist was a natural development for her. But after her father's death, it became even more of a struggle for her to deny his good, caring, aspects in order to keep her hatred of him pure and strong. *Bulimia nervosa* was one result of this increased struggle.

During therapy, Sonya came to realize that her father was not all bad. After she had grieved his death she lost most of her rage towards him. Some of the blocks on acknowledging and expressing her emotions and her sexuality were lifted. Her bulimia was largely resolved. She became more flexible. She even began, in the safety of the consulting room, to experience sexual feelings towards a man. But this seemed to challenge her lesbianism, which she had no desire to abandon. At this point, she chose to cease therapy.

Of course, there are other paths to lesbianism and radical feminism than that taken by Sonya. But most are based, at least in part, on unconscious psychological mechanisms of the kind that Sonya's case illustrates. In discussing these, I have no wish to seem critical of radical feminism, which I greatly value. It is a force that has helped women to find a voice. It has been a vital impetus for collective action, and has benefited women in numerous ways. The object of this discussion is not to criticize radical feminists, but to point out that they are ultimately *dependent on men*. Their position is one of polarity. Men occupy one pole, radical feminists the other. Radical feminism exists primarily as a reaction against men and the stereotypically masculine. Without men, radical feminists could not exist: they are as dependent on men for their identity as are traditional women. Ultimately, radical feminism is a false path to independence.

Women Who Live Without Men

The Superwoman Syndrome and the retreat of superwoman tell us that competing directly with men to achieve greater economic independence is not an easy task for women. Unless it includes a refusal to accept patriarchal myths of wifeliness and motherhood, it is an almost impossible one. Achieving true independence through radical feminism is equally difficult. What other paths toward independence from men are available for women?

An obvious solution is to live alone, or with other women. It is easier in some ways for women to choose this option than it is for men, because there is comparatively little prejudice toward older unmarried women. But if a woman chooses to live alone, especially in a town or city, she has to cope with the fear of being sexually assaulted by men. She is at risk of being followed home by a man and observed to be living alone. In some urban areas, women living on their own are in constant fear of male intruders. Although sexual assaults on solitary women by male intruders are statistically quite rare, they are given much exposure in the media. Ostensibly, the aim of this exposure is to warn women living alone. In reality, it has the effect of greatly increasing their fearfulness.

Economic factors also make it difficult for women to live alone, especially if they are in poorly paid jobs, which is still true of far more women than men. Unlikely ever to be able to buy their own home, they are forced to rent. Since single women have virtually no access to state subsidized housing, they are required to rent privately. This means that they have no long-term security. They are the natural prey of unscrupulous landlords. Women, then, cannot easily escape from male oppression by living alone.

Unmarried men over the age of thirty or so who live together are widely assumed to be homosexual. This prejudice makes it difficult for older men to feel comfortable about living together, whether they are homosexual or not. Older women who live together are less likely to be stigmatized as homosexual. Even if they are, it may be of little or no concern to them, because English-speaking societies are relatively tolerant of female homosexuality. But financial obstacles to women living together are almost as great as those confronting women who choose to live on their own. Two working-class women who decide to live together will be doomed to insecurity in privately rented accommodation unless they have enough combined assets and income to buy a home. Given the poor pay and security of tenure of most women's jobs, this is unlikely.

In reality, a woman cannot easily live contentedly and with dignity alone, or with another woman, unless she can afford to buy her own home. This choice is restricted to that minority of unmarried women who have well paid and reasonably secure jobs. But that minority is gradually increasing in size, and as it does more and more women are likely to choose living alone, or with other women, on a long-term basis.

Women who choose to live independently of men are generally well adjusted. As we saw in Chapter 1, single women report much lower levels of psychological symptoms than either married women or older unmarried men. The superior psychological and social adjustment of single women, especially older ones, owes much to their ability to create social support networks. They are far better at this than men, whose homophobia is but one of many impediments to the task. Most women who live alone, or who share a house with one or two other women, have a network of female friends. Women in these networks understand each other's need for practical and emotional support, and they are generally vigilant for opportunities to give it. Unlike men, they do not need to obscure love and affection for each other with compulsive task-sharing and shared sporting or recreational activities. They are happy to just sit and talk, without the need for alcohol as a social lubricant. They are not frightened to hug, kiss or caress each other when the need is there.

Most unmarried women, together with women in general, have ready access to their inner world and their creativity. Unlike most men, they have not had to bury their feminine, creative attributes as part of managing envy and guilt. Women who choose to be unmarried are generally content to spend time alone, sustained rather than frightened by the richness and complexity of their inner lives. Comfortable with their creativity, it is natural for them to enjoy a wide range of solitary, creative pursuits, including needlework and other handicrafts, painting, sketching, designing, music and pottery. Men are far less able to enjoy such solitary activities, and also less creative ones, like reading for entertainment. This contributes much to men's greater difficulty in being alone.

Women who live without men may have more chance than married women of defining their own sexuality, but meeting their sexual needs may be more difficult. Homosexual women who live together are, of course, as capable of meeting each other's sexual needs as heterosexual couples, and perhaps more so. Heterosexual women do not generally need regular sexual intercourse to make them feel like women. Sex is therefore much less compulsive for them than it is for men, and they rarely use up much time and energy in pursuit of it. None the less, most single heterosexual women enjoy sex and value relationships with men that allow their sexual needs to be gratified. But achieving such relationships is not easy. This is mainly because men and women have such different attitudes to sexuality, a topic to be discussed later in this chapter.

Unmarried women in their thirties probably agonize more about having babies than about having sex. They live in a world that places great emphasis on having children, and which portrays childbirth and child-raising as the ultimate fulfilment for women. The reality of having children is systematically obscured, and the reasons for this have been explored in Chapter 6. Patriarchal myths and stereotypes of motherhood still hold sway, and single women must grapple with these. Few are willing to have babies unless they are married or living with the father. But this usually means sacrificing independence. Many unmarried, childless women in their mid-thirties to early forties alternate between envy of women who have children and relief that they themselves are free of such responsibilities.

Envy tends to predominate, and a powerful and painful ambivalence about having babies often persists until either pregnancy or the arrival of the menopause resolves the issue.

It seems then, that women who live alone or with other women in their own homes have a good chance of leading happy and fulfilled lives independently of men. But even women like this are not usually free of male oppression, in the form of patriarchal ideas and values. Although less constraining than the personal, daily oppression of an unhappy marriage to a partriarchal husband, it is none the less a tyranny. It can be removed only by challenging the patriarchal world view on which it is based. Some feminists believe that this is their most important task.

Challenging the Patriarchal World View

Since the early 1980s, feminist theorists have written increasingly about the all-pervasive nature of patriarchy. As part of this, some have rejected philosophy as a useful mode of enquiry, arguing that it is simply an extension of patriarchal thought. Others have questioned the whole basis of knowledge creation, suggesting that the way we perceive and comprehend the world is subject to an overwhelming male bias. Only by redefining the world in non-patriarchal terms, they argue, will it be possible to free women from male oppression. Redefining the world means questioning our most basic assumptions. We must challenge the structure of language, and the way we use it. We must challenge not only the way that we think, but the building-blocks of thought. We must ask questions about the creation of knowledge itself.

This brand of feminism has not yet been popularized to any degree. It is fairly new; it is complex, abstract and difficult to grasp; and some of its most convincing protagonists, such as Julia Kristeva and Luce Irigaray, have written in French, limiting their impact on the English-speaking world. But so powerful and potentially constructive are these ideas that they deserve to be spread as widely as possible. A central theme of this approach is the abandonment of dualism. Traditionally, it is argued, we structure our world in terms of opposites, for example male-female, good-bad, object-subject. Because challenging these dualities is a major aim of this style of feminism, I will use the term *unitary feminism* to describe it.

Unitary feminism reaches far back into Western history for an understanding of how knowledge is created. Records of Memphite and Babylonian myths dating from 3,000 BC reveal the existence even then of a fundamental split between male and female. The themes are strikingly consistent: the male deities were responsible for order, reason and logic. Female deities contributed chaos, emotion and the irrational. Originally, this male-female split was part of a fairly equal, complementary balance. But gradually the female element came to be regarded as inferior and subordinate to the male. I outlined this process of subordinating the feminine principle in Chapter 5, but did not consider at that point its impact on the creation of knowledge.

The Ancient Greeks were very active in subordinating the feminine principle. The myth of Pandora is an example: Zeus wished to punish the race of men that lived on earth because they had stolen the gift of fire. He ordered the creation from clay and water of a woman whose beauty matched that of the gods. He sent this woman, Pandora, down to earth with a box, the lid of which she opened. Out of it flew all that was bad: disease, pestilence, plague, all the sources of human chaos and suffering. Only hope remained in the box. The similarity of this myth to the Old Testament story of Adam and Eve is apparent.

Greek philosophy also was disparaging of women. Aristotle, an important model for later Western philosophers, believed that the highest human state that could be achieved was Theoretical Wisdom. But only men could achieve it. This male bias continued in the work of most later philosophers, including Emanuel Kant, an eighteenth-century writer whose influence on modern philosophy is still great. Thus, the unitary feminists argue, the very fabric of Western philosophical thought is permeated with the idea that the male is superior to the female, and that male qualities are more desirable than female ones.

Unitary feminism also points out that the fundamental duality of Western thought helps to oppress women by enshrining them as objects to be acted upon by men as subjects. Women are defined only as the objects of men's thought. This difficult concept is vividly illustrated by the following quote from M. Tax (*Woman and Her Mind* p. 28):

A young woman is walking down a city street. She is excruciatingly aware of her appearance and of the reaction to it (imagined or real) of every person she meets. She walks through a group of construction workers who are eating lunch in a line along the pavement. Her stomach tightens with terror and revulsion; her face becomes contorted into a grimace of self-control and false unawareness; her walk and carriage become stiff and dehumanized. No matter what they say to her, it will be unbearable. She knows that they will not physically assault her or hurt her. They will only do so metaphorically. What they will do is *impinge* on her. They will demand that her thoughts be focused on them. They will use her body with their eyes. They will evaluate her market price. They will comment on her defects, or compare them to those of other passers-by. They will make her a participant in their fantasies without asking if she is willing. They will make her feel ridiculous, or grotesquely sexual, or hideously ugly. Above all, they will make her feel like a *thing*.

The full impact of this quote is appreciated when one tries to imagine it being said not in relation to a woman, but to a man who is being observed by a group of women. This underlines the profound difference between women's experience of themselves mainly as objects, and men's experience of themselves mainly as subjects.

Unitary feminists are not alone in challenging the duality of Western thought. Ever since Einstein's Theory of Relativity replaced Newtonian laws as the guiding principal of theoretical physics, duality has been under attack by physicists, philosophers and metaphysicians. The notion of objective reality is in decline. We live in an age where people can 'create their own reality' as part of a unitary world where rigid boundaries between observer and observed – or subject and object – no longer exist. As our thinking in the West becomes less dualistic, and perhaps more Eastern in nature, it may become easier for us to stop thinking in terms of mutually exclusive categories. Male and female will cease to be polar opposites. Instead, they will be seen as qualities that are fluid and flexible, merging one into the other; qualities that may peacefully coexist within both men and women.

The question of language is fundamental to some leading unitary feminists, who emphasize that the basic structure of language is patriarchal. By this they mean that language is used mainly to control and manipulate the objects that it defines. Language coerces, controls and organizes far more than it liberates and creates. It is concerned mainly with the external rather than the internal world. Language is essentially male, and it has subsumed and subverted that which is female.

Although these ideas about language are very important, their protagonists have great difficulty in creating convincing alternatives to existing language structure and usage. But this is not crucial to their argument. The main point is that the structure of language itself makes it difficult for women to define and experience themselves in ways that are not imposed upon them by patriarchal men.

I have devoted some time and space to unitary feminism because I believe that it represents the best chance that women have of achieving true independence from men. The essence of unitary feminism is that it invites us to understand. It seeks to explain the nature of men's control over women from many perspectives. It underlines the powerful, pervasive and persisting nature of that control. Yet it offers hope for constructive change. But the change that it proposes is of a fundamental kind that concerns the way in which we perceive ourselves and the world that we inhabit. To make such changes will be arduous, and will require a long-term commitment. It will require enormous patience and perseverence. The aggressive, confronting, separatist approach of the radical feminists, although it has played a vital part in the modern feminist movement, is not the answer. It enshrines dualism. If women are to achieve true independence from men, it must be based on a clear understanding of the real issues, and a willingness to try and make the space between male and female smaller, not greater.

The Sexuality of Independent Women

According to the unitary feminist view, Western women do not have an identity that is truly their own, but one that has been constructed by the operations of patriarchy. This idea extends to women's sexuality. In fact, women have worked hard over the past thirty years or so at reclaiming and defining their own sexuality. They have had some success at this, which offers hope that women will be able to reclaim other aspects of their identity in the future. The way in which women have begun to define their own sexuality is an exciting story, and it can perhaps be thought of as a blue-print for action in other areas.

The systematic study of psychosexual development emerged toward the end of the nineteenth century. Freud was at the forefront of this new field, and his views dominated psycho-analytic thinking about sexuality until at least the 1960s. Unfortunately, Freud's views on female sexuality were misleading. He studied mainly middle-class women living in a profoundly patri-archal society, and his data were based on a fairly small number of detailed case studies. He wrongly assumed that his findings could be universally applied as part of a comprehensive theory of women's sexuality. Because men had such power to define women, and women's sexuality, Freud's views became widely accepted.

Freud suggested that women experienced two kinds of sexuality. One was immature, and was focused on the clitoris. The other was mature, and was centred on the vagina. Healthy sexuality required women to relinquish the clitoris as an erogenous zone and a means of orgasm. Only if they did this could they achieve mature sexuality, focused on the vagina. Only orgasms that occurred through vaginal stimulation, such as that which occurred during heterosexual intercourse, could be con-sidered a full and healthy expression of female sexuality. Women who relied on clitoral orgasms were thought to be fixated at the phallic phase of psychosexual development. Psychotherapy was required to remedy the situation.

This false idea of women's sexual response was rooted in a phallocentric view of sexuality. According to this, the main object of sex (other than procreation) is to permit men's gratification through orgasm. Sexually, the woman is of interest to the man only as a receptacle for his penis, which is the exclusive focus of male sexual pleasure and response. Since the vagina is the natural receptacle, it was considered to be also the natural centre of woman's sexual response.

It will be recalled from Chapter 8 that a general expectation of sexual enjoyment within marriage did not emerge until toward the end of the nineteenth century. Up until then, marital sex was strictly for procreation. Men usually sought sexual pleasure outside marriage, mainly from prostitutes, who were freely and widely available. Once the expectation of sexual pleasure and fulfilment *within* marriage became widespread, which it had done by the early twentieth century, the initial focus was on men's sexual enjoyment and how to enhance it. But increasing men's pleasure meant enhancing the sexual responsiveness and enjoyment of their wives. This was a profound challenge to traditional patriarchal society, since it had long sought to control women's fertility through suppressing and confining their sexuality.

Patriarchy managed this difficult situation by putting women in a classical double-bind. Women were allowed to have orgasms during heterosexual intercourse. But they had to be vaginal orgasms, induced by the thrusting of the male organ. Clitoral orgasms were forbidden, ostensibly because they were 'unhealthy', but in reality because they were not dependent on penile thrusting. They could be induced by manual stimulation. This carried the risk that women might begin to recognize and manage their own sexuality, thereby escaping from men's control. In fact, the vaginal orgasm is largely a myth. Psychophysiological research has shown that its existence as an independent phenomenon is questionable. Although it probably does occur, it is rare. Women were expected to do the impossible. It is not surprising, therefore, that they failed to respond to their husbands' desire that they should be more responsive sexually. Neither is it surprising that men began to blame women for being 'frigid'. Frigidity became a new focus for psychotherapy, although it was conveniently linked with Freud's ideas of fixation at the phallic phase. Psychotherapists, usually male, overlooked the fact that false ideas about women's 'phallic fixation' were an original cause of their frigidity.

This pattern of events will by now be familiar to readers. It is reminiscent of projective identification. Male sexuality was limited and constrained by phallocentricity. Instead of recognizing

238

this problem, men projected it on to their wives, who then became responsible for delivering their husband's sexual pleasure. When the arrangement proved to be unsatisfactory because of wives' lack of sexual responsiveness, they were blamed for being 'frigid', even though the frigidity had been created mainly by a male, phallocentric view of female sexuality. The stage of projective identification was reached when women actually perceived themselves as 'frigid', coming to believe and feel in accordance with men's projections.

Uncovering the Truth About Women's Sexual Response

The truth about women's sexuality began to emerge in the 1960s. This owes much to the pioneering work of Masters and Johnson, who had the courage to set up a laboratory for the objective study of human sexuality. Their findings not only discredited phallocentric myths of female sexuality, but helped to make sex a legitimate subject for scientific enquiry and rational discussion. Masters and Johnson established a data base that enabled women to begin in earnest the task of reclaiming their sexuality.

They showed that the clitoris and the penis were remarkably similar in terms of their nerve supply and responsiveness to stimulation. They demonstrated beyond doubt that the clitoris, and not the vagina, was central to female orgasm.

The revelation of these important facts coincided with the start of the modern feminist movement. Feminists put much time and effort into educating women about the real nature of their sexuality. Women were encouraged to take pride in their genitals rather than be ashamed of them. They were encouraged to explore them visually and manually, and to learn about their structure and function. Most importantly, they were encouraged to masturbate. It is a paradox that this emphasis on masturbation first arose from an awareness that at least 10 per cent of women had never achieved orgasm during sexual intercourse with their husbands. Another 10–15 per cent reached a climax only occasionally. Much thought and effort went into teaching these women how to have regular orgasms during marital sexual intercourse. This meant first teaching them to reach reliably a climax through masturbation. Such programmes were widely available, especially in the more progressive American states. They were very successful in allowing women to become orgasmic, and their methods and results were widely publicized. This had a dramatic and unexpected side-effect: it changed women's attitudes toward masturbation in general.

This change in attitude has had a profound effect on women's sexuality. Whereas thirty years ago women masturbated with as much guilt and furtiveness as men, many now practise it and talk about it freely and without embarrassment. In this regard they have left men far behind. Now that women are more willing to manage their own sexuality, they have become less sexually dependent on men. They have begun to redefine their sexuality in a non-patriarchal way. A heterosexual woman who chooses to live independently of men has the option of self-gratification as a valid, enjoyable alternative or addition to sexual intercourse. Of course, most heterosexual unmarried women enjoy sexual intercourse with a compatible partner more than they enjoy solitary masturbation. But having masturbation as a legitimate alternative helps them to wait for the right person at the right time. It introduces an element of choice that might not otherwise exist.

The Daughters of Independent Women

What happens to the daughters of independent women? Here I use the term independent to mean women who do not share their homes with men, and who are not directly dependent on them financially. This question is an important one because many children are now raised in single-parent families, of which 80–90 per cent are headed by women.

If we accept that psychoanalytic theories of psychosexual development are broadly correct, then daughters raised by single mothers should be spared the task of resolving an Electra complex. Without the need to suppress their internalized male attributes, they should have relatively few problems in being assertive and competitive in their adult relationships with men. But, in the absence of a relationship with a father or father figure, they may internalize a false, sex-role stereotyped version of masculinity, as outlined in Chapter 6. This internalized male stereotype requires them to develop attitudes and behaviour

240

based on the reciprocal female stereotype. Such a development would inhibit rather than encourage competitiveness with men.

It is not clear which pattern occurs most frequently. Presumably, the attitudes of independent mothers toward men is the most important factor in deciding this. Research could be undertaken to compare the psychosexual adjustment of young women raised by single mothers with that of young women raised in two-parent families. Unfortunately, this cannot be done with any scientific validity, because of the complicating effect of socio-economic status. Most single mothers live in socially deprived circumstances, often in housing projects with a high proportion of similar families. Their daughters are exposed to a whole range of social difficulties which more affluent children escape, and their opportunities for a good education are greatly limited.

With all these major social disadvantages, it would be expected that the psychological adjustment of daughters of single mothers is relatively poor. What data exist show that this is not so. Overall, the psychological adjustment in late adolescence and early adulthood of these young women is comparable with that of young women from more affluent two-parent families. Presumably, there have been enough *psychological* advantages for daughters raised by single mothers to compensate for their socio-economic disadvantages. The precise nature of these psychological advantages remains uncertain, but the absence of an Electra complex could be a major one.

The idea that daughters of independent women may be unusually comfortable competing in the world of men has important implications. If, as seems likely, their numbers steadily increase, they might represent a significant new development in the area of sex roles. Their impetus toward competitiveness and equality with men is not determined directly by feminist ideas and influences. It is based instead on the removal of a traditional impediment to women competing directly with men, namely the Electra complex with its internalized guilt and envy. Women like this should be fairly free of conflict over sex roles. They were raised by women who combined motherhood with independence, and who had to struggle alone in the world to survive. Such a background should give them a realistic view of mothering, and this will help them resist the idealized images of wifeliness and motherhood that still oppress so many women. If all this is going to happen, we should know about it fairly soon. Perhaps it has started to happen already.

Independence Versus Conservatism

I have mentioned in previous chapters the failure (in 1982 and again in late 1983) of the Equal Rights Amendment to achieve enough support for passage through the United States legislature. Phrases such as 'all men are equal', omitting mention of women, remain unmodified in the United States Constitution. The failure of the Equal Rights Amendment (ERA) owed much to the opposition of conservative women's groups. For those feminists and others who worked so hard and for so long to achieve the ERA, its failure was an unexpected and bitter blow. Since then, the feminist movement in the United States seems to have lost momentum.

The failure of the ERA was a salutary experience for American feminists. It was a clear statement that a majority of the American people had remained largely uninfluenced by feminist ideas. Several reasons for this have been proposed in earlier chapters. It seems that most women do not want more independence from men, or to enjoy full equality with them. Most women still trust men to look after their interests in the financial and political world. This appears just as true in other English-speaking countries as it is in America.

It is not clear to what extent women have polarized around feminist issues. But whatever proportion of women is actively feminist, at crucial moments politically the influence of feminism appears to be almost equally balanced by women who are actively conservative. With the help of conservative men, conservative women currently have the edge. Presumably, a majority of women fall between the two extremes. Feminist hopes for a revolution in popular thought about sex-role issues have clearly not been realized. Perhaps we should not be surprised about this. For a revolution to be successful, a majority of people must feel strongly oppressed by a tyranny that they clearly recognize. For people to join a fight for freedom and independence, it must be obvious to them that their freedom and independence have been taken away.

For a majority of women, the conditions for revolution do not exist. But this will not stop individual women seeking to become more independent. The greater their number, the greater will be the momentum for change. As the failure of the ERA so clearly attests, fundamental and widespread changes in sex-role attitudes have yet to take place. Thirty years of active and vigorous feminism in the English-speaking countries, and especially in America, have had a very limited impact. If American feminists are still licking their wounds after the defeat of the ERA, let us hope that they will soon rejoin the fray. If European feminists are struggling to find a theory and practice of feminism that meets the challenges of the 1990s and beyond, let us hope that they will persevere.

10

Changing Men, Changing Women

Five of the previous nine chapters have been concerned mainly with men, and four have focused mainly on women, although one of these is relatively long. I said in the Introduction that I would try and give equal weight to women's and men's issues. If I have devoted a fraction more space to men, I hope that women will not begrudge this. After all, far more has been written in recent years about women's issues than about men's, in the popular press as well as in professional and academic publications.

Writing about men and women in separate chapters, and from a historical perspective, has been essential to this book. But in doing so I have had comparatively few chances to focus on the *interaction* between modern men and women, although some of the case histories serve such a purpose. This final chapter is primarily devoted to relationship issues. In emphasizing the interaction between men and women, I preserve unconscious psychological mechanisms as a central theme. These mechanisms, and especially projective identification, are the key to understanding compulsory marriages and other destructive relationships.

Jealousy is perhaps the most common single theme in contemporary relationship problems. It can be a dangerous emotion, especially for those women who are the objects of it. Men are responsible for nearly all murders of women, and a high proportion of these homicides are the final outcome of relationships characterized by extreme forms of jealousy. For these reasons I have chosen abnormal jealousy as the initial theme of this chapter.

Morbid Jealousy

Morbid jealousy is a clinical term used to describe the experience of jealousy in an extreme, pathological form. Descriptions of

244

morbid jealousy can be found in classical literature, in newspapers and magazines, and in professional journals. I recall a case of my own in which the bonds that tied the couple together, normally of an invisible, psychological kind, were actually visible. The husband locked his wife's leg to his own with a plastic-covered chain when they went to bed at night. Only in this way could he be protected from acute anxiety over his irrational belief that she would be unfaithful to him while he slept.

A British psychiatrist, Michael Shepherd, writing in the *Journal of Mental Science* (July 1961: 687–753), provides further clinical examples. He describes a middle-aged man:

> He was dominated by the idea that his wife was planning to get rid of him. He accused her repeatedly of promiscuous behaviour; on occasion he struck her . . . In his calmer moments he admitted to the irrational nature of his ideas, but from time to time he became dominated by their force and intensity (p. 709).

Referring to another middle aged man:

> He became upset if his wife looked at anyone, looked for stains on her clothing, examined her underclothes and occasionally tore up her dresses. He made frequent, increasingly absurd accusations of infidelity . . . but was usually contrite after his outbursts (p. 707).

Finally, a 56-year-old man:

> He became irritable, and would strike his wife, sometimes hurting her and even threatening her life . . . He entertained the belief that his wife was being unfaithful to him . . . In hospital and away from his wife he admitted that there had been very little evidence to support his accusations of infidelity, but that he could not prevent these ideas from coming into his mind (p. 710).

Although a majority of descriptions given by Shepherd in his classical paper are of men, morbid jealousy in women is described also.

Morbid jealousy is by no means confined to psychiatric patients. It is probably widespread throughout the community, and it may affect the most creative and successful people. A recent example of this is vividly portrayed in the book *Be My Baby* by Singer Ronnie Spector, one of the original Ronettes, and her co-author Vince Waldron. Ronnie talks of her marriage to Phil Spector, a Hollywood legend who became rich and famous as a brilliant record producer and manager of performing artists in the 1960s. She alleges that Phil kept her a virtual prisoner in his Hollywood mansion for seven years, destroyed her career, pushed her towards alcoholism, and tormented her almost beyond endurance. Occasionally, Ronnie says, he would allow her to go for a drive alone, as long as he knew exactly where she was and when she would be back. But Phil insisted, apparently, that he accompany her in the form of a life-sized inflatable mannequin that looked exactly like him, wore his clothes, and was strapped into the passenger seat beside her! If she was late back, she would be exposed to tirades of abuse and rage. If Phil could not accompany Ronnie on tour, he apparently insisted that the phone line to her room be kept open all night so that he could ensure no one was with her: he would listen intermittently throughout the night until she awoke in the morning.

A more sinister example is detailed in the recent book *Sleeping With the Devil* by Suzanne Finstead. It is based on a true story of Barbara, a beautiful and intelligent young woman who believed that 'somewhere in the world was the man that God had chosen for her, the other half of her soul.'

Barbara met Richard, a wealthy, handsome and charming businessman, while skiing. They fell in love within days, and within weeks were sharing an expensive city apartment. Richard had said that he was divorced, but he was still married, and his relationship with Barbara precipitated an acrimonious legal dispute with his wife. During this, he showed that he was utterly unscrupulous and ruthless in pursuing his own ends, to the extent of systematically 'framing' people, and threatening to kill them.

Richard began to abuse Barbara physically. She blamed the stress of his divorce for this, and tolerated it until, during one violent episode, he almost killed her. Although Barbara still loved Richard, she moved out of their apartment for her own safety. Richard's response was to systematically harass her, including tapping her phone, making and arranging abusive phone calls,

246

slashing her tyres, and having her followed. Unable to possess her, he was determined to make her unhappy and afraid, and to stop her from replacing him with another man. Barbara could not find a lawyer to take on her case, apparently because of Richard's dangerous reputation.

A few months after the separation, Barbara was shot four times by a masked man while sitting in her car. She was left permanently paralysed from the chest down. Her assailant escaped, but evidence was eventually found that appeared to connect the attempted homicide with Richard. By this time he had gone to live overseas, and could not be extradited to face charges.

More than ten years after the attempt on her life, Barbara remained fearful that Richard would try once again to kill her: 'As long as he's running around the world free, there will always be fear in my life.'

In *The War Against Women* Marilyn French says:

> Almost every day, a man kills a woman who has left him for beating her, who has struggled *within the system*, getting a court order enjoining him from approaching her . . . Department of Justice statistics show that 75 per cent of reported assaults against wives or lovers are committed *after* separation (p. 191).

This form of violence toward women is currently receiving much attention in the popular media. Reports of it appear almost weekly in the press and other news media. Documentaries or fictionalized accounts appear frequently on television and in the cinema. Books on the topic are published regularly. But it is rare for any of these representations of the problem to attempt a real understanding of why it happens. Commonly, the victim is blamed. Most people simply cannot comprehend why a woman remains for many months or years in a relationship that almost daily threatens her physical well-being, even her life. From the absence of understanding emerges blame.

Men like Richard, as portrayed in *Sleeping with the Devil*, are seen as inhuman monsters, deserving the severest punishment for their hideous crimes. Of course, such crimes are utterly abhorrent and unacceptable, and should be punished. But portraying men who seriously injure or abuse women merely as evil monsters serves only to increase public rage towards them, and the rage of some women to men in general. Adding to women's rage increases the gulf between men and women, and makes it even more difficult for them to communicate with each other. Progress will be made only if rage and blame are softened by understanding, however difficult this may be. The following case history is written with this in mind.

Case 8: Gina and Tod

Gina and Tod were referred to me by their family physician after Gina had admitted to her that a recent broken nose was not, as she had first claimed, the result of an accident. It had been broken by her husband Tod in the course of a domestic argument. The doctor had urged Gina to leave Tod at once, but she was adamant that she still loved him and wanted to save their marriage. Gina thought that Tod could be persuaded to join her for marriage therapy, and he subsequently agreed to this. I first interviewed Gina and Tod separately, starting with Gina.

Gina's Tale

Gina described her family background as very happy. Her parents, she said, were still in love, and had never argued. The family atmosphere had always been one of peace and quiet. As she talked, it became clear that peace prevailed because Gina's mother had always totally acquiesced to the wishes of Gina's father. This had not been a major problem for Gina's mother, because she rarely disagreed with her husband, an achievement that owed much to the fact that they lived almost entirely separate lives.

Gina's mother was exclusively responsible for all domestic tasks and activities, including child-raising (Gina had two younger sisters). Her husband was the sole wage-earner. He did absolutely nothing around the house and was not expected to. As long as his domestic needs were fully met, he was happy to leave household matters to his wife. He did not interfere.

Although this arrangement seemed to work well for her parents, it left Gina effectively fatherless. When she was young, her father avoided having anything to do with her, referring

Gina's requests back to her mother. To his emotional remoteness was added physical absence: he worked long hours, and had interests that took him out of the house a great deal. When Gina got older, there was an awkwardness between them that hindered communication, and they continued to spend little time together.

Because her parents seemed so happy, Gina dreamed of early marriage to a man who perfectly met her needs, just as her father seemed to meet her mother's. Unable to identify with her own father, or to internalize any of his 'masculine' attributes, she had fantasies about men that were based on stereotyped, romanticized and unrealistic images of manhood. She came to view herself also in a stereotyped way, a self-image that was reinforced by her mother's very traditional ideas and behaviour. Academically average, Gina had no incentive to study at school because she craved only marriage and full-time motherhood.

When Gina met Tod at work, she thought that he was both good-looking and exactly the kind of strong, silent man on whom she could depend. They married ten months later, after a passionate courtship. Gina was twenty-two and Tod twenty-five. At the time, Gina was working in a bakery on production lines. She wanted to stop this boring, tedious work, but both she and Tod agreed that she should carry on until they had saved enough money for a deposit on a house.

Tod's Story

Tod's story was remarkably similar to Gina's – until he was ten. At this time his father had suddenly and unexpectedly left his mother for another woman. Tod's mother was shattered by this brutal termination of a marriage that to her had seemed idyllic. Being a full-time mother and housewife had suited her well, and she had no idea that her husband was in any way dissatisfied with the marriage.

Tod, who had a younger brother, had never seen much of his father. Even when they were together, Tod felt that his father spent time with him reluctantly, always wishing to be elsewhere. He claimed not to miss his father very much after he left the family.

Tod had always been very close to his mother, who waited hand

and foot on him and his brother, just as she did on her husband. Her mothering of Tod intensified after his father left. Instead of looking for paid work, she stayed at home, supported mainly by child maintenance and alimony payments. She redirected on to Tod and his brother most of the energy that she had formerly spent on looking after her husband.

Once into his teens, Tod began to think of himself in a very macho, stereotyped way. He became rude and aggressive at school and towards his mother, especially if she did not give him exactly what he wanted. Just as she had always yielded to her husband's wishes, so did she to Tod's. Increasingly, Tod mixed with boys who thought and behaved as he did. Never very successful academically, his grades suffered, and he left high school without graduating. He got a job on the production floor of a local factory.

As part of his stereotyped, macho view of himself, Tod often fantasized about meeting the perfect woman. Not only was she physically attractive, but she adored and worshipped Tod completely. When he first met Gina, she seemed exactly what he was looking for.

The Marriage

Once they were married, Gina believed that Tod would become even more like her ideal man. In particular, she hoped that he would enjoy talking with her freely and spontaneously, and be affectionate and supportive. But, at least when he was with Gina, Tod continued to be the rather silent man that she had first met. The more that Gina sought communication and affection, the more silent and withdrawn Tod became.

From the start, Tod had expected Gina to do all the housework. As he explained to me: 'Housework is women's work. My job is to earn the money. When I'm at home, I'll do what I want when I want.'

Because of her traditional, stereotyped view of women's role, Gina had agreed to this arrangement. Although she continued at the bakery, she went part-time, working three days a week. She tried hard to please Tod and to live up to her idealized, unrealistic idea of wifeliness. But the harder she tried, the more critical Tod

250

became of her efforts. Gina thought of stopping work so that she could devote herself full-time to looking after Tod, but their urgent need to save kept her at the bakery.

Gina had two good friends at work, and she confided in them about her problems at home. Both agreed that the situation was very unfair. Not only should Tod do some housework, but he should also stop demanding that Gina respond immediately to his every whim. These views helped Gina to see the injustice of her situation. One evening, when Tod asked for another beer from the fridge, she told him to get it himself. Gina had never done this before, and her unexpected refusal caused something inside Tod to snap. He leapt from his chair in front of the television and screamed: 'I told you to get me a fucking beer, you stupid bitch. Now get it.'

Gina was so shocked that she couldn't move. Tod, assuming that she was refusing to obey him, walked up to her and slapped her face, hard. Gina burst into tears. Tod started yelling at her again: 'Cry you bitch, that's all you're fucking good for. If you don't shut up and get me a beer, I'll hit you again. Harder. Then you'll really have something to cry about.' Gina got his beer. Then she went to the bedroom and cried herself to sleep. Tod continued to drink beer and watch television.

The next morning, Tod was remorseful. He explained that he was being victimized at work by a foreman. Only his lack of any training, and very limited job prospects, stopped him from leaving. Rather than risk unemployment, he would stay where he was. Gina forgave him. His state of contrition persisted, and, for a while, their relationship blossomed. It was, said Gina, a bit like a second honeymoon.

But about six weeks after the first violent episode, there was a second one. It started with Tod complaining that Gina hadn't finished his laundry on time. Instead of apologizing, Gina suggested that he might consider doing his own laundry some-times. An argument began. Uncharacteristically, Gina stood up for herself, and the argument escalated. Tod became more and more enraged until he ended the disagreement by punching Gina in the stomach. Winded and retching, she retreated once again to her bedroom, where she sobbed uncontrollably. Mercifully, Tod left her alone.

Similar episodes occurred quite regularly, with Tod always remorseful and begging forgiveness. He always had an excuse, and Gina always forgave him. This was followed by increasingly brief honeymoon periods, during which Tod was helpful around the house and generally more considerate.

Matters improved when, after two years of marriage, the couple bought a small home with the help of a bank loan. But the repayments and costs of unexpected repairs increased the financial pressure on them. The fights resumed and became more bitter. For the first time, Gina consistently refused to have sex with Tod, and this increased his violence toward her. He started accusing her of having an affair at work: 'If you don't want sex with me, you must be getting it somewhere else.' It was during an argument about Gina's alleged infidelity that Tod broke her nose.

Therapy

After assessing them both separately, I began to see Gina and Tod together. The first two sessions revealed that Tod's world view was very fixed. He truly believed that sex-role stereotypes were the only proper basis for relationships between men and women. It was his unshakeable conviction that only women should do domestic work. He believed also that he should be free to do exactly what he wanted when at home, without consulting Gina. This included getting drunk most weekends. It became clear that Tod viewed women as second-class citizens, basically inferior creatures who should revere men and obey them without question. These views, he insisted, were shared by all his friends. He found it almost impossible to believe that any man might think differently.

Once Tod's world view was clarified, the cyclical nature of his violence toward Gina could be understood. During their honeymoon periods, although he tried to do what Gina wanted, he resented it because it was *unmanly* for him to behave like that. As his resentment increased, so did the likelihood that he would hit her again.

Gina told me that she had stayed in the marriage so far because she loved Tod. But in reality she was trapped in it by guilt, fear and uncertainty. Her own very stereotyped ideas about sex roles

252

meant that she blamed herself when she failed to live up to Tod's unrealistic expectations. However, her ideas were not fixed. Rather, she was never sure if she was right to try and change them. In sharp contrast, Tod was certain that his own views were correct. This certainty made it even more difficult for Gina to question her own traditional beliefs. As well, constant anxiety and fear of violence had eroded her self-confidence and left her fearful of managing alone. Her marriage had become compulsory. To keep hope alive, she clung to the idea that Tod would change, an idea that was reinforced by their brief honeymoon periods.

During the third conjoint session I suggested that if Tod was able to change some of his ideas about sex roles, the marriage might improve. Gina agreed, and we talked about the matter at some length. But at the end of the session, Tod said that he didn't really want to change, and could see no point in coming to see me again. Gina said that she would like to see me on her own, and, because I was concerned about her safety, I arranged an appointment for the following day. During this session I told Gina that I did not believe that the situation would improve, and explained why. I urged her to leave the marriage for her own safety, and gave her detailed information about the resources available to help her if she did choose to separate. But Gina was adamant that she wished to stay in the marriage. She thought that the three conjoint sessions had been salutary for Tod, and that he would not hit her again. Only if he did would she seriously consider leaving the marriage. She decided not to make a further appointment.

Although neither Gina nor Tod consulted me again, both were later admitted at different times to the general hospital where I had a part-time appointment. In this way I was able to find out what happened to them.

The Dissolution

About three months after their last interview with me, Tod's violence toward Gina began to escalate again. This was partly because she tried to stand up for herself more than she had done previously. Tod became increasingly jealous of her, and forced her to stop work, even though this risked falling behind with the house payments. Gina became virtually housebound, because

253

whenever she went out alone Tod would accuse her of infidelity, and a fight would usually result.

After one such fight, Gina was so badly injured that she had to be admitted to hospital. From there she went to a women's shelter, where she agreed to separate from Tod. Gina's absence put Tod into a frenzy of anxiety and rage, and he searched relentlessly for her whereabouts. He could think of nothing except finding her. Finally, eight weeks after their separation, he discovered her address through a mutual acquaintance. He went straight round. Through the screen protecting Gina's front door he begged to be allowed in. He wept and pleaded with her, swearing that he still loved her and could not live without her. He promised that if she came back to him he would really change, and they would have the happiness they had always hoped for.

Gina resisted. She told him firmly and clearly that she had no wish ever to see him again. She wanted him to leave. Eventually he did. But he came back twice more to repeat the performance. Only when Gina said that she would get a restraining order did he agree to stop calling. However, he continued to harass her. He chose ways that were mainly indirect and subtle, making it impossible for Gina to obtain a restraining order. She knew that he was watching her house, and thought that he was also following her. He showed remarkable ingenuity in his attempts to make her life a misery. So disturbing and frightening was this harassment that Gina decided to move. But shortly before she did so, Tod had a serious motor-vehicle accident. He had a blood alcohol level of almost three times the legal limit.

While recovering in hospital, Tod became very depressed and he sought to commit suicide by jumping from the roof of the building. He had his leg in plaster, and his progress toward the roof was so noisy and slow that he was apprehended before he reached it. He subsequently agreed to have psychiatric treatment, in the course of which he gradually relinquished his preoccupation with Gina. His harassment of her ceased. Finally, he accepted that she was now fully independent of him, with no wish ever to see him again. He was able to let her go.

Implications of the Case

In a psychological sense, Gina and Tod had problems that matched perfectly. Unable to identify with her father, Gina had failed to internalize any of his masculine attributes. In developing a sex-role stereotyped view of herself, she came to believe that she needed a man to manage for her all those things that belonged in the separate realm of the masculine.

Like Gina, Tod had been unable to identify with his father, or to internalize his masculine attributes. This left a vacuum within him that grew when his father left. This vacuum was filled with macho, stereotyped images of manhood drawn mainly from the popular media. With the onset of puberty and its sexual urges, Tod had to work even harder to bury his primary identification with his mother, who represented the feminine within him. His internalized feminine attributes had to be ruthlessly suppressed, because they were totally incompatible with the harsh, macho image of himself that he was compelled to create.

Gina could not access the masculine because she believed that it belonged only to men. This left her submissive toward them, and reliant on them for help in all matters beyond the domestic. Tod could not access the feminine, because it was buried too deeply within him. In their early, passionate love for one another, they fused psychologically: Gina identified with Tod's masculine attributes, and he projected his feminine attributes on to her. Gina shouldered the burden of Tod's denied femininity, and Tod took on the weight of Gina's forbidden masculinity.

This arrangement failed later because of Tod's need to deny totally his femininity. In unconsciously projecting it on to Gina, he had to keep full control over it. Only in this way could it remain completely disguised. But this meant trying to exert total control over Gina. When she began to resist this control, the very core of Tod's identity was threatened. This threat to his sense of self explains why 'something snapped' inside him when Gina refused, for the first time, to obey his command.

The more that Gina tried to stand up to Tod, the more he was compelled to force her into submission. Physical violence, and the constant threat of it, became an indispensable part of this process. As Tod's abuse of Gina increased, he was forced to believe that she deserved it. This was the only way that he could avoid seeing himself as a brutal, vicious bully. By persuading himself that Gina was bad, and therefore in need of correction and punishment, Tod could see himself as righteous. But this meant that those denied feminine attributes which he had unconsciously projected on to her became bad also. This increased his need to deny and project them, creating a monstrous vicious cycle: the more that Tod abused Gina, the more he hated those parts of himself which he had projected on to her, and the more, therefore, he felt compelled to abuse and humiliate her.

This vicious cycle was broken only after episodes of severe physical abuse when Tod could not avoid a sense of guilt and remorse. At such times, he was contrite, vulnerable and anxious to please Gina. Fearful that she might leave, he did his best to become the kind of man that she wanted him to be. This created their brief honeymoon periods, during which Tod idealized Gina's femininity, at the same time transforming from bad back to good his own projected feminine attributes. But Tod's resentment and anger steadily accumulated until released by another episode of violence.

Tod's accusations of infidelity arose primarily from his idea that Gina could not survive without a man to support and protect her. If she did not want him, then there must be someone else. The more that she rejected him, the more Tod became convinced that there was another man in her life. This irrational belief was strengthened by her lack of sexual responsiveness to him. Because he believed that, like him, she could not meet her own sexual needs, then another man must be having sex with her. These illogical ideas were given strength by Tod's unconscious envy of Gina. She had something that was, although he did not consciously recognize it, basic to his survival as a human being: his femininity. If he lost her, he would loose this also. Tod's envy of Gina, with her double quota of femininity, fuelled his jealousy, increasing his need to control and demean her. If he could demean and humiliate her enough to make her life a misery and turn her into an object of pity, then he was protected from the pain of envy.

Why Harassment Persists

One of the most sinister and puzzling aspects of morbid jealousy is its persistence after the victim of it has managed to escape from the relationship. The case of Gina and Tod illustrates why this happens.

Once a woman has escaped from a morbidly jealous man, she has taken with her a fundamental part of him, namely the denied femininity that he projected on to her. Naturally, he wants it back. But, because the projection is unconscious, he experiences instead an overwhelming desire to find and reclaim his lost partner. Often, a man in this situation becomes obsessed with the search, thinking of little else, and devoting all his time and energy to it. The rest of his life may collapse around him.

On finding his former partner, he uses a combination of pleas and threats to persuade her to return. If it becomes clear that she will not come back, then systematic harassment may begin. The main object of this is to make the woman as unhappy, anxious and frightened as possible. This protects the persecutor from such feelings within himself. As well, he wants her to believe that he will always find her, wherever she goes. She might then believe that the only way to escape her suffering is by returning to him.

Although many women eventually move to a location which remains unknown to their persecutor, they often live in fear for many years that he will find them. But most morbidly jealous men appear to give up the search for their former partners within two or three years. Often, they find a woman to replace her. Sometimes, they become able to accept the feminine within them, so that they no longer need to try and reclaim it from elsewhere. In Tod's case, incapacitating physical injury interrupted his persecution of Gina. He then had to experience for himself the pain that he sought to inflict on her, becoming overtly depressed and suicidal as a result. Fortunately, he found the courage to accept psychiatric treatment. This allowed him to accept his own feminine attributes and finally to let go of Gina.

Morbidly jealous men are prone to the abuse of alcohol and other drugs. This adds to their self-destructiveness, which can be expressed indirectly through accidents, or directly through deliberate self-harm. For some, the pain of morbid jealousy is so great that it can be relieved only if its object is destroyed. But in killing their former lovers or wives, these men are left to manage their pain alone. Often, rather than do this, they kill themselves.

Morbid Jealousy and Patriarchy

In microcosm, the morbidly jealous man's behaviour and attitudes mirror exactly the attempts of the larger patriarchal society to define and control women's sexuality. The morbidly jealous man, in a very real sense, is simply doing what he has been trained to do. But he has absorbed his training too well. He can see no reason to behave differently.

Most men, although strongly influenced by sex-role stereotypes, can distance themselves from them enough to modify their attitudes to sex roles when it is clearly appropriate to do so. For morbidly jealous men, sex role stereotypes are a fixed and literal basis for conducting relationships. These residua of nineteenth-century patriarchy are, to morbidly jealous men, commandments etched in stone.

Once this is understood, it becomes possible for us to soften a little our rage toward these men. Like the women they brutalize, they also are the victims of patriarchal ideas. It is these ideas, subtly distorted, that help them to justify their brutal persecution of women. In becoming persecutors, they degrade and dehumanize themselves to an extreme degree. Sometimes, when they recognize this, it becomes impossible for them to go on living.

How can we use an understanding of morbid jealousy to prevent it? If sex-role stereotypes are central to the problem, then modifying these is a logical starting point. But we have seen in previous chapters how difficult this is. Much of modern industry relies on creating markets through emphasizing and exaggerating the differences between men and women. The popular media and advertising industry work at this task hard and relentlessly. Perpetuating sex-role stereotypes is a crucial part of the whole process. Feminists constantly challenge the perpetuation of sex-role stereotypes. However, as we have seen, the feminist movement has been so successfully marginalized by the popular media that it has had little direct influence on the majority of women. But men, too, are beginning to publicly challenge sex-role stereotyping. Perhaps the best hope is for men and women to work at the task together, an idea that I will return to later in this chapter.

Morbid jealousy is by no means exclusive to men. Women experience it also, and perhaps almost as often as men. The basic mechanisms are the same for both sexes. Morbidly jealous women unconsciously project their masculinity on to men, and then seek to control them. But women have very little power to control men, especially in a patriarchal society. A man who is in a relationship with a morbidly jealous woman can resist her attempts to control him relatively easily. In the absence of effective control, her projection cannot develop into projective identification. This is a crucial point. When women are the victims of morbid jealousy, their very survival may depend on total obedience to their husband's wishes. Once the object of unconscious projections comes to behave in accordance with them, the stage of projective identification has been reached. From this point onward, it is extremely difficult to make any positive changes in the relationship. The victim, already in danger, will continue to be at risk even if she manages to escape.

Morbid Jealousy and Agoraphobia

A woman married to a morbidly jealous man often finds it difficult to get help. Her husband may try and stop her leaving the house without him, because this provokes his irrational beliefs. If she defies him and goes out alone, she is likely to be the subject of an abusive cross-examination, or worse, when she returns. Many women living in such circumstances become virtually housebound. If they are able to seek professional help for the problem, they may neglect to mention the husband's morbid jealousy, either because they are fearful of possible domestic repercussions, or because they think that the doctor (especially if he is male) will not believe them. They may even fear that a male doctor will fail to see anything greatly wrong with their husband's extreme jealousy. Some wives attach credence to their husband's belief that his jealousy is the legitimate expression of a powerful and exclusive love. All this makes it difficult for them to work out precisely what the problem is, or even whether there really is a problem. A common outcome is for them to describe the problem as belonging to them alone, and this may result in a diagnosis of agoraphobia.

Agoraphobia, once referred to as the 'Housebound Housewife Syndrome', affects women 4–5 times more often than it does men. Only a small proportion of sufferers are totally confined to the home. Most can travel some distance, although often they are restricted to within a mile or two. If they try and go further away from home, they experience severe anxiety or devastating panic attacks. The Epidemiologic Catchment Area survey mentioned in Chapter 1 has shown that agoraphobia is one of the most common psychiatric disorders in women. It is most frequent in women aged 25–44: at any one point in time it affects 5–6 per cent in this age group. Agoraphobia affects only 1–1.5 per cent of men in the same age group. In a city of one million people, 30,000–40,000 women are likely to be suffering from agoraphobia. It is a major social problem.

Because of their reluctance to disclose the truth about their husbands' behaviour, it is impossible to know what proportion of women with so-called agoraphobia are restricted primarily as a result of their husbands' jealousy. But it is probably in the region of 20 per cent. Even when abnormal jealousy is absent, agoraphobia can lead to a compulsory relationship, and this happens in the following way.

Many married women with agoraphobia are similar psychologically to the 'superwomen' described in Chapter 9. They believe that they must put the needs of their husbands and children before their own, but at the same time they want to lead their own independent lives. This internal conflict over sex roles is a major factor in precipitating agoraphobia. Because it reaches a peak when women have young children, this is the commonest point at which agoraphobia begins. Once the agoraphobia is established, the sufferer usually abandons her efforts to lead her own life. This reduces her sex-role conflict and related frustrations. The reduction of conflict paradoxically reinforces the agoraphobia, setting up a vicious cycle that often sustains the symptoms for many years: agoraphobia is a notoriously persisting condition. Inevitably, women feel very guilty about being agoraphobic, usually because it places great limitations and demands on their husbands and others. They usually blame themselves for their agoraphobia, a blame that is commonly reinforced by their husbands. This represents an exaggeration of the usual mechanisms for managing guilt discussed in previous chapters, whereby men project it on to women, who internalize it; women's guilt then helps to keep them confined to the traditional roles originally imposed upon them by men. Agoraphobia can be seen as a compulsory version of women's traditional role.

Ordinary Jealousy, Open Marriage, and Unfaithfulness

Morbid jealousy is the extreme expression of an emotion that is universal. A certain amount of jealousy is ordinary in all human relationships. Within marriage or between lovers, troublesome jealousy most commonly arises from the threat – real or imagined – of sexual infidelity.

It is timely at this point to return to the topic of sexuality within marriage. Nearly everyone assumes that marriage represents a commitment to sexual fidelity. But surveys have repeatedly suggested that, during the entire course of a marriage, faithfulness is achieved by only a minority of men. Women appear to be better at remaining faithful, but as many as 40 per cent do not manage it. Of course, the figures vary from survey to survey, and cannot be considered reliable in a truly scientific sense. None the less, few would disagree that maintaining sexual fidelity throughout a marriage is, for many people, very difficult.

Open Marriage

By open marriage I mean the willingness of both partners to let the other develop a sexual relationship with someone else. The idea of open marriage has never been popular in the English-speaking world, although it became more acceptable in the relatively permissive era that began in the 1960s. But even at the height of permissiveness, it was a practice that appealed to comparatively few people. It was restricted mainly to large, cosmopolitan cities, and even in those that were notorious for it, such as Los Angeles, it was not a widespread practice.

261

In the 1960s, the idea of open marriage came to include 'swinging' or 'wife-swapping'. This involved the regular exchange of marriage partners, either with another couple or as part of group sex. It was hailed by some as a creative and healthy alternative to monogamy. But research into this type of open marriage has shown that it nearly always had a damaging effect on relationships. Often, it also had an adverse effect on one or both partners individually. Perhaps because of this, 'swinging' became unfashionable even before the end of the permissive era. It is now a practice carried out by a very small number of people for whom the advantages of it appear to outweigh the disadvantages.

It is likely that 'swingers' are very different from those who practice open marriage in the more 'traditional' sense. For the latter, the choice of extramarital sexual partners is an essentially personal, private matter. The idea of 'wife-swapping' is as distasteful to such people as it is to most. Because 'traditional' open marriage is so private, very little is known in a scientific sense about its problems and benefits. But it seems clear that only a tiny number of people can make it work successfully. For most of those who try it, the negative effects appear to outweigh the positive ones.

Whatever the precise nature of an open marriage, the main obstacle to its success is likely to be jealousy. It is common for one partner to become jealous of a particular relationship formed by the other. Often, once this problem is resolved, a similar one emerges with the other partner, and so on. Problems with jealousy usually create so many difficulties that the experiment with open marriage is abandoned. Commonly, long-term negative effects are left in its wake.

The advent of AIDS has made open marriages of any kind even more risky and difficult to manage. Although they may still work for a very small number of people, they are clearly not the answer for a great majority of those who find it difficult or impossible to be monogamous.

Extramarital Affairs

By keeping an extramarital liaison secret, the unfaithful partner seeks to avoid confronting directly those issues that first drove him or her toward infidelity. For most people, an affair simply postpones having to deal with serious marital and personal problems. But avoiding problems by postponement usually makes it even more difficult to deal with them when, finally, they can be avoided no longer.

Having an affair very rarely improves a marriage. If the liaison remains undiscovered, the unfaithful partner's guilt is often a lasting obstacle to greater marital intimacy. Since a lack of intimacy is one of the problems that leads to an affair, its continuing absence increases the likelihood of further infidelities. If an affair is discovered, the anger and pain of the deceived partner may never be fully resolved. This is another potent obstacle to greater marital intimacy and harmony.

There is one aspect of an affair that is perhaps more dangerous and destructive than any of those above: the risk of infection. This risk is especially high because the deceived partner will be unaware that it exists, and will therefore take no precautions. The list of sexually transmitted diseases is long. It includes some that are incurable, several that are very dangerous, and one that is fatal, namely AIDS. Even if there were no other reasons, the risk to both partners of contracting one or more of these diseases makes an affair unacceptable. It is not a solution to the problem of managing sexuality in modern marriage. Better ways are needed.

Making Monogamy Easier

Although monogamy is such a struggle, especially for men, current alternatives generally create more difficulties than they resolve. Can monogamy be made easier?

In Chapter 8 I outlined ways in which men might become less reliant on women to gratify their sexual needs. The essence of such a change is for men to accept celibacy as a valid and enjoyable alternative to sexual intercourse, if only for limited periods of time. For most men, celibacy is made easier by masturbation. But, as *The Hite Report* so clearly illustrates, there is a profound prejudice against male masturbation. For most men, it is something that they do reluctantly when sexual intercourse is not available. Its main object is the relief of sexual tension rather than enjoyment. Feelings of guilt, alienation and emotional frustration are commonly left in its wake.

For reasons discussed in Chapter 9, there is much less prejudice against female masturbation. This allows women relative freedom to gratify themselves sexually, making it easier for them to lead celibate lives and to be sexually independent of men. Of course, many women still have negative attitudes to masturbation, and do it reluctantly with little enjoyment or satisfaction. But the proportion of such women is relatively low, and is certainly smaller than in the case of men.

Men's widespread rejection of celibacy as a state that is at times desirable arises from historical ideas of manliness. Men's deep prejudice against masturbation has similar origins. These historical ideas are perpetuated by sex-role stereotypes, which hold that regular heterosexual intercourse is fundamental to true manliness and to male well-being generally. Such ideas help to keep men sexually dependent on women. But this sexual dependency is incompatible with monogamy for many men, and perhaps for most. If monogamy is to work better, men must become more willing to manage their own sexuality. The same is true of women, although to a much lesser extent. The greatest obstacle to changes of this kind is sex-role stereotyping. We have seen that it has many other negative effects also. The rest of this chapter is concerned mainly with ways of resisting or ameliorating these negative effects.

Changing Men

Political and economic power in English-speaking countries is still overwhelmingly male. The proportion of women in the legislative bodies of America, Britain, Canada and Australia remains tiny. Although Britain has recently had its first woman Prime Minister, the likelihood of that happening in Australia, or of a woman becoming President of the United States, appears remote. At least in America and Britain, feminism has failed to significantly increase the number of women with direct political power and influence. Similarly, the boards of most major business companies still include few women, although resistance to change here appears less than in politics, and the appointment of women to senior business positions is becoming steadily more frequent. Ultimately, this trend has occurred because it makes good business sense: excluding women has meant excluding at least half the available talent, and companies cannot remain competitive if they continue to do this.

Although the progress toward economic independence that women have made in the past thirty years has been of undoubted benefit to them, it has occurred in the absence of any widespread, fundamental changes in sex-role beliefs and attitudes. The advances that women have achieved are based mainly on industrial changes rather than on ideological ones. Sex-role ideology in the English-speaking world remains fundamentally traditional and patriarchal. Perhaps we should not be surprised about this. If men have most of the political and economic power, why should they voluntarily abandon it?

In so far as feminism represents a women's revolution, it has not yet required men to struggle fiercely to resist it – at least not at a collective level. But individually, many men have struggled with feminism. Some have successfully managed to resist it; others have reached a compromise; a few men have embraced it. Certainly, there is a small but growing number of men who believe in feminist principles and who are willing to act upon their beliefs.

The real challenge for men is three-fold. First, they must recognize that they have been corrupted by the power which they have over women. Second, they need to recognize clearly the benefit of sharing this power more equally. And third, they must understand what changes are necessary and how to make them. Each of these tasks is a major one. Together, they represent a challenge that is profound.

Reclaiming the Feminine

When Victorian men projected their denied femininity on to the women whom they had subjugated so effectively, this corrupted not only their own masculinity, but also the feminine principle. Almost a century has passed since the end of the Victorian era. What exists, now, for men to reclaim from women? How much of it has been reclaimed already? What have been the effects of this reclamation, and what might they be in the future?

Robert Bly has written thoughtfully about these matters, and in *Iron John* he has this to say about contemporary young men who try to avoid behaving in a sex-role stereotyped manner:

> There's something wonderful about this development – I mean the practice of men welcoming their own 'feminine' conscious-ness and nurturing it – this is important – and yet I have the sense that there is something wrong . . . Many of these men are not happy. You quickly notice the lack of energy in them . . . Ironically, you often see these men with strong women who positively radiate energy (pp. 2–3).

If these young men have indeed reclaimed the feminine, what is it doing for them? According to Bly, it has turned them into pleasant, caring, likeable men – but men who are 'soft', lacking substance and vitality. Perhaps what has been reclaimed is not true femininity. Perhaps it is a *stereotype* of femininity, inevitably lacking freshness, substance and vigour. During those generations in which men have been denied legitimate expression of their own femininity, they have relied on women to express it for them. But what women expressed for men was not true femininity. It was the corrupt, stereotyped version that patriarchy had imposed on them. In reclaiming it, these young men have freed the young women in their lives, allowing them to radiate natural strength and energy. But in comparison, the men themselves seem like pale shadows.

There is another problem with the kind of femininity that men are reclaiming from women. Much of the impetus for men to change – to become more like women – has been a reaction to criticism by feminists, and especially radical feminists. This criticism naturally focuses on the *negative* aspects of manhood. These include: men's destructive aggression, manifested in rape, domestic violence and other violent crimes, in warfare, and in the uncontrolled exploitation of natural resources; men's insensi-tivity, manifested in their failure to communicate with women; and men's emotional constriction, shown by their inability to be openly affectionate, caring, loving or emotionally supportive.

Men are beginning to internalize these negative images of masculinity on a significant scale. At a conference that I recently attended, one of the speakers – a man – had this to say about masculinity: 'Like garlic, it has its uses, but a little of it goes a long way, and a heavy dose is nauseating.' It was clear from the audience response that most of the men present agreed with the speaker's sentiments.

It seems then, that in abandoning the male sex-role stereotype and seeking to become more like women, men are at risk of becoming bland, guilt-ridden, self-disparaging softies. If this is the alternative to being a 'macho man', then it is impossible not to sympathize with men who cling to sex-role stereotypes.

Recreating the Masculine Principle

It appears that simply reclaiming the feminine will not recreate a masculinity that is strong, vibrant and attractive. But unless the image of the 'new man' is at least as positive as the traditional, stereotyped image, most men will resist change. Before masculinity in English-speaking nations became constricted and stereotyped, what were its qualities? If we rediscover these and find them to be positive and attractive, then perhaps we can find ways of resurrecting them in the modern world. This represents the search for a true masculine principle, without which a true feminine principle could not exist, and vice versa. I found a description of key elements of the masculine principle in David Gilmore's book *Manhood in the Making: Cultural Concepts of Masculinity*. Although Gilmore does not talk about a masculine principle as such, it seems that what he says captures much of the essence of it:

> Again and again we find that 'real' men are those who give more than they take; they serve others . . . Men nurture their society by shedding their blood, their sweat, and their semen, by bringing home food for both child and mother, by producing children, and by dying if necessary in faraway places . . . This, too, is nurturing in the sense of endowing or increasing. However, the necessary personal qualities for this male contribution are paradoxically the exact opposite of what we Westerners normally consider the nurturing personality (p. 229).

It is noteworthy that Robert Bly also emphasizes nurturing when

267

he discusses what is lacking in modern, non-stereotyped ideas of manhood. He describes a male initiation ceremony among the Kikuyu of Africa. First, the young man is separated from his mother and taken to a secret place for men some distance from the village. So far, this ceremony parallels the prepubertal initiation ceremonies in Papua New Guinea, described in Chapter 7. The young man then fasts for three days before he is introduced to a circle of older men sitting round a camp fire. He is frightened, hungry and thirsty. Each of the men in turn takes a sharp knife, opens a vein in his arm, and lets a little of his blood flow into a bowl. The young male is then offered the bowl as nourishment.

This ceremony includes much that is tender and compassionate, in marked contrast with initiation ceremonies in Papua New Guinea (although it will be recalled that the period of obligatory homosexuality had a nurturing element). It allows the young man to recognize that men, as well as women, can be nurturing and caring. It elevates rather than devalues the status of the feminine principle, which therefore does not need to be harshly suppressed. In such a society, men can be nurturing, caring and compassionate toward each other, as well as being fierce warriors.

The true masculine principle includes the capacity to be nurturing in a tender, sensitive way as much as it does the willingness to be fiercely aggressive and competitive. But Western man has lost the ability to nurture in a close, intimate way. In being separated from the home by the Industrial Revolution, men were separated from their capacity to nurture in a 'feminine' way. Instead, they nurtured their children and families *indirectly*, by working hard and long in mines, mills and factories. To survive in that harsh and dangerous world, they had to bury the pain that they felt about being inhumanly exploited and separated from their families. In burying this pain, they buried their capacity to nurture.

If the capacity to nurture directly is the key element of the feminine principle that men need to reclaim from women, how might this be done? We know from research surveys that most married men contribute very little to child care. True role-sharing is still uncommon, and role-reversal remains very rare. Only about 10–15 per cent of divorced men gain sole custody of their children and function as heads of single-parent families. Thus, in today's English-speaking world, most men spend very little time directly nurturing their children, although if we accept Gilmore's broader definition of nurturing, men do it indirectly through the breadwinner role. But the breadwinner role is often draining and exhausting, especially if it involves boring, menial, repetitive work. As one man put it: 'I feel like I spent forty years of my life working as hard as I can to become somebody I don't even like.'

Directly nurturing children can be boring, frustrating and repetitive also. But as long as it is balanced by other activities, it includes much that is stimulating, challenging and rewarding. Playfulness can be especially energizing at an emotional level. Of course, the focus of nurturing is not restricted to children. Women tend to be good at nurturing each other and also the men in their lives. Most men are more nurtured than nurturing. Modern, non-stereotyped women have both the capacity to nurture and the opportunity to do it on a voluntary rather than on a compulsory basis. Perhaps this contributes to the strength and vitality that seems so often to be lacking in their male counterparts.

If men acquired the same capacity to nurture as women, and the same opportunities to exercise it, then the true masculine principle might begin to re-emerge. Modern, non-stereotyped men might gain strength and vigour. Of course, this would require truly equal role-sharing to become the norm, something that could not happen without massive changes in existing social and industrial attitudes and practices. If such changes were made, they would be profoundly liberating for men. Much of the basis for sex-role stereotyping would disappear. It is this *overall* liberation that might allow men to develop the rich and robust depth of character that is an essential part of the true masculine principle. Although the capacity to nurture directly is just one aspect of this, it appears to be a crucial one.

Increasingly, men are confronting these issues in their personal lives, some in gatherings like those run by Robert Bly, others in the context of men's groups. A few are confronting them in social and political arenas, often collectively with other men. These activities represent the beginnings of what might be called the men's liberation movement.

269

Men's Liberation

If a men's liberation movement exists, it owes much to women's liberation. In the 1970s, a few mainly middle-class men started to meet together regularly in small groups because their female partners had already started to do so. Initially, these men's groups focused on consciousness-raising. Members would frequently berate themselves for having been so patriarchal and insensitive to women's issues. They promised each other, and their wives, to try and do better. Their guilt was eased, and the women in their lives were placated.

As the women's movement gained momentum, the rather patronizing nature of men's groups was replaced by a mixture of anxiety and anger. Increasingly, women were ending their marriages, leaving husbands who were often very confused, frustrated and resentful. With their greater economic freedom, middle-class women especially were insisting on genuine equality with the men in their lives. Middle-class men needed help in coming to terms with all this, and they found some of this help in men's groups.

It was quite new for men to form groups with the sole aim of talking about personal problems and giving each other support and encouragement in resolving them. Gradually, a significant number of men came to realize what a profoundly helpful and liberating experience this could be. They were learning to nurture each other.

Although men's groups led appreciable numbers of men to realize that patriarchy was truly oppressing some women, it did not always appear to be oppressing their wives. In fact, many men in these groups thought that their wives led more interesting, pleasant, varied and rewarding lives than they did, and seemed happier than they were. At this point, some of these men began to question their own lives: as part of this, they often experienced feelings of frustration and dissatisfaction, even of oppression. Usually, these feelings focused on their full-time breadwinner role, which did not seem to be valued or appreciated by their wives or children. But the notion of being *oppressed* by this role was unacceptable, since it clearly conferred so many privileges on them.

The absence of any obvious, large-scale oppression of men has stunted the growth of the men's liberation movement. If men are not oppressed, they cannot be liberated. The links between radical feminism and lesbianism gave the women's movement early impetus: these links were possible because both groups felt oppressed and persecuted. But men's liberation has not joined hands with gay liberation. Many gay men not only feel oppressed and persecuted, but freely talk about this. Although heterosexual men often feel the same way, it is difficult for them to publicly articulate these feelings with any credibility or conviction.

This difficulty has given rise to a paradox. In its public, sociopolitical manifestations, the men's liberation movement has not been primarily concerned with men's issues. Instead, it has tended to focus on women's problems. The vigour of groups such as Men Against Rape and Men Against Sexual Assault clearly attests to this. These groups are of vital importance, because they insist that men take personal responsibility for their violence to women, instead of blaming women for provoking it. But they fail to emphasize the reasons for men's violence, and the need to make social changes in order to reduce men's destructiveness not only to others, but also to themselves.

To be successful, men's liberation must find a way of allowing more men to talk with conviction and credibility, and in public, about their true feelings. Although men are not economically oppressed, at least in relation to women, many experience *emotional* oppression. When this is talked about, it is usually described as 'alienation'. The interaction of patriarchy and sex-role stereotyping alienates men from their feelings; from their capacity to nurture children, each other and women, and from much else that is central to the true masculine principle. But 'Men Against Alienation' is unlikely to become a rallying-cry (its acronym sounds like an appeal to the maternal!); the concept of alienation is too complex and diffuse to provide a suitable focus for publicity. The fight against it is unlikely to give men's liberation the impetus that it needs to deal directly and vigorously with men's problems.

In spite of all these difficulties, the importance of the men's liberation movement cannot be overestimated. If enough men show publicly their dissatisfaction with patriarchy, and the

271

sex-role stereotyping that helps to perpetuate it, then other men will begin to listen. If the power of sex-role stereotypes to oppress women and alienate men is to be successfully challenged, then this challenge must come from men themselves.

Changing Women

The feminist movement has been unsuccessful in creating widespread changes in attitudes to sex roles. The main reason for this has been the sheer power of patriarchy to preserve a traditional, stereotyped perspective on the relationship between men and women.

Between 40 and 45 per cent of married women age 18–60 do not have paid work outside the home. As we saw in Chapter 1, these women experience levels of anxiety and depression 3–4 times higher than do their husbands. In absolute terms, about one quarter of them have clinically significant anxiety and depression, equating with formal, treatable psychiatric disorders. This huge burden of emotional pain and suffering is, as we have seen, intimately connected with sex-role stereotyping, a form of oppression that contributes not only to psychiatric disorder, but to many other forms of female suffering. Domestic violence is the most obvious of these.

Feminists are acutely conscious of the plight of these women, and have done much to increase community awareness of it. But thus far they have been able to do little to change it. As long as a large majority of women are reasonably content with traditional sex-role attitudes and behaviour, this situation is unlikely to alter. Just as men need a powerful incentive to recognize the oppressive nature of stereotyped, patriarchal attitudes, so do women. If feminism has failed to generate this incentive, can it be created in other ways?

Women and Power

I have noted previously the tiny proportion of women occupying seats of power in the legislative, judicial and business arenas of English-speaking nations. When a woman achieves high status in any of these traditionally male domains, she is commonly thought to have psychological attributes that belong more to the masculine than to the feminine. Margaret Thatcher, the first woman to become Prime Minister of Britain, is a good example. As a woman of the political right, many of the sentiments that she expressed were linked with traditional, patriarchal values. This reinforced the popular perception of her as a masculine woman, whether or not it was really true.

Such a view of powerful women makes it difficult for ordinary women to identify with them and accept them as valid, realistic role models. But this is not true of the increasing number of women who achieve more modest status in the business world and in the professions. Most of these women are able to preserve an image that is predominantly feminine, although not in the traditional, patriarchal sense. As I hope to show in what follows, it is these women who offer the best chance for a major change in attitudes to sex roles.

In her introduction to Susan Faludi's superbly documented book *Backlash: The Undeclared War Against Women*, Joan Smith suggests:

> The greatest achievement of feminism in the last two decades . . . is the change it has brought about in female consciousness . . . the founding aims of the women's movement – reproductive choice, equal pay, access to child care and freedom from sexual abuse – are now supported by vast numbers of women who might not, especially in the present repressive climate, identify themselves as feminists (p. xv).

Smith argues that it is precisely this change in women's attitudes and expectations that has generated the patriarchal 'backlash' which Faludi demonstrates so brilliantly.

But the crucial point is that although very many women have achieved 'the founding aims of the women's movement', *most do not see themselves as feminists*. As I have argued throughout this book, it is mainly economic liberation that has allowed a real change in women's expectations over the past thirty years. For the first time in Western history, nearly all women have the opportunity for paid work outside the home. They can earn money that is truly their own. It is this money that has bought them the beginnings of freedom from patriarchy, and the chance of creating their own hopes and expectations. So far, feminist ideology has been largely irrelevant to them.

The most devastating patriarchal backlash against women was the Inquisition, during which millions of dissident women were burned at the stake. This backlash was primarily a response to women's increased economic power, power that arose from their intimate involvement in the cottage industries that were flourishing at that time. Combined with their collective power, this economic power gave women the potential to redefine themselves in non-patriarchal terms.

Exactly the same thing is happening now. No longer isolated in the home, women are living and working together in the larger community. They are regaining collective power. Combined with their growing economic power, this is creating for women a chance to redefine themselves in terms that defy or transcend patriarchy.

Dissident women are no longer burned at the stake. Instead, as Faludi shows so well, they are pilloried, trivialized or misrepresented by the popular media. Currently, a fierce ideological battle is raging. But it is not recognized as such in the popular mind. It is not seen as a war between feminism and patriarchy. The popular media have debased and concretized the issues so that they appear to revolve around 'family values'. By locating the battle in the family arena, the forces of patriarchy have found women's Achilles heel: their guilt. Guilt about not meeting the needs of their children and husbands as well as they should. Guilt about putting their own needs before those of their family. Guilt about almost anything that might make them believe that they have a valid place in the world beyond the home.

It is for these reasons that professional women, and other women who have achieved some power and status through their own efforts, are so important. Women like this often compete directly with men. They know what men are really like, especially when their power and status are directly challenged. But their position allows them to resist male intimidation, especially when they fight it collectively. These experiences, and their intelligence and education, allow them to see the real nature of the battle for women's hearts and minds. Comparatively few of these women regard themselves as feminists. But their contribution to women's liberation is now more vital than it has ever beem. Through the example of their own lives, and by articulating the real issues, they can help women less fortunate than themselves to resist the forces of patriarchy and sex-role stereotyping.

Reclaiming the Masculine and Recreating the Feminine

As we have seen, sex-role stereotyping requires women to deny their masculinity and project it on to men. If a true feminine principle is to re-emerge in the English-speaking world, women must reclaim their projections. At a psychological level, true liberation for women will not occur until this happens. But just as men have mistaken a false, stereotyped version of femininity for the real thing, so have women erred with regard to the masculine. In its harsh, one-dimensional, stereotyped form, masculinity is not an attribute that most women wish to incorporate. This helps to explain why, so far, they have shown little desire to reclaim it from men.

As more women compete directly with men, or work closely with them as equals, they become aware that their relationships with the opposite sex need not be determined by sex-role stereotypes. As they get to know better the men with whom they work, they learn that many of them have 'feminine' attributes, even though the men themselves may not recognize this. In effect, a woman in this situation is resolving her Electra complex. She comes to recognize that true masculinity includes a feminine element. This makes it easier for her to acknowledge and reclaim her own masculinity. One effect of this is to allow her to feel less guilty and fearful about competing directly with men.

If she is married to a traditional man, he may find it difficult to accept her increased assertiveness. Problems of this kind are a major contributor to the current high divorce rate. The more that women abandon their guilt and fear about competing directly with men, the more will traditional marriage be threatened.

The issue of women's assertiveness is a crucial one. Women are commonly exhorted to be more assertive as part of personal development, and a sizeable industry has arisen to help them. But most manuals and training courses on assertiveness emphasize techniques rather than ideology. They fail to recognize the need for ideological change. Without this, a woman rarely maintains the new assertion techniques that she has learned, especially if those close to her do not wish her to be more assertive. If she changes her beliefs about sex roles – and that means a change of ideology – she is much more likely to persevere with the task of defining and asserting her real needs and desires.

Reclaiming the masculine by entering the work-force and competing directly with men is very hard work. Moreover, it is a path that is not yet open to many women. Most still work either as men's subordinates, or in gender-segregated industries where they compete mainly with other women. But it is the step of returning to the work-force that is the crucial one. Once back, it is almost impossible for a woman not to meet other women who have reclaimed the masculine, or who have begun the task. With their support and understanding, she can begin the task herself.

Some women believe that the true feminine principle can be created anew without the need to reclaim the masculine. This approach has much in common with the men's mythopoetic movement. It relies on the celebration of femininity through myth and ritual. Recently, there has been a remarkable flourishing of popular books in this area. Their titles include: *Laughter of Aphrodite: Reflections on a Journey to the Goddess*; *The Witches' Goddess: The Feminine Principle of Divinity*; and *Motherpeace: A Way to the Goddess Through Myth, Art and Tarot*.

All these books have similar themes. Most are well researched, easy to read and persuasive. Some make explicit links with feminism, others do not. They emphasize that the feminine principle was the original organizing force for humankind, manifested in the worship of female deities. They trace, as I have done in Chapter 5, the attempts of patriarchy to suppress the feminine principle. In various ways they encourage women to recognize and celebrate the true feminine principle. One of these ways includes specialized meditation techniques, an example of which is the Waxing Moon Meditation (one of many provided) from *The Spiral Dance* by Miriam Samos:

Ground and center. Visualise a silver crescent moon, curving to the right. She is the power of beginning, of growth and generation. She is wild and untamed . . . Feel your own hidden possibilities and latent potentials; your power to begin and grow. See her as a silver-haired girl running freely through the forest under the slim moon. She is virgin, eternally unpenetrated, belonging to no one but herself. Call her name 'Nimuel' and feel her power within you (p. 78).

Such meditations have therapeutic value for many women. But they do not address directly that most important psychological task of reclaiming the masculine. The *original* feminine principle that these meditations embody was untamed and powerful, and included much of the masculine. It represented the experience of Western women before the feminine principle became corrupted and distorted by the collective projections of patriarchal men. This original, true feminine principle has been lost, perhaps never to be found. It cannot be resurrected simply by meditating upon it. But such meditations allow women who practise them to feel stronger and more powerful. This may give them the strength to make positive changes in their lives, and perhaps also to confront men when they have previously avoided it. Once this starts to happen, they have a chance of reclaiming the masculine.

Working Together

In order to gain initial momentum, the women's movement had to be largely exclusive of men. It has remained so. But a growing number of men have become feminists. Many of them would like to take an active part in the women's movement. They very rarely do so, primarily because feminist women exclude them. The basis of this exclusion is the belief that only women can be true feminists, because only women really know what it is like to be oppressed by men.

Although a large majority of actively feminist women still favours excluding men, the majority is getting smaller. If this trend continues, it might eventually become possible for feminist men to take an active, central and visible part in the women's movement. This can only be a good thing, although it is likely to be fiercely resisted by radical feminists. If this resistance is absolute, the mainstream women's movement will have to exclude radical feminists in order to admit men. Rather than risk such a damaging split, the movement may be forced to continue excluding men.

Radical feminism, one of the movement's greatest strengths in its formative years, may now have become an obstacle to its further growth and development.

Has the men's movement excluded women as actively as the women's movement has excluded men? This is certainly true of what may be called the personal or 'therapeutic' men's movement, which includes the mythopoetic approach. It is argued that men cannot 'be themselves' in the presence of women, who are therefore excluded.

That part of the men's movement which operates in a public, socio-political context is less exclusive of women. Some groups of this kind actively seek the direct involvement of women. A few women find the courage to join them, and probably their numbers will increase. If this happens, it will surely add richness and vigour to the men's movement.

A logical end-point of these trends in the men's and women's movements is their coalescence into a people's movement. Of course, there have been people's movements before. The most popular ones, such as Socialism and Communism, have been ideologically based. But their leaders have always emphasized the *tangible benefits* that will emerge from realization of their goals. These benefits are mainly economic in nature, easily recognized and measured.

The men's and women's movements have goals that, if achieved, are likely to be of great benefit throughout the community. These benefits include a vast improvement in women's *psychological* health and well-being, and a great improvement in men's *physical* health – together with something that men should hold most precious, namely an increase in their longevity. But none of these benefits can actually be promised. Even if they could be, they might have less immediate impact than promises of better living standards.

This leaves only ideology. But translating the inequities and negative effects of patriarchy and sex-role stereotyping into a marketable ideology is not easy. The relevant ideas are complex and, to be fully understood, require a certain degree of psychological-mindedness. But only if these ideas become popular will they have any real impact. Making them popular is the real task of both the men's and women's movements. As we have seen, the popular media work hard and relentlessly at reinforcing sex-role stereotypes. Halting and reversing this process is a huge challenge. The chances of success would be much increased if liberated men and women worked at the task together.

The End of Marriage?

We have seen how, largely as a result of the Industrial Revolution, marriage was transformed from a mainly economic institution into a mainly psychological one. Marriage and romantic, passionate love became inextricable, and remain so today: at least 80 per cent of English-speaking Westerners give 'falling in love' as their main reason for getting married.

We have seen also that falling in love requires an unconscious psychological manoeuvre. The essence of this is the man's projection of his buried, unwanted 'feminine' attributes on to the women of his choice. To reciprocate his love, the object of his desire must project her unwanted 'masculine' attributes on to him.

As the case of Gina and Tod demonstrated, this arrangement is naturally unstable, because the man's need to deny and project his feminine attributes is nearly always much stronger than the woman's need to deny and project her masculine attributes. Especially for men, projection can be very hard work. It requires that its object behaves in a stereotypically feminine way. Men whose wives threaten to depart too much from patriarchal ideals of wifeliness often spend huge amounts of energy trying to make them conform. If the wife refuses, the husband's adjustment may be destroyed. That this can happen to the most powerful and eminent of men is clearly shown in the article 'The marriage of the "collapsible" man of prominence' summarized in Chapter 2.

The more that married women work outside the home and achieve financial independence, the more they can resist their husband's attempts to control them. But sometimes they choose not to, and this is most likely to happen when women themselves rely on projection to manage their denied masculinity. Such women tend to idealize their husbands. But as we saw in case five, *The Abandoned Wife*, idealization can be a means of exerting considerable control over its object.

Romantic Love and Equality of the Sexes

Can romantic, passionate love survive true equality of the sexes? I believe not. But we remain so far from true sexual equality that this prediction is unlikely to be put to the test, at least in the near future. Let us look briefly at two of the *minimum* requirements for true sexual equality.

First, all families must have ready access to high quality, safe and affordable child care. The current situation is concisely stated by T. Brazelton (*American Journal of Orthopsychiatry*, 1986; 56: 14–25):

> Even under the present conditions, the choices in child care for over 50 per cent of working mothers are grossly inadequate. Poor, vulnerable people are unable to find care of any quality and must leave their small children in dangerously inadequate circumstances . . . we must provide vital safeguards if we mean to protect the future development of small children of working parents. These are costly, and cannot be paid for by parents alone. Our responsibility as mental health and child care professionals requires that we work toward development of a national policy with a national subsidy (p. 24).

Since this statement was published, there have been no significant overall improvements to child care for working mothers in either America or Britain. In some respects the situation has deteriorated, mainly because of cut-backs in government funding.

Second, all men must have ready access to part-time work. Many men would like to be able to work reduced hours at particular times in their lives, and especially when their children are young. But current work practices mean that at this stage of the family life-cycle their wives are likely to be out of the work-force, or working only part-time. Money is short. Therefore instead of working reduced hours, men generally have to work longer and harder than usual when their children most need them. Better opportunities for job sharing between men and women, and perhaps especially between husbands and wives, would help remedy this gross inequity for men. But gender segregation in the work-force remains the rule, and this makes job sharing between men and women almost impossible. Data gathered in 1991 showed that women made up 99 per cent of secretaries, 96 per cent of house cleaners and domestic servants, and 93 per cent of nurses. Men made up over 90 per cent of construction workers, mechanical and electrical engineers, miners, woodworkers, and, for some mysterious reason, dentists. Sex-role stereotypes perpetuate gender segregation, and vice versa. This is just one of the many circular interactions that help to preserve the patriarchal *status quo*.

Clearly, we remain a very long way from creating even the most basic requirements for true equality between the sexes. But, should we ever achieve it, what might we expect of relationships between men and women?

With true equality between them, both sexes would be able to more freely acknowledge and express their opposite gender characteristics. There would be little need for men to project their denied femininity on to women, or for women to project their unwanted masculinity on to men. Romantic, passionate love would largely vanish. Marriage, if it survived, would be based primarily on the desire for companionship and emotional intimacy.

A world in which romantic, passionate love barely exists may not be very appealing to most people. Perhaps that is why we cling to our traditional ideas of love so fiercely. Perhaps we choose to live with sex-role stereotypes because, deep down, we fear that the alternative will be bland and boring.

In Chapter 1 I mentioned the trend toward postponing marriage. If this trend continues at the same pace, by the year 2000 almost 25 per cent of women will not marry before the age of thirty-five. By the year 2020, the proportion will be nearly 40 per cent. Perhaps this represents the beginning of the end of marriage, and with it the demise of romantic, passionate love. If so, new kinds of relationships between men and women will naturally emerge. I hope that they will not be bland and boring. Rather, I hope that they will be as exciting and interesting as those based on falling in love. And safer. Much safer.

Selected Bibiography

R. Ardrey, *African Genesis. A Personal Investigation into the Animal Origins and Nature of Man*, Collins, London, 1961.

E. Badinter, *The Myth of Motherhood*, Souvenir Press, London, 1981.

J. Barrett and R. Rose, *Mental Disorder in the Community*, Guilford Press, New York, 1986.

R. Bly, *Iron John*, Element Books, Dorset (UK), 1991.

N. Chodorow, *The Reproduction of Mothering: Psychoanalysis and the Sociology of Gender*, University of California Press, Berkeley, 1978.

C. Christ, *The Laughter of Aphrodite: Reflections on a Journey to the Goddess*, Harper & Row, San Francisco, 1987.

H. Creekmore, *The Satires of Juvenal*, Mentor, New York, 1963.

M. Daly, *Pure Lust. Elemental Feminist Philosophy*, The Women's Press, London, 1984.

S. Faludi, *Backlash: The Undeclared War Against Women*, Chatto & Windus, London, 1992.

J. & S. Farrar, *The Witches' Goddess. The Feminine Principle of Divinity*, Robert Hale, London, 1987.

S. Finstead, *Sleeping With the Devil*, W. Morrow, New York, 1991.

J. Frazer, *The Golden Bough*, Macmillan, London, 1976.

M. French, *The War Against Women*, Hamish Hamilton, London, 1992.

B. Friedan, *The Second Stage*, Sphere Books, London, 1983.

D. Gilmore, *Manhood in the Making: Cultural Concepts of Masculinity*, Yale University Press, New Haven, CT, 1990.

R. Graves, *The Greek Myths*, Penguin, London, 1960.

E. Grosz, *Sexual Subversions*, Allen & Unwin, Sydney, 1989.

R. J. Hafner, *Marriage and Mental Illness*, Guilford Press, New York, 1986.

F. Harrison, *The Dark Angel: Aspects of Victorian Sexuality*, Sheldon Press, London, 1977.

S. Hite, *The Hite Report on Male Sexuality*, Knopf, New York, 1981.

B. Johnson, *The Lady of the Beasts*, Harper & Row, New York, 1988.

R. Johnson, *He: Understanding Masculine Psychology*, Harper & Row, New York, 1977.

J. Klaits, *Servants of Satan: The Age of the Witch Hunts*, Indiana University Press, Bloomington, 1985.

P. Laslett, *Family Life and Illicit Love in Earlier Generations*, Cambridge University Press, New York, 1977.

T. and R. Lidz, *Oedipus in the Stone Age*, International Universities Press, Madison, 1989.

K. Lorenz, *On Aggression*, Methuen, London, 1966.

V. Noble, *Motherpeace: A Way to the Goddess Through Myth, Art and Tarot*, Harper & Row, New York, 1983.

R. Norwood, *Women Who Love Too Much*, Arrow Books, London, 1986.

P. O'Connor, *Understanding Jung, Understanding Yourself*, Methuen, London, 1985.

I. Pauly, Adult Manifestations of Male Transsexualism. In *Transsexualism and Sex Reassignment*, eds R. Green and J. Money, Johns Hopkins Press, Baltimore, 1969.

P. Resick, Sex-role stereotypes and violence against women. In *The Stereotyping of Women*, eds V. Franks and E. Rothblum, Springer, New York, 1983.

C. Russell and I. Megaard, *The General Social Survey*, 1972–1986, Springer–Verlag Inc., New York, 1988.

P. Russianoff, *Why Do I Think I am Nothing Without a Man?* Bantam Books, New York, 1982.

M. Samos, *The Spiral Dance: A Rebirth of the Ancient Religion of the Great Goddess*, Harper & Row, San Francisco, 1979.

A. Samuels, *Jung and the Post-Jungians*, Routledge & Kegan Paul, London, 1985.

M. Schatzmann, *Soul Murder: Persecution in the Family*, Random House, New York, 1973.

E. Shorter, *The Making of the Modern Family*, Fontana, London, 1976.

R. Spector and V. Waldron, *By My Baby*, Macmillan, Sydney, 1991.

M. Stone, *When God Was a Woman*. Harvest/HBJ, San Diego, 1978.

M. Tax, 'Woman and Her Mind.' In *Radical Feminism New York*, eds A. Koedt, E. Levine and A. Rapone, Quadrangle Press, New York, 1973.

United States Department of Commerce, *National Data Book and Guide to Sources*, 108th Edition. Bureau of the Census, 1988.

W. L. Williams, *The Spirit and the Flesh: Sexual Diversity in American Indian Culture*, Beacon Press, Boston, 1986.

M. Wittig, *Les Guerilleres*, translated by D. Le Vay, Avon Books, New York, 1971.